PLANET STRANGE

THOM POWELL

HANGAR 1 PUBLISHING

CONTENTS

INTRODUCTION

There's something going on beneath our feet. I first became aware of it as I investigated the Sasquatch phenomenon. I struggled to answer the question of where exactly they went when they wanted privacy and shelter.

For two decades, I studied this mystery. I wrote a few books and attended countless conferences. I met people who comb the wildernesses in search of Sasquatch evidence. Frequently, such folks happen across mysterious structures in the woods that look like teepees without the hide covering. I'd seen them many times myself, and they just didn't look like adequate shelter from the elements. I was also fortunate to meet and learn from Native Americans who offered an alternative. They told me that the tribal perspective was that the Sasquatch live within the Earth; they have subterranean refuge from which they emanate.

I wanted to study this possibility, like the Sasquatch mystery in general, as scientifically as I could. I was never a scientist, but I was a science teacher for my entire career, and I always believed and taught that science, correctly done, could always generate accurate answers to important questions. I found out I was wrong. It was explained by one particularly great thinker named Henry Franzoni that, as much as we would like to, we cannot apply science to the Sasquatch question for two reasons: they are intelligent, and they are rogue (they wish to remain hidden).

Henry patiently explained for my benefit, "You cannot do science on intelligent, rogue beings. They're actively concealing their whereabouts, and they are often employing trickery and deception that can confound attempts to be purely scientific."

Think about how the CIA finally caught up with Osama bin Laden. They gathered numerous bits of information, most unverifiable, and searched for patterns that may offer some small amount of predictive value. They applied a lot of outside-the-box thinking and ultimately came to the tentative conclusion that he was hiding in plain sight; as long as 'plain sight' was a compound in Abbottabad near the Pakistani equivalent of West Point. Bin Laden was caught through a process that was as much spying as science, and this is a very important point when we look for answers to many questions that fall into the category of paranormal phenomena. My friend and retired scientist Ron Meyer observed that science and spying are not really opposites. The scientific method has evolved since the time of Galileo, and it continues to do so. The scientific method, laboratory experiments, pattern recognition, statistical analysis, and noticing the unusual are all part of practicing science, and spies use these same tools whenever they can. Ron observed that, in the case of killing Osama bin Laden, gut intuitions did play a role, but a lot of statistical analysis, particularly focused on pattern recognition, helped the CIA figure out where he was hiding.

On the other hand, Ron also agrees that the paradigms and models of science, particularly physics, cannot explain anomalous events and mysteries I discuss in this book. Whether the mystery involves UFOs, Sasquatches, crop circles, or other phenomenon, one must remember that, as much as we wish we could do science, not only is it difficult to do science on intelligent, rogue beings, but science as it is currently defined and practiced cannot do much with paranormal events.

I want to be a scientist. I may be a spy or simply a reporter. I began my spying/reporting by collecting all the information that might be relevant. Then combing through it, like a science-minded spy, teased out patterns that may have predictive value. I formed conclusions that seemed to answer all the questions even though I could not really test them. I did write it all down, and that is what we have here. My conclusion is that we essentially share the planet with other intelligent beings that probably have the ability to come and go from our world, but when they are here, they reside in spacious underground citadels that have been modified and greatly improved over the drippy, cold caves that we sometimes explore.

Each chapter of this book explores a separate line of evidence and reasoning to support this overarching view. The final two chapters attempt to unify all the distinct pieces of evidence and explore their implications. Still, the general direction of this book should be clear by now.

Astrophysicists have this high-profile scientific effort called SETI or Search for Extraterrestrial Intelligence. Radio telescope arrays are pointed into the cosmos in hopes of detecting intelligent signals from distant civilizations that we cannot visit in person. Logically, it seems like a worthwhile avenue of investigation. However, I would argue that this worthy project is doomed to failure because its fundamental assumptions are flawed. It is assumed that the aliens are "out there" somewhere and that if we listen to radio frequencies, we will eventually detect the electromagnetic signatures of distant alien civilizations.

A fundamental flaw is the assumption that the entities we seek are no more sophisticated than we are and, therefore, use familiar and detectable radio signals as we do, so we should be able to detect whatever communication frequencies they are using. I once had dinner with a SETI director named Seth Shostak when he visited Portland. I was given to understand that the SETI directors see no reason why the intelligent life forms we seek would wish to conceal their presence. If this assumption, or any of the previous ones, is mistaken, then the whole SETI program may be 'barking up the wrong tree.'

I'm rooting for them, but I doubt the SETI program will ever produce the evidence it seeks. Not because we are alone in the cosmos; we most certainly are not. We just have to figure out where to look and what we are looking for. Our biases and preconceived notions take us in some wrong directions. Consider, for example, that the place to search for other intelligent life is not somewhere in the emptiness of space but somewhere a lot closer to home.

This book presents the conclusion that intelligent 'off-planeters' (they are no more *alien* than we are) presently co-inhabit our Earth, and if the SETI program wants to find detectable evidence of any so-called 'alien' existence, then they need to do some outside-the-box thinking. Instead of pointing their radio telescopes out into the voids of interstellar space, they might try turning their radio telescopes around, in a manner of speaking, for the beings they seek are *behind* them. They're already here. As we listen intently to the murmurs of the cosmos, the beings we seek may be looking right over our collective shoulders.

Enrico Fermi, father of the hydrogen bomb, came up with the 'zoo hypothesis' to explain why we cannot find any evidence of off-planet intelligent life. We may be like the animals in a zoo, he speculated, blissfully unaware of the visitors who observe our comings and goings from concealed vantage points. Zoo keepers know that animals are less stressed and behave more naturally if the zoo patrons, and even the zoo keepers, are kept out of sight. Therefore, increasingly, zoo pens are fitted with two-way mirrors so that spectators and workers can see the animals without being seen. By this analogy, intelligent 'off-planeters' have been observing human activities with a certain interest. The keepers of our terrestrial zoo, for the most part, remain in the shadows, safely behind the figurative two-way mirrors of human perception. They can easily see us, but from our side of the glass, we cannot easily see them.

There are clues as to what *is* really going on. One just has to figure out what and where to look for. The clues may not be definitive, and they aren't always obvious, but they are there, and they point to one over-arching conclusion: we are not alone, and we probably have not been since the very dawn of humanity.

Charles Fort was an author and paranormal researcher in the first decades of the twentieth century. He was the first to suggest that the UFO sightings that were happening back then were indications that we were being visited by intelligent beings from somewhere beyond Earth. Not only was he ahead of his time in this regard, but he went even farther to speculate that the extraterrestrial activity was more than casual visitors from another planet who were just passing through. "The earth is a farm," Fort used to say, and at least one of the crops that is produced here is *us*.

What or who is down in the Earth? Are there living beings down under, or is the Earth itself alive and intelligent? For me, this is the ultimate mystery of Nature. Is Nature itself alive and intelligent, or is a group of hidden beings running the show? In my search for answers, I am betting on spying rather than science because, as Max Planck, a Nobel Prize-winning scientist famously said:

"Science cannot solve the ultimate mystery of nature. And that is because, in the last analysis, we ourselves are a part of the mystery we are trying to solve."

1

NOTHING NEW

I f we share the planet with aliens, off-planeters, or whatever you want to call them, they may even reside among us here on Earth. They probably didn't arrive recently. Our understanding of the whole UFO deal is relatively new, dating back to the late 1800's. Before that time, encounters with aerial phenomena were more likely regarded as divine in origin. Things changed when Percival Lowell, a wealthy businessman, mathematician, and astronomer built a pretty sizable telescope on a hill outside of Flagstaff, Arizona and used it to begin studying Mars. In his European travels in the mid-1800s, Lowell was fascinated by the sketches of canals on the surface of Mars that were produced by an Italian astronomer. Giovanni Schiaparelli directed an observatory in Milan, and he felt that he was seeing structures on Mars that were not natural features. Lowell also became aware of similar work and similar conclusions by French scientist Camille Flammarion, who published a book on Mars.

To satisfy his curiosity about Mars, Lowell founded the observatory in Arizona that still bears his name. The 24-inch diameter refracting lenses of Lowell's telescope were primitive by today's standards, and they were certainly not good enough to accurately view the details of the Martian surface. Lowell did, however, pioneer the idea of placing a telescope in a remote location, away from city lights so as to improve its resolution of faint amounts of light that would be drowned out by urban light pollution.

Lowell published his first book, *Mars,* in 1895 and *The Canals of Mars* in 1906. At the time, many astronomers doubted the accuracy of Lowell's observations of putative canals on Mars, but Lowell went even further. He postulated that the canals were indicative of not just a civilization but a civilization that was in decline, maybe even collapse. Knowing what we now know about Mars, it is easy to ridicule such ideas, but the science of telescopic observations was still in its infancy, even though it seemed like Lowell had achieved a breakthrough in observatory siting and operation, which he indeed had. As telescopes improved in later decades, Lowell's ideas about Mars and the alleged canals were, of course, convincingly refuted.

Meanwhile, a whole bunch of fiction writers seized upon Lowell's radical ideas to craft some compelling novels. The first and most spectacular of these fictional masterpieces was H. G. Wells' *War of the Worlds* (1897). Not only did Wells build on the idea of other civilizations in our solar system, but he also, for the first time, developed the terrifying idea that a civilization poised on the brink of collapse would invade its neighbors (namely us) in its desperate quest for survival. A whole bunch of other authors exploited similar themes right up to the dawn of the space age. *The Red Planet* by Heinlien (1949), *The Martian Chronicles* by Ray Bradbury (1950), and *The Gods of Mars* by Edgar Rice Burroughs (1918) are perhaps the most well-known examples of the profound impact that Percival Lowell had on popular literature and popular thinking about neighboring planets and the life forms they ought to harbor. All the Flash Gordon shows of the 1950s are similarly attributable to the compelling but spectacularly wrong-headed thinking of Percival Lowell that persisted for decades after his death. Perhaps Lowell's mis-observations about Mars persisted for not just years but decades because he made such enduring contributions to the field of astronomy. For example, Lowell was convinced that the orbits of the outermost planets then known, Uranus and Neptune, had orbital fluctuations that indicated the presence of an unknown planet that he dubbed "Planet X." Although Lowell died in 1916, well before any more planets were discovered, Lowell did lay the groundwork for a big discovery. Lowell's 'Planet X,' namely Pluto, was discovered in 1930 by Clyde Tombaugh at the Lowell Observatory.

Also, Lowell did develop the model for siting observatories that has not been improved upon since; equipment as specialized and expensive as modern telescopes are, as they MUST be, located away from the light pollution of population centers and as high in the atmosphere as is possible to minimize atmospheric distortion. Taken to its logical conclusion, the best place to locate a telescope would be outside of Earth's atmosphere altogether. This would render the equipment immune to the effects of atmospheric distortion, air pollution and light pollution. It does make the telescopes a bit tougher to use and maintain, but the Hubble and, more recently, the Kepler space telescopes do perform spectacularly better than any Earth-based telescope of similar size, and they can be operated day and night, unlike all terrestrial telescopes except solar telescopes (which look only at the Sun). It is sometimes said that Percival Lowell was the single astronomer who had the most impact on public opinion before Carl Sagan in the late 20th century.

Not only did Percival Lowell popularize the science of astronomy more than any person prior to Carl Sagan, he popularized the notion of other worlds that contained other civilizations. This idea had not been much considered, not to mention written about, by the population at large before the time of Lowell. Western religious thought was adamant in the view that we on Earth were God's one and only chosen people. Western religious thought uniformly drew from scripture the view that all of Heaven and Earth was for the benefit of humanity. The Earth was the only habitable planet, not just in the solar system but the whole of the cosmos. Lowell was among the first to tender the suggestion that this was definitely not necessarily the case.

In this way, Lowell laid the groundwork for a transformation in literary and even scientific thinking. One of the first to take this ball and run with it, scientifically, was New Yorker Charles Fort. As early as 1919, Dutch American author Charles Fort wrote books arguing that unexplained aerial lights (now called UFOs) represented visitors from other worlds. Fort's *The Book of the Damned* was published in 1919, followed by *New Lands* (1925) and *Lo!* in 1931. Fort was perhaps the earliest collector of accounts of anomalous events, which became known in those days as Fortean phenomena. Fort would collect any and all accounts of anomalous phenomena and file them in shoe boxes. He had dozens of shoe boxes full of file cards, each with a separate account of a UFO, a hairy beast, a dinosaur-like bird, a ghostly spirit, a human abduction, missing time... you name it. Then, Fort would attempt to make sense of the whole constellation of 'Fortean' phenomena, which ultimately led him to the inescapable conclusion that not only was the Earth being visited and observed by beings from other planets, but that we humans were being manipulated for some unknown purpose by these presumably super-sophisticated beings. One of Fort's most profound and succinct conclusions was that "the Earth is a farm," the implication being that we humans were, for whatever purpose, the crop.

Fort's most profound conclusion may have been his fundamental challenge to the so-called objectivity of the scientists of the day. Fort's overarching view was that the dismissive and inherently skeptical nature of scientists was sometimes counterproductive, especially when attempting to explore what he called 'marvels' and what we now call paranormal events. Fort wrote:

> "People with a psychological need to believe in marvels are no more prejudiced and gullible than people with a psychological need NOT to believe in marvels."

Bear in mind that "marvels" as Fort used the term, is essentially synonymous with that which we today describe as 'paranormal' phenomena. The word "paranormal' did not exist in the lexicon when Fort was writing in the early twentieth century. Instead, they referred to scientifically unexplainable phenomena as Fortean phenomena or sometimes just 'marvels.'

While Fort died in 1932, others carried the torch, especially in the years after the watershed UFO sighting over Mt. Rainier, Washington, by pilot Kenneth Arnold in June of 1947. Several factors make Kenneth Arnold's particular sighting more important than anything short of the Roswell incident. First, Kenneth Arnold was a serious and sober pilot who was not just out flying a plane on a Sunday afternoon. He was actively searching the wilderness of northwest Washington for the remains of another plane that mysteriously vanished in the area. He was essentially on a mission of mercy. Further, he witnessed not one but nine discs flying in formation, in daylight conditions, and in unlimited, cloud-free visibility. Arnold estimated the speed of the formation at a thousand miles an hour.

Arnold was a highly experienced pilot with thousands of hours of flight time in his CalAir A-2. Much of his time was spent doing search and rescue missions and other mercy missions. Arnold described the formation of objects he saw as saucer-shaped and "moving like a saucer skipping across the water." The media took the ball and ran with it from there, and ever since then, we have been calling them 'flying saucers.' Arnold remained active in UFO research and even appeared at UFO conferences until his death in 1984. Arnold's principal frustration with the UFO problem seemed to be not the question of whether they exist but what exactly it would take to get people to take the subject seriously.

> "I've seen something and hundreds of other pilots have seen something. We have dutifully reported these things...and we have to have fifteen million witnesses before anybody is going to look into this problem?...Seriously? Well, this is utterly fantastic. This is more fantastic than flying saucers or people from Venus or anything, as far as I'm concerned."
>
> (Notice the similarity in logic to that which Fort expressed some forty years prior.)

Not long after the forceful assertions of Kenneth Arnold, the extraterrestrial hypothesis (ETH) began to gain traction. Jacques Vallee published a very articulate examination of UFO evidence and the implications thereof entitled "Challenge to Science." Meanwhile, some official government and military departments WERE secretly and not-so-secretly looking into the matter. Predictably, the not-so-secret reports, like Project Blue Book, trotted out the same preposterous conclusions: mass hallucination, swamp gas, mistaken observations of the planet Venus, and so on explained away virtually all UFO sightings. Less discussed were the studies that arrived at different conclusions: A West German study conducted between 1951 and 1954 concluded that other planets are the most likely origin of at least some of the UFOs witnessed in European skies. Another study, Project Sign, was sponsored by the newly created U.S. Air Force. In 1948, they issued a concluding document entitled The Estimate of the Situation, stating that the ETH was the best explanation for unidentified flying objects. The report was rejected by General Hoyt Vandenberg for lack of proof. A Major Fournet in the Pentagon also dismissed the report as "extreme extrapolation based on scant evidence." The project was disbanded in 1949, and the personnel were reassigned to Project Grudge. All copies of the report went to the incinerator. However, Project Sign and the resulting "Estimate of the Situation" is still thought of as the Holy Grail of Ufology. Despite the fact that no known copies survived, its existence has been confirmed by well-known government-hired UFO research consultants like Jerome Clark and J. Allen Hynek.

At this point in time, we are well past the need for more government and military studies, not to mention more debate and discussion of whether UFOs exist. We may also be past the need to further debate the origin of the crafts, at least in the general sense. Certainly, some of them are interplanetary in origin, although that conclusion may be misleading in one important aspect. While the mysterious crafts and their occupants may *originate* from other planets, it does not necessarily follow that they are traveling from afar on an ongoing basis. Some modern researchers have come to the conclusion that interplanetary beings have been investigating the Earth for centuries.

One of the original arbiters of this view is Swiss researcher and author Erich Von Daniken. Although his 1968 magnum opus *Chariots of the Gods* and the sequels have been criticized as an example of the sloppy research and distorted truths that so often characterize UFO literature, von Daniken did open the floodgates for some further research that has become increasingly difficult to dismiss out-of-hand.

Perhaps the most noteworthy of the post-*Chariots of the Gods* researchers is Zecharia Sitchin. Born in Azerbaijan in 1920, he was raised in Mandatory Palestine (which became Israel in 1948), educated in London, and relocated to New York in 1958. Sitchin's multicultural and multilingual background positioned him uniquely to study Sumerian culture and then teach himself to read and translate cuneiform, the original written language used in Mesopotamia and Sumer (modern-day Iraq and Syria). Cuneiform is generally regarded as among the world's first, maybe even the very first, written language. Clay tablets containing cuneiform (Latin for 'wedge-shaped' alphabet) inscriptions have been unearthed by the thousands in palaces and temples in Iraq and Syria. Many have yet to be translated. The University of Pennsylvania holds the largest collection of cuneiform tablets in the U.S. Larger collections exist in England and Iraq. Cuneiform tablets as old as 3200 B.C. have been found, but the language was more primitive then, relying more on pictographs than an alphabet, per se. Tablets on the order of 2600 B.C. show a much more sophisticated alphabet of about 600 signs and symbols.

The translation of cuneiform tablets is a bit easier than when it was first attempted in the late 1600s by Roman traveler Pietro Della Valle and English scholar Sir Thomas Herbert around 1638. French and English scholars made sustained efforts to translate cuneiform as more tablets were discovered and found their way back to Europe. By the mid-1800s, Assyriologists like Henry Rawlinson in England and Edward Hincks in Ireland were making huge progress. Proper names were obviously the most difficult things to figure out, but more clay tablets were being steadily unearthed, and names from new tablets were deciphered more easily using the older ones. By 1857, a panel of experts examined the translations of the leading experts and, upon being satisfied that there was general agreement, especially between the translations of the two leading experts, Hincks and Rawlinson, and it was declared that the translation of Akadian cuneiform was a done deal.

Meanwhile, the sheer number of newly discovered clay tablets was becoming enormous. One library in Iraq was discovered around 1850 that contained tens of thousands of tablets. Such discoveries have continued into modern times, and the number of clay tablets now stored in museums sits at anywhere from 500,000 to two million, depending on whether you want to consider broken fragments to be separate tablets. The British Museum holds the largest collection, followed by The Louvre in France, Istanbul Archaeology Museum, National Museum of Iraq, then Yale and University of Pennsylvania in the U.S. Most tablets just sit there in museums and have never been closely looked at, much less translated. Maybe only 30 or 40 thousand tablets have been translated worldwide out of the half a million that have been discovered so far. Most tablets are detailed records of transactions, but some, such as the famous Epic of Gilgamesh, tell fascinating stories or describe aspects of Sumerian and Mesopotamian society. Even today, there are only a few hundred cuneiformists in the entire world who can competently translate these priceless historical texts.

One now-deceased cuneiformist was Zecharia Sitchin. Probably as a consequence of his multilingual upbringing, Sitchin was able to achieve the remarkable feat of teaching himself cuneiform. This is where things get interesting.

When Sitchin was doing his translating, there were very few others who could verify the accuracy of his translations. It is much easier for others to cross-check each other's translations, especially since the publication of one particular book entitled, *Sumerian Lexicon* in 2008.

But in Sitchin's day, he was going it alone. After teaching himself cuneiform, he set about translating some of the enormous number of clay tablets in the British Museum, specifically certain pre-Nubian and Sumerian texts and one particular seal (cylindrical tablet) known as VA 243. Sitchin then claimed that these texts indicate that the Sumerians had interactions with a group of beings from another planet in our solar system called Nibiru. This planet was said by Sitchin to have a very oblong orbit that carries it out past Neptune, then across the orbit of the other planets, and back around the Sun every 3,600 years or so. In the book which summarized his translations, Sitchin related that Planet Nibiru also had a problem. Its atmosphere was deteriorating (sound familiar?) in a way that threatened the very survival of the resident beings, the Anunnaki. Their leader, Anu, dispatched his two sons, Enlil and Enki, to Earth to direct and supervise the extraction of large amounts of the only substance that could repair the atmospheric damage to Nibiru, namely gold. Specifically, Anu sent a squad, led by his two sons, to gather the rare, single-atom isotope of gold known as monoatomic gold.

The crew that worked under the direction of Enlil and Enki was too small for the big job of mining and transporting large amounts of gold from the rich gold fields of southern Africa. Consequently, they rebelled, and Enlil faced an acute labor shortage. Fortunately, Enki was able to use his advanced knowledge of gene splicing to create a replacement labor source. Enki took the DNA from the indigenous primates, which we know from the fossil record to be Homo erectus, also known as Java Man. He spliced their genes with their own extraterrestrial Anunnaki DNA to create a new species, namely, us.

This new species, as described in clay tablets according to Sitchin, was known at the time as 'the Adamu,' which not-coincidently hearkens to the biblical first human known as Adam. Needing a mate for Adamu, Enki took tissue from Adamu and created his companion, who we all know from the Old Testament as Eve. According to the Sumerian version of the story, which predates the Old Testament but bears tremendous similarities, the serpent in the Garden of Eden was not Satan but rather the incarnation of a more benevolent entity who advocated for the enlightenment of Adam and Eve. In any case, Adamu and Eve were relocated to the gold fields of Africa, which is why that very region of Africa bears the fossils that identify it as the birthplace of humanity. The story goes on and on, the Anunnaki gods are portrayed in the same ruthless, brutal manner as the deity we understand from the Old Testament.

Sitchin's interpretation of Sumerian texts bears many other similarities to Hebrew, Arabic, and Christian scripture. Spiteful gods, bitter rivalries, epic floods and destruction of cities all manifest in Sumerian clay tablets, according to the works of Sitchin. Cain and Abel, the brothers of Old Testament infamy, were Enlil and Enki of Sumerian lore. As with Abraham's sons, Enlil and Enki were rivals; in the end, one kills the other. At another point in the Sumerian version, the ruthless Anunnaki god Enlil tried to wipe out the fledgling human race by somehow initiating a great flood. Fortunately, Enki warns his favorite son (Noah), who survived the flood by building some sort of boat that could withstand the deluge. The Nephilim in the book of Genesis are indeed the Anunnaki themselves, who came down from the skies and took human wives. Many more details of the interaction between Anunnaki and the fledgling human race are described by Sitchin in his nine books, the first one being *The Twelfth Planet*. According to Sitchin, Sumerians were aware of all nine planets, including Pluto, and the Moon and Sun were also seen as planets. This left Niburu, the home of the Anunnaki, as the twelfth planet.

All specific details of this convoluted story could not be refuted when Sitchin first published his translations of Sumerian cuneiform texts beginning in 1976. After 2006, it became much easier for amateurs to translate cuneiform. Suffice it to say that the more other scholars attempted to verify or refute the translations of Zecharia Sitchin, the more his interpretations and translations were called into question. Not only were his translations considered overly loose and sometimes just plain wrong, but the science behind his claims was also challenged. The Sumerians were aware of only five planets, experts insisted, not eleven or twelve. The very idea of a large planet that took over a thousand years to complete one highly elliptical revolution around the Sun is seen by astronomers as laughable. It would be a world of perpetual darkness and cold. Whatever atmosphere such a planet held would be much thicker than Earth, and no one can think of an atmospheric issue that could be repaired with gold, monoatomic or otherwise. The list of disputes with Sitchin's descriptions of terrestrial interaction with interplanetary beings goes on and on, to the point where Sitchin's credibility is non-existent in the eyes of science. Still, the words of Charles Fort have a certain relevance here:

"People with a psychological need to believe in marvels are no more prejudiced and gullible than people with a psychological need NOT to believe in marvels."

Sitchin may not have much credibility in the eyes of his fellow cuneiformologists, not to mention mainstream astronomers, but he does enjoy a strong following among 'ancient alien theorists.' He may even be the leading voice among those 'New Agers' who favor revisionist histories, including alien visitations to Earth, especially in ancient times. Sitchin most assuredly got many details of his cuniform translations wrong, but he certainly was not wrong about everything. There are even some big elements that, in hindsight, Sitchin absolutely nailed. There are even a few authors who feel they have verified some of Sitchin's extraordinary claims. The existence of a large, undiscovered planet with an elongated orbit is not laughed at now, even though it may have been when Sitchin was still alive. Also, the idea of a worldwide flood of biblical proportions was an absurdity to geologists and paleontologists of Sitchin's day. The existence of such a flood is now a virtual certainty.

Planet X

Sitchin claimed the Sumerian texts described the Anunnaki as a god-like race of beings that originated from a distant planet in our solar system with a highly elongated orbit that brought it around the Sun once every 3600 years. Astronomers rolled their collective eyes at such an improbable suggestion, explaining the impossibility of sustaining life on such a planet.

While I tend to agree that lack of sunlight would render life as we know it impossible, others argue that only internal radioactive decay on such a planet or some unknown heat source could render conditions that could sustain life under otherwise impossible conditions. Regardless, at the time of Sitchin's death in 2005, our most advanced scientists had absolutely no evidence that such a planet existed or even could exist.

Then, in 2015, the thinking suddenly changed. Caltech astrophysicists Konstantin Batygin and Mike Brown announced that their study of orbital perturbations of the outer planets, plus some detailed mathematical modeling, suggested (they used the word "proved") that a planet that was ten times the size of earth with an extremely elliptical orbit actually existed. They predicted its orbit would take it around the sun every 10,000 to 20,000 years. Since the name of any newly discovered planet is determined by the discoverer, they could not go so far as naming a planet that was still unproven. So they labeled their theoretical planet Planet X, which would have pleased Percival Lowell.

You better believe that Batygin, Brown, and a whole bunch of others are today using the world's most powerful telescopes to be the first to prove such a planet exists. Despite the much-increased power of modern telescopes, the challenge of training such equipment on the exactly correct patch of sky at the exactly correct moment is quite daunting. While Sitchin may not be completely off the hook on his claims of an unknown planet Nibiru with its hyper-elongated orbit, it's fair to say nobody in the astrophysics community is laughing at the idea that such a planet, that Sitchin was the first in modern times to suggest, may actually exist. Time will tell.

The Flood

Recall that Zecharia Sitchin also claimed that, according to ancient Sumerian clay tablets that he translated, the Sumerians circa 3000 B.C. described a worldwide flood of positively epic proportions. Again, such a fantastic claim caused the scientific community to heap ridicule onto Sitchin, even though the book of Genesis also depicts a flood of positively biblical proportions. In fact, informed ethnologists and archeologists will tell you that every single ancient culture worldwide that kept records of significant historical events also has accounts of a mega-flood. To anyone who doubts the validity of these admittedly unverifiable historical accounts, I have two words to look up on Google or YouTube: Younger Dryas.

According to Sitchin's admittedly far-fetched narrative, the newly developed human race had become a little too big for its collective britches in the eyes of its creators. The interbreeding between the original Anunnaki gold miners and Enki's surprisingly attractive human species led to an emerging race of beings that were smarter and more prolific than was ever intended. Things were getting out of control, especially in the eyes of Enki's petty and ruthless brother, Enlil. So, Enlil decided to wipe out the proto-species that had been created by his talented brother. Enki got wind of Enlil's plan and warned a select few, specifically one Noah-like character, to prepare for a terrible flood by building a specialized boat that could be tumbled in the surf. According to the Sumerian version of this biblical story, the craft wasn't really the familiar ark of the book of Genesis, but rather a boat that would enclose the inhabitants and enable them to survive a really rough ride. Also, the animals to be loaded aboard were not the 'two of every species', but rather a bunch of livestock that would serve as a food source and the seed of an animal husbandry operation that would be critical to the survival of the handful of poor saps who had to repopulate the post-flood wasteland.

Flood Science

In the 1940s, a geologist at the University of Washington in Seattle published a paper declaring that strange landforms throughout eastern Washington pointed to an enormous flood that inundated the region at the end of the last ice age, some fifteen thousand years ago. As with the radical ideas of Zecharia Sitchin, the radical ideas of J Harlan Bretz were met with uniform skepticism and outright ridicule from most of the geologic community at the time.

Bretz had three problems. First, he could not explain where all of the water would have come from that he was claiming for such a sudden and destructive event. His second problem was that no other geologist had spent the time carefully surveying all of the nooks and crannies of this vast and remote corner of the continent that is eastern Washington. Bretz had spent several summers touring the landscape with his family in tow. He knew the details of the landscape like the back of his hand and the features he explored and documented pointed clearly to a wide swath of land, which he called the Channeled Scablands, being suddenly and utterly devastated by an enormous rush of water. The area was and still is so remote and desolate that this very area of eastern Washington was chosen for the site of the Hanford Nuclear Reservation, a super-secret facility that would perform the super dangerous process of enriching the uranium and plutonium that would be the fuel of the world's first atomic weapons. Since the whole region was so unfamiliar to the rest of the world, when Bretz tried to describe the features that all pointed to his proposed flood, no one else in the scientific community could relate.

Perhaps Bretz's biggest hurdle was the popularity of uniformitarianism; the prevailing view in geology at the time that gradual processes, not sudden catastrophes, were the sole means by which all terrestrial landscapes were shaped. Bretz, on the other hand, was proposing something quite sudden and dramatic, even cataclysmic. There just wasn't any support for such unconventional theories. Not only did Bretz's flood fly in the face of accepted geologic principles that were in vogue in the 1940s and 1950s, but still worse, it harkened to one particular cataclysm that no mainstream geologist wanted to endorse: Noah's flood.

The very idea that every landmass on planet Earth could have somehow been covered with water at the same time was so preposterous that any geologist who even hinted that such an event might happen would be committing professional suicide. And yet, this was what Bretz was doing. For the next two decades, Bretz, a respected geology professor at the University of Washington in Seattle, had reduced himself to the laughing stock of the national geologic community. One geologist who worked for the U.S. Geologic Survey, J.T. Pardee frequently mocked Bretz' ideas. Another particularly vocal critic of Bretz's then-radical idea was James Gilluly, also of the U.S. Geological Survey. His criticism of Bretz stemmed from the fact that Bretz's ideas ran counter to the always gradual changes espoused in the uniformitarian doctrine that was widely accepted at the time, but also that Bretz was espousing a theory that was more scriptural than purely scientific. Despite the harsh criticism Bretz refused to recant and always insisted that other scientists would grasp his thinking if they would just visit the landscape, which admittedly wasn't on your way to anywhere.

The ridicule went on for decades but this tragic story has a rare happy ending. Pardee and Gillully finally accepted an invitation to view the evidence in person. They joined a well-attended field trip to the Channeled Scablands of eastern Washington, which Bretz himself did not attend. The trip gave Bretz's critics their first personal exposure to the dramatic landscape that Bretz had personally studied and described for twenty-five years. Gillully was humbled. At one point, he was heard uttering, "How could I have been so wrong?"

Bretz was not one to rub it in. There was a geologic consortium at which the evidence for the Missoula Flood (as it is sometimes called) would be presented. Specifically, a couple of grad students just published a paper that answered the open question of where all the water came from. They had found unmistakable evidence of a vast impoundment of water in west-central Montana around the town of

Missoula. Bretz was still alive and invited to attend the conference where he would finally achieve vindication. He knew he was right all along. He skipped the conference and stayed home.

When scientists suggest new and radical ideas, they are seldom, if ever, vindicated in their lifetime, even if they happen to be right. Galileo was correct about the orbital paths of the solar system but his work was not verified until Newton's math verified it a hundred years after his death. Alfred Wegener died some fifty years before his theory of continental drift was verified. Bretz must have derived some small satisfaction from the fact that his radical idea was confirmed, but he himself observed that he had no interest in I-told-ya-so's. He famously observed, "All my detractors are dead."

This brings us to the Younger Dryas, the new flood myth that may not be as mythical as critics allege. Authors Randall Carlson and Graham Hancock have been arguing for years that geologic evidence found throughout the planet points to an epic, worldwide flood some 12,800 years ago. The event is nick-named Younger Dryas because it is the younger of two times when pollen from an arctic plant known as the dryas flower positively proliferated in the ice core samples taken from Greenland and elsewhere in the Arctic. Ice cores are like tree rings; they are highly accurate representations of ancient climates and climatic shifts to those who know how to read them. Ice cores are new but unassailable testimony to climatic conditions thousands of years ago. Analysis of such cores indicates that the planet was thrown into a 'nuclear winter' of drastically colder temperatures precisely 12,800 years ago, and it stayed that way for 1200 years. During this time, one of the very few plants that was able to proliferate was the dryas flower. What Randall Carlson and Graham Hancock have been saying is not just that an object from space collided with the Earth and plunged us into winter, but that the object or objects that hit the Earth struck the vast continental glaciers that covered Greenland and North America, melting enormous quantities of ice in a matter of hours or days. Ice chunks were ballistically projected all over the northern hemisphere and everything on land was pummeled by huge chunks of flying ice that rained down from the sky. Forty species of mega-fauna like mastodons, mammoths, tigers, and horses, as well as the Clovis-era human culture, were wiped out in an instant. The melted ice pack inundated Earth and sea levels rose sixty feet overnight, worldwide, and eventually as much as three hundred feet. If there was once an Atlantis, it was submerged 12,800 years ago.

As always, main stream science wants nothing to do with such new and radical suggestions that something like Noah's flood actually happened on a worldwide basis. That said, some courageous researchers have taken up the cause and newer and stronger evidence is being found all the time that supports the idea that the Younger Dryas event 12,800 years ago did happen and the biblical flood of Genesis is not a myth. Graham Hancock likes to say that what historians call myths are better thought of as memories, and he points out that every ancient culture, worldwide, that was keeping records or preserving oral traditions has an account of an epic flood.

Randall Carlson points to elliptical depressions in the southeast U.S., called the Carolina Bays, as indications of the pummeling of the surface by ballistically projected ice chunks of enormous size. Similar indentations are found in Nebraska, where they are called the Nebraska Rainwater Basins. In both cases, the orientation of these depressions points toward Saginaw Bay off of Lake Huron, suggesting that Saginaw Bay is, in fact, an impact crater. Scientist Antonio Zamora published a book about impact geology entitled *The Neglected Carolina Bays,* in which he presents a strong case that numerous geologic features throughout the continent are attributable to the Younger Dryas' impact event. As always, when a scientist suggests a catastrophic event, the scientists who favor uniform earth processes over periodic catastrophes will raise the same objection: "where is the water?" was also the principal objection to Bretz's suggestion of a flood. In the case of impact catastrophes, the sustained objection has always been, "where is the crater?"

So far, there are not one but three candidate craters for the Younger Dryas Event. One candidate is, of course, Saginaw Bay off of Lake Huron, another is a curious circular feature that lies at the bottom of eastern Lake Ontario, and the newest one is a thirty-mile-wide crater that was discovered with ice-penetrating radar beneath the Hiawatha Ice Sheet in northern Greenland. Indeed, Carlson and Hancock have also argued that the Younger Dryas Event was so sustained that there were probably multiple impacts that rendered most of the surface of the Earth completely unlivable for the better part of a century between 12,800 and 11,600 years ago. Perhaps the most compelling new find (besides the Hiawatha Crater) that supports Carlson and Hancock's view are the 'black mat' layers found in the recent rock record. Within the rock record at various places around North America are found thin layers of high carbon (presumably from widespread forest fires) as well as traces of unique substances like shock quartz and microdiamonds, which are known to be associated with high-velocity impacts, and rare elements like platinum and iridium which are more common in space than on Earth. These are the same substances that Luis Alvarez used to support the theory that dinosaurs were wiped out by an asteroid impact some 65 million years ago. Alvarez's theory was widely disputed, and as usual, skeptics demanded to see a candidate crater, which he did not have. Eventually, petroleum geologists working around the Yucatan Peninsula stumbled upon a curious region-wide crater we now call Chixulub. Alvarez's once-radical theory of dinosaur extinction is now mainstream. Luis Alvarez was the first to suggest that asteroids or comets strike the Earth with devastating consequences. This idea is not only more accepted today, but it is being suggested that the Earth is impacted at regular intervals of 12,000 to 15,000 years.

Still more interesting is Randall Carlson's opinion that the Missoula Flood was triggered by the same Younger Dryas Event, as was a whole bunch of other flooding on a virtually global basis. Not only is he unifying mega-flood theory, but he is validating old testament scripture AND the seemingly specious translations of Sumerian clay tablets by Zecharia Sitchin. While I agree with the view that Sitchin might have been a bit loose in his translations of cuneiform tablets, he did get a few things right, like the flood, and probably the mysterious planet, and maybe one more thing: Earth may have been visited by off-planeters a long time ago. Sitchin went even further, claiming that, according to the cuneiform texts, Earth was just not visited. Rather, Sitchin was adamant that Earth was essentially taken over as a resource colony for a beleaguered but technologically advanced extraterrestrial civilization. This is where Sitchin's translations seem like a bit of a stretch, although South African author Michael Tellinger has found evidence of gold mining in southern Africa that dates to a time that has always been regarded as the stone age of humanity.

In his book *Slave Species of the Gods,* Tellinger agrees with Sitchin that humanity was not even close to being able to extract and purify lode deposits of gold and that only by being directed could humanity have been able to accomplish such a feat as long ago as 200,000 years, or more. Tellinger grew up in the gold fields of South Africa. His investigations have identified mine tailings, mine shafts, and addits that date to an almost impossibly old date of 200,000 B.C.! This is precisely the time at which Sitchin claims that the Anunnaki gene-spliced the human race from Homo erectus. Further, Tellinger correctly disputes the view that stone-age humans could have ever developed the sophisticated processes of not just gold mining, but gold *ore* mining. Alluvial gold could have been easily collected from surface deposits and rivers, but digging for gold in subterranean veins and lodes would have been way beyond any stone-age human sophistication or motivation. Further, the process of purifying and processing the gold using cyanide and mercury heap-leach extraction would have been impossibly sophisticated to have been developed by humans even 50,000 years B.C. In Tellinger's view, and certainly Sitchin would agree, only with outside direction from a much more intelligent set of beings could such primitive humans ever have figured out how to extract and purify subterranean gold deposits. Not to mention figuring out what to do with gold once they obtained it.

Whether Earth was once simply visited or full-on occupied by off-planeters, a logical step must be explored as a consequence. From a purely logical perspective, it stands to reason that if Earth was visited once, then at the very least, they return periodically, and quite possibly, they never left. That naturally implies that they are still here, or at least they, whomever they are, come back every once in a while to check on things. We humans don't go to all the trouble to visit distant planets and moons just once. We plan multiple visits to conduct increasingly sophisticated tests. Why wouldn't they?

If they are here, why then, don't we see *them*? Well, we do. We see them all the time. Whenever the UFO phenomenon manifests, we may be seeing our off-planet overlords. It may also be that they have decided to take a back seat to human evolution and development, so we see indications that they are around, but it is a bit presumptuous to assume that they have any intention of stepping out of the shadows to shake our collective hands. They're here alright, they just stay in the shadows. Maybe there is even a rule, like the 'prime directive' that was featured in Star Trek episodes: Do not interfere. Let the locals find their own way.

Extraterrestrials were regarded as gods to early humans. At some point, humans ought to be left to develop with a minimum of outside interference. That would be in keeping with a prime directive. Some day, we may be sophisticated enough as a species that we are allowed to view the galactic community in which we are a small player. We are not there yet. Hopefully, we are getting closer.

There's some potentially good news here: If the Earth has been visited and still is visited, perhaps on a routine basis, at least that takes alien invasion scenarios off the table. After all, why would off-planeters invade us if they already lived here and had been doing so for a long time? It would be like the U.S. Army invading the San Diego Zoo. Why invade something you already own? Maybe we can count on our extraterrestrial overlords to help out with some of our planetary maintenance issues. If another asteroid or comet threatens the Earth, they might prove to be very helpful in deflecting it. Maybe they already are.

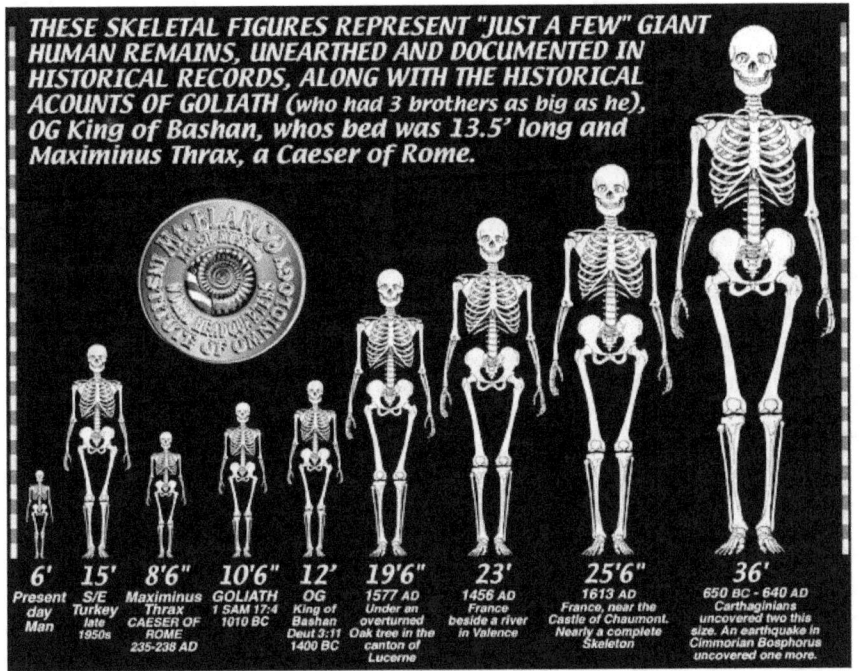

THESE SKELETAL FIGURES REPRESENT "JUST A FEW" GIANT HUMAN REMAINS, UNEARTHED AND DOCUMENTED IN HISTORICAL RECORDS, ALONG WITH THE HISTORICAL ACOUNTS OF GOLIATH (who had 3 brothers as big as he), OG King of Bashan, whos bed was 13.5' long and Maximinus Thrax, a Caeser of Rome.

6'	15'	8'6"	10'6"	12'	19'6"	23'	25'6"	36'
Present day Man	S/E Turkey late 1950s	Maximinus Thrax CAESER OF ROME 235-238 AD	GOLIATH 1 SAM 17:4 1010 BC	OG King of Bashan Deut 3:11 1400 BC	1577 AD Under an overturned Oak tree in the canton of Lucerne	1456 AD France beside a river in Valence	1613 AD France, near the Castle of Chaumont. Nearly a complete Skeleton	650 BC - 640 AD Carthaginians uncovered two this size. An earthquake in Cimmorian Bosphorus uncovered one more.

2
_____

GIANTS

Tidal waves of European immigrants crashed over eastern North America in the mid-1700s, displacing whole tribes of natives from their homeland. The displaced tribes allied themselves with the French and launched the French and Indian War against the invading colonists and their British sponsors. George Washington, then only a colonel, commanded an American militia in northern Virginia. He was given the task of defending colonists in and around Winchester, in Virginia's Shenandoah Valley. Toward this end, Washington directed the construction of Fort Loudon as a refuge for colonists and a garrison for Colonel Washington's troops. As they dug the foundation for this fort, Washington's men unearthed several strange skeletons that measured seven feet long and more! The fort still remains as a tourist attraction, but nobody knows what happened to these remarkable skeletons that were unearthed by Washington's men during the French and Indian War (1754-1763).

Fast forward to 1848. Another future president of considerable repute was heading home to Illinois from his congressional duties in the nation's capital. Abe Lincoln was still a congressman when he detoured to Niagara Falls on his way back to Chicago. After admiring the impressive cataracts, Lincoln gave a speech with some curious references:

"When Columbus first sought this continent, when Christ suffered on the cross, when Moses led Israel through the Red Sea—nay, even when Adam first came from the hand of his Maker, then, as now, Niagara was roaring here. The eyes of that species of extinct giants, whose bones fill the mounds of America, have gazed upon Niagara as ours do now. Contemporary with the whole race of men, and older than the first man, Niagara is as fresh today as ten thousand years ago."

Being a native of Illinois, Lincoln was fully aware of the numerous gigantic skeletons that had been exhumed from mounds in his home state and in neighboring states all over the Midwest. Lincoln was doubtlessly aware of the fact that the largest collection of 'Indian mounds,' as well as the largest single mound in all of North America, was in his home state of Illinois. Monk's Mound dominates the site of an ancient city we now call Cahokia. No one knows the original name of this sprawling complex that once existed at the confluence of the Ohio and Mississippi Rivers near present-day Collinsville, Illinois. Though many mounds have been destroyed at the hands of development, Cahokia once contained over 120 man-made piles of earth, the largest one being the fourteen-acre Monk's Mound, so named for an order of monks who took up residence on the flat top of the hundred-foot high mound. It must have been an impressive view for the monks atop the earthen mound that is more massive than Egypt's Great Pyramid of Giza. If there is any truth to the idea of 'pyramid power,' they must have felt it.

As curious as the mounds were, the hundreds of skeletons that were unearthed almost every time someone took a spade to the ground around Cahokia and elsewhere were the big news. Bones were similarly unearthed in Ohio, Indiana, West Virginia, and New York, including in the vicinity of Niagara Falls near present-day Buffalo, New York.

Not only were there bones seemingly everywhere, but they were, as often as not, much larger than modern humans. They were often observed to have double rows of perfectly formed teeth in both the upper and the lower jaws. They were often buried in peculiar sitting or standing positions, sometimes in the mounds themselves, but usually somewhere near a mound. Strangely, the skeletons, as often as not, crumbled to dust as soon as they were exposed to air. Along with the bones of giants, early white settlers were unearthing finely made tools that were so heavy they could barely be picked up. Copper tools, some hammered, some cast, jewelry like finely crafted copper beads, stone disks, arrowheads, spear points, and more were being unearthed and sold to collectors at the Cahokia site, as well as countless other mound locations throughout the eastern United States.

These finds of giant skeletons, in association with mound sites, were not a secret. Everyone who read local newspapers, including Abe Lincoln, had seen the accounts of giant skeletons and accompanying artifacts. It was common knowledge of the day, though somewhere along the way, this common knowledge got plowed under and lost along with countless mounds that suffered the same fate. Industrious settlers with no particular respect for the past human history of the landscape to which they felt entitled were busy transforming this landscape into farms and towns. Not only were all those mounds in the way of progress, but when they were leveled, it was discovered that the mounds often contained particularly fertile soil.

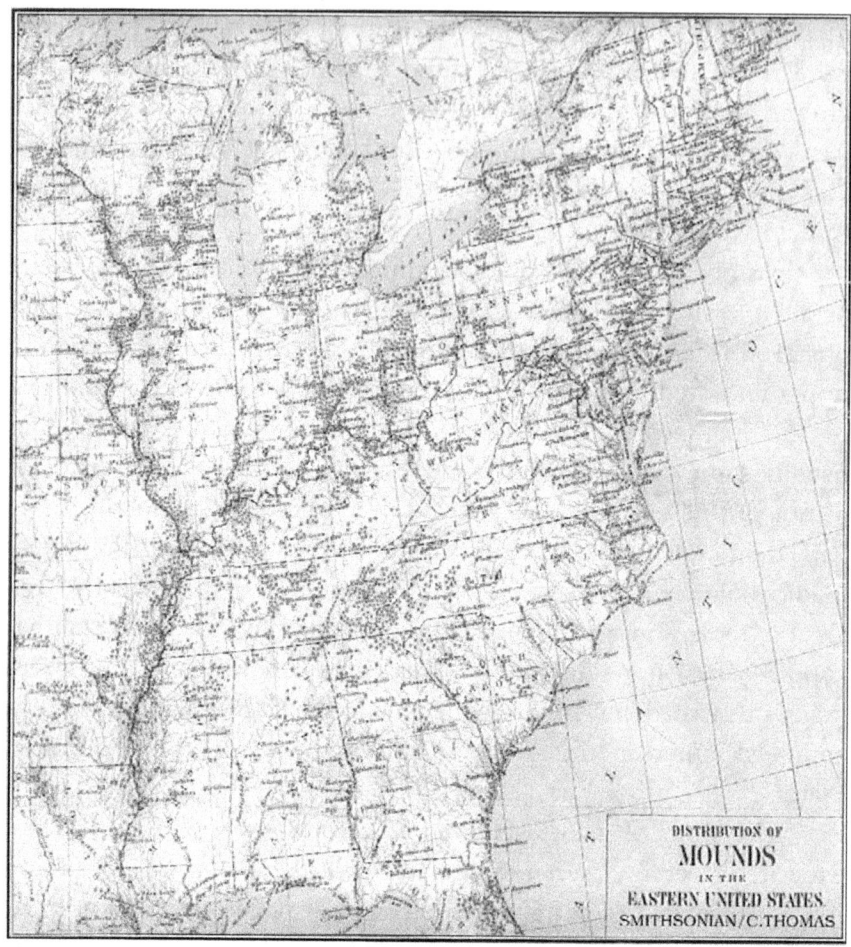

Countless thousands of earthen mounds were obliterated in the name of progress. It is barely possible to fully comprehend how many mounds fell to the plow. Virtually every state in the eastern half of the United States had hundreds, if not thousands, of earthen mounds, big and small, forming designs and geometric patterns, especially in the fertile bottomlands along rivers, large and small. The exact purpose of the mounds is still not fully understood. They are often called burial mounds, and while many mounds have produced bones, many more have produced no bones at all. It is even observed that the giant bones were interred deep beneath the mound, as if the mound had been built at some time after the burial. More often, burial chambers were not a part of the mound, and the bones were found only because someone was digging a foundation or excavating a road cut.

Giant skeletons were being exhumed so often that digging up the bones and collecting the accompanying artifacts became a popular pastime on what was then the frontier. There were no laws against it, and the artifacts were seen as a source of extra income. Such ruthless 'pot-hunting' was so ubiquitous that some people were starting to raise objections to this unscrupulous behavior. By the late 1800s, though archaeology was still in its infancy, the desecration of the ancient sites was stirring outrage from the aspiring archaeologists of the time. Even the academically oriented archeologists of this era were not very careful excavators. By today's standards, their technique was little better than that of undisciplined artifact-hunters. Still, by the late 1800s, a view was emerging that argued it was necessary to preserve these sites and the antiquities they contained for careful future study. After yet another century, yet another view found favor, that the sites were sacred and should not be disturbed at all.

But throughout most of the nineteenth and even into the twentieth century, not only was there a steady loss of priceless cultural artifacts, but the skeletons that came out of the ground in association with the artifacts were carelessly treated, often destroyed, by doing nothing more than exposing them to air. In other cases, amateur archeologists wanted to make some kind of contribution to science, so whatever skeletal remains were not immediately destroyed were turned over to the newly formed Smithsonian Institute in Washington. Soon after the end of the Civil War, the Smithsonian was dispatching teams to mound complexes with the mission of collecting as much material as possible. Their main interest was in the giant bones, particularly the skulls from the giant skeletons. So where are these giant skeletons now? Why are we not able to go to the Smithsonian in Washington D.C. or some other museum and view the skeletons of these beings who might qualify as Sasquatches by today's standards?

The tireless efforts of contemporary researchers like Jim Vieira, Hugh Newman, Fritz Zimmerman, L.A. Marzulli, and Richard Dewhurst have produced at least a partial answer to this mystery. These authors have reconstructed the story of what happened to many of the missing giant skeletons. They have done so by collecting and studying archived museum documents, collecting newspaper accounts by the thousands, anecdotal accounts, and the few rare photographs that date back to the earliest attempts to photo-document the early explorations of the American West.

While it can be argued that all of this collected information still does not rise to the level of scientific proof that giants once inhabited North America, it is rather compelling due to its sheer consistency. It all paints a very clear and very damning portrait of a ruling American scientific institution, the Smithsonian Institute, that diligently collected thousands of giant skeletons over a period of at least eighty years (from the 1850s to the 1930s) and then made them all disappear.

In this age of perpetual conspiracy theories, it might seem a stretch to consider yet another conspiracy theory, this time to conceal the mysterious past human history of North America. What exactly is a conspiracy theory? The legal definition of a conspiracy is any time two or more people agree to break the law. A theory, in the scientific sense, is a carefully constructed hypothesis that has been tested and verified through multiple experiments. But *theory, as it is more commonly used, is synonymous with a guess (or a hypothesis) that has not undergone rigorous testing.* An act of *conspiracy* that rises to the level of a *theory*, in the original sense of the word, would be a very well-verified conspiracy, indeed.

But we all understand that the word "theory" has been misapplied to the realm of guesswork for so long that even most dictionaries carry a second definition that accepts that 'theory' in another use, is synonymous with 'guesswork.'

Now, let's clarify 'conspiracy.' Legally speaking, a conspiracy happens any time two or more people make a plan to break a law. Do conspiracies really happen? Of course, they do. They happen all the time. A bank robbery involving two or more crooks must, by definition, start with a conspiracy. Do *government conspiracies* happen? Can you say Watergate? Did Trump conspire to hide secret documents after he left the presidency? Was the American public kept in the dark about the true costs and casualties of the Vietnam War? Was Lee Harvey Oswald really the one and only perpetrator of the Kennedy assassination? Did the CIA under Ronald Reagan sell cocaine on the streets of American cities to raise money for black projects like funding the Contras military efforts in El Salvador? That happened. Did the weapons of mass destruction that were invoked to initiate the invasion of Iraq really exist? No, and that has been subsequently admitted by senior state department officials since then. One of the newest examples of something that certainly qualifies as evidence of a 'conspiracy theory' is the release of video footage of UFOs by military pilots. These pilots who are speaking out in the media appear to have the full support of their top brass.

Any UFO researcher or reader knows that the government denied any and all alleged UFO activity from the end of World War II right up until these newly public videos and accounts that surfaced with the Pentagon's blessing in 2021. One of my UFO buddies feels that the change in the historic military mindset came from a softening of attitude that was happening in other countries in Europe and South America. Indeed, England, perhaps our staunchest ally, has released UFO files previously held secret by their military. I do not even wish to see punishment or rebuke fall upon the government and military circles that kept and still keep the UFO secrets from public inspection. I include this discussion only to illustrate that 'conspiracy theories,' and still worse 'government conspiracy theories,' have happened in the past and still do. Anyone who argues otherwise is patently naïve. The only question for me is just how deep the pool really is. What other secrets are still being kept or were kept in the past, maybe with considerable success?

The most important one for me is the giant skeleton mystery. Verification of their existence completely rewrites the human history of the North American continent and probably the entire Earth. There is a clear, if incomplete, paper trail of artifacts and giant skeletons that entered the realm of the Smithsonian. Newman and Vieira have unearthed official Smithsonian catalog cards that accompanied giant skulls, which in some cases were signed by Ales Hrdlicka himself. Further, there is no denying that the official story of today is that such skeletal material does not exist in museum archives. Is this prima facia evidence of a 'conspiracy theory'? Only if it was illegal for Smithsonian officials to destroy archived material. Maybe it still exists and is just being kept away from prying eyes. Whether or not it rises to the level of a conspiracy theory (whatever that is) there is definitely every indication of a cover-up.

Why would the Smithsonian do such a thing? The answer lies in a couple of sociological principles that were very important elements of domestic policy in the late 1800s and early 1900s. What seems improbable by today's standards becomes probable in light of the perceived importance of these two ideas back then. 'Manifest destiny' and 'eugenics' are the ideas that were used to justify historically epic mis-applications of science.

Manifest Destiny was the term used to describe what was seen as an almost genetic predisposition of humanity, specifically white European humanity, to move ever westward across the North American continent. This inherent tendency, this compulsion, as it was described by historians of the time, was used to justify the fairly unscrupulous acquisition of 'unsettled' land without regard for the present occupants of that land. In order to justify this theft and the genocide that accompanied it, it became morally expedient to regard the First Nations people as nothing more than uncivilized sub-humans. The term 'savages' was regularly used to describe Native Americans throughout this era, and this degrading moniker enabled settlers to justify all manner of ruthless behavior that was directed toward the native people. But, in order to deny that the Native American occupants of the continent were in any way civilized, it became necessary to promote the view that, prior to the arrival of Christopher

Columbus in 1492, there was no civilization whatsoever on the North American continent.

"No pre-Columbian civilization in North America" became essentially the official government policy at the federal level. This official view gave white European settlers, and the federal government, leeway needed to declare official sovereignty over all Native American lands. The Smithsonian, and the Bureau of Ethnology, became instruments of this policy because they were expected to scientifically buttress this bullshit policy.

The Smithsonian was founded in 1864 as a national repository for the prehistoric artifacts and skeletons (mostly giant) that were being steadily unearthed by European settlers. The very first Smithsonian publication was a report prepared by Squire and Davis, two of the earliest scientifically minded individuals to study the mound phenomenon as it existed continent-wide. Their view was that the mounds were created by a lost, prehistoric race that was in many ways superior to the indigenous people (Indians) of the time. Squire and Davis emphasized the fact that even the Indians themselves acknowledged that they did not build the mounds. This is still seen as true today. Indigenous Native Americans largely believe that the mounds and the giant skeletons that accompany them were already there when their ancestors arrived. Indeed, the mounds were seen as sacred sites, and the bones were respected and left undisturbed.

Meanwhile, lawmakers and policymakers needed support for the idea that the federal government was entitled to claim sovereignty over all historically tribal lands. They turned to the reigning scientific body, the Smithsonian, for quasi-scientific support. There, they found a sympathetic ear in John Wesley Powell, a Civil War veteran and famed explorer who headed the U.S. Geological Survey, then the Bureau of Ethnology at the newly minted Smithsonian Institution. Powell achieved fame as the original explorer of the Colorado River through Utah and then through the treacherous Grand Canyon in Arizona. This made him a bit of a national hero and, as founder of the Bureau of Ethnology in 1879, and a white guy, who spent a lot of time among various Indian tribes out west, he was seen as a national expert on Indian affairs.

As director of the Bureau of Ethnology, Powell was fully aware of the mountains of artifacts and the giant skeletons that were coming into the possession of the Smithsonian. Indeed, Powell delegated squads of Smithsonian-appointed collectors to actively collect these artifacts and skeletons before they were lost. Toward this end, Powell appointed Cyrus Thomas to direct the study of mounds and presumably the giant skeletons associated with them. Before he went to work for the Smithsonian, Thomas was a big supporter of the Lost Race origin of the mounds, as opposed to the view that the mounds were built by ancestors of the indigenous tribes.

It was Cyrus Thomas who was put in charge of the program to aggressively collect the giant skeletal material that was being constantly unearthed, with priority placed on the acquisition of the skulls. Yet, in the process of studying this material, numerous artifacts were acquired that contained linguistic references to European, Hebrew, and Asian cultures. Such artifacts (like the Newark Holy Stones of 1860) seemed to suggest that this Lost Race of giants were seafarers who had contact with other cultures, worldwide. This was an extremely dangerous suggestion if the view that Native Americans were savages was to be maintained. The Newark Holy Stones, with their Hebrew inscriptions, simply could not be reconciled with the official view that no pre-Columbian civilization existed in North America. This view was a necessary underpinning of the other official view that Manifest Destiny was justifiable and legitimate. Discoveries like the Newark Holy Stones were ultimately dismissed as fakes and hoaxes. Eventually, even Cyrus Thomas came around to Powell's view that the mounds were products of a simpler culture.

If John Wesley Powell was the first Smithsonian official to deny Native American claims to sovereignty, the director he appointed to succeed him finished the job. Ales Hrdlica (pronounced: 'ales' like the beer, herd-LICH-ka) did more than any other single individual to bolster the federal policy of denying Native Americans their claim not only to their sovereignty but also to their status as fully human beings.

One of the Newark Holy Stones with presumptive Hebrew inscription.

Hrdlicka, a Czech immigrant, was the first to develop the theory that all Native American tribes, in North and South America, colonized North America just three thousand years ago by way of the Bering Land Bridge. Hrdlicka was appointed the first curator of physical anthropology at the Smithsonian in 1903, and he was a guiding force in that eminent institution until he retired in 1942. Hrdlicka inherited all the skeletons and skulls that had been so dutifully collected by Powell and Thomas. It is a simple fact that, under his direction, all of the meticulously collected skeletal material that documented the ancient and giant race totally disappeared, never to be seen again. Why? Because Hrdlicka was a big proponent of the bogus concept of eugenics: the view that the Caucasian race was in some way superior to Indian or African races. Mind you, this is the very same idea that Hitler seized upon to justify his program of genocide. Many of the skeletons in the Smithsonian collection by 1915 suggested that the mound builders were not just a very tall race but a race with rather Caucasian features. This fact could be used to suggest that Native Americans shared a common ancestry with

European Caucasians, and artifacts like the Newark Holy Stones with the ancient Hebrew inscriptions further bolstered that view. Obviously, if ideas like Manifest Destiny and eugenics were going to hold water, the skeletons had to go away, and so they did.

To this day, the official view of ethnologists is that the mounds were constructed by the ancestors of the present Native American tribes, even though tribal members with historical knowledge dispute this. Authors Hugh Newman and Jim Vieira do see signs that the old-guard views are beginning to crumble in light of current discoveries and more reasoned thought. Specifically, Kennewick Man, found in a sand bar along the Columbia River in 1996, has helped force a long-overdue revision in the accepted view of the ancient history of North America. At first, it was said that the 9000-year-old skeleton had Caucasian features. Then, another anthropologist named Powell decided that it most closely resembled either members of the Ainu from coastal Japan or natives of Polynesia. In either case, the nearly complete skeleton was seen as further evidence of multiple migrations into North America, both by sea and by land.

It is refreshing to know that contemporary thinking in anthropology and archeology is finally recognizing the revolutionary but compelling data that goes back as far as two centuries. Yet, it is discouraging to read the equally compelling case that Newman and Vieira built to support the view that hundreds, maybe thousands of giant skeletons were systematically acquired by the Smithsonian, only to be destroyed. Just as interesting, and certainly more uplifting, is the picture that Vieira, Newman, and many others have assembled as to what the giant skeletons of the past are telling us about human history.

The first, and perhaps most important, contribution by these revisionist researchers is the view that humanity is much older than the so-called experts of our day have ever realized. Conventional thinking is largely of the view that humanity arrived in North America via Siberia and the Bering land bridge, but only in the aftermath of the Ice Age, 12-15 thousand years ago. Based on recent archeological finds, this number becomes laughable. In 1896, a skull was discovered in

Buenos Aires and inspected by Ales Hrdlicka himself. After a close examination of the skull and the geologic strata from which it originated, Hrdlicka had no choice but to agree that the rock layer it came from was 1.5 million years old. Hrdlicka examined yet another skull that looked way too modern to qualify as ancient in origin, though it too was dug from a rock layer in Argentina that bore an estimated age of 3-5 million years old.

Fossilized skull fragments and leg bones from New Jersey were extracted from a rock layer that was dated at 107,000 years old, which predates the oldest human bones ever found in Africa by at least 7,000 years. This too was shown to Hrdlicka, who endorsed the authenticity of the find, though he did so without knowing the age of the rock layer it came from. Hrdlicka might not have been so quick to endorse the find if he had known the approximate age of the rock layer. Remember, Hrdlicka espoused the view that nobody lived in North America until the first paleo-Americans arrived via the Bering land bridge just three thousand years ago. Long after Hrdlicka's death, the date of the New Jersey find was placed at 107,000 years old.

Numerous other finds in North and South America support the view that humans have been in the new world much longer than previously thought. Newman and Vieira even go so far as to suggest North American skeletal remains are so old that it is possible humanity may have actually originated right here in North America. Rather than migrating *to* North America in relatively recent times as we have always been taught, humanity may have arisen from Homo erectus in the New World first, *then* spread out to other parts of the world. Several recent findings are used to support this view. Sandia Cave in New Mexico has produced finely made stone tools and arrowheads that were dated at 250,000 years. Other tool finds in Calico, southern California and Toca da Esperanca, Brazil have similarly been dated over 200,000 years ago. Meanwhile, academians continue to insist that humans arose from Homo erectus ancestors only 100,000 years ago.

And then there are the finds like the 13,000-year-old female skull from near Mexico City with distinctly Caucasian features. Patagonia has also produced skulls that were not only giant in proportion but Caucasian in appearance. Giant skeletons with Caucasian features have been exhumed from the Channel Island off California. Giant skeletons and dozens more giant skeletons with red hair were taken from Lovelock Cave in Nevada. Many tribes in the northeast U.S. have European features. Chief Joseph of the Nez Perce tribe in present-day Idaho insisted some of his ancestors were white. His most cherished possession was a pendent that bore Mesopotamian cuneiform inscriptions. He said it had been passed down from his ancestors.

Cro-Magnon skulls from America also pre-date what is thought to be the first arrival of Cro-Magnons in Europe, some 40,000 years ago. Cro-Magnon skeletons are more robust than Homo sapiens, topping out at more than seven feet tall. A Cro-Magnon skull from Sunnyvale, California, was dated 70,000 years old, and stone tools from the U.S. that were dated 48,000 years match or exceed the age of the oldest tools found in Europe.

All these new finds have forced anthropologists to consider some completely different ideas about how humanity originated and how they eventually spread out. Werner Mueller suggests in his 1990 book that Cro-Magnons, along with another race of tall, bearded Caucasians migrated to Europe from North America about 44,000 years ago. Another researcher, Jeffery Goodman, Ph.D., has long argued that humans originated in North America before spreading out to Europe as well as Asia. He claims that DNA analysis shows a match between ancient Neanderthals in Europe, Denisovans in Siberia, and modern humans in the New World.

Just as revolutionary as the new thinking about dates, the new thinking about these early humans is really strange. The giant skeletons found throughout the continent suggest that the first Paleo-Indians in North America were Caucasian, not Mongolian in origin. Anthropologists were coming to this conclusion as far back as the 1940s. Bear in mind that the term 'Caucasian,' as it has been used in anthropology circles, refers to skull and bone features, not skin color. Caucasian features are seen in human populations in Africa, Asia, and Europe.

Many Native American tribes have legends of interacting with what they usually call the Tall Ones. They didn't always get along. There are stories of wars with the Tall Ones, but they were also seen at times as very helpful, and even god-like. Eventually, the Tall Ones are said to have died out, gone to the clouds, or "resumed their form as thunderbirds." Some tribes have legends describing the ability of the Tall Ones to completely change form.

It is this god-like status afforded to the Tall Ones in Native American oral histories that causes me, and even some academics, to wonder about the origins of the Tall Ones. Over and over, new evidence is being found that suggests that the race of giants was very advanced in many ways. The mounds and the artifacts that they have produced show that the giants, rather than the later-arriving average-sized Indians, built the mounds. Giant skeletons are inextricably linked to the mounds. Native American oral histories are in complete agreement on this. As previously stated, they say their ancestors did not build the mounds. The giants did. Then the giants went away. Cherokee legend states that the tall, "moon-faced" white people were forced to relocate to underground residences as more and more Native Americans moved into the region. This took place about the same time that the mega-fauna disappeared 13,000 years ago (around the time of the Younger Dryas Event).

When they were around, the giants produced tools, artistic pieces, and earthen structures that show high degrees of sophistication in agriculture, mathematics, and astronomy, as well as more shamanic matters like magic. Other North American tribal legends assert that the Sasquatch are similarly talented medicine men who live underground. Tribal stories, unverifiable as they may be, describe tall ones who could control weather, control crop fertility, speed up plant growth, and do lots of other neat shamanic tricks. In the Southwest, Pueblo Indians and their ancestors, the Anasazi, speak of lizard-like "Ant People" who reside underground. They can cross realms through the Sipapu, which is a small hole in the circular kiva structures that are found in virtually all cliff dwellings and pueblos throughout the Southwest.

Now, the thinking is coming around to embracing the idea that the mounds themselves are capable of imparting energies that do things like improving the fertility of seeds. Vieira and Newman found a newspaper account from 1903 describing corn kernels found sealed in a jar next to a giant, eight-foot skeleton buried *sixty feet deep* in the soil of Kentucky. Just digging a grave that deep is a remarkable feat, but when the seeds were unsealed and planted, they grew exceptionally well. Consequently, the original seeds, as well as the seeds of the offspring, were distributed among the local farmers.

Researchers John Burke and Kaj Halberg had heard so many stories about seed fertility and magnetism associated with mounds that they decided to test the idea. During the 1990s, they put many different types of seed in proximity to mounds and found that they could indeed measure an improvement in crop yield, frost hardiness, disease resistance, and, of course, overall plant size. Mind you, crop circle researchers have found the same thing to be true for seeds taken from plants that are laid down inside crop glyphs. Also, like crop circles, the Burke and Halberg experiments yielded strong indications that the mounds and megalithic sites had perceptible effects on feelings of well-being, consciousness, and vagaries that mainstream scientists want absolutely nothing to do with.

Not being shy about floating speculative thoughts, Vieira and Newman even suggest that the mounds may have so much telluric energy that they were used to enhance not only the size of plants, but the size of giant people as well. If true, then the ancestors of the giants created the mounds, and then the mounds created the giants. Some work done by a few Japanese researchers shows an increase in animal size when the same critters are exposed to extremely low frequency (ELF) electromagnetic force (EMF). The Japanese researchers also point out that pulsed EMF has been used for many years to treat skeletal disorders like delayed fracture healing and non-unions. EMFs also appear to help *in vitro* bone growth.

Quetzalcoatl as represented in Mayan stone sculpture.

Vieira and Newman persuasively argue that the giants who built the mounds knew that they harnessed the geomagnetic energies of the earth, creating concentrations of natural magnetism that enhanced plant growth, human growth, longevity, and other matters relating to human consciousness and spiritual well-being. This potent power, sometimes called the Orenda principle, is mentioned by Burke and Halberg as a possible explanation for the impressive stature of the Tall Ones in North America as well as other places around the globe. They observe that tall, robust, and intellectually advanced humans existed in many places globally as recently as 5 or 6,000 years ago, though these attributes have been gradually absorbed into and, to some extent, exterminated from modern society.

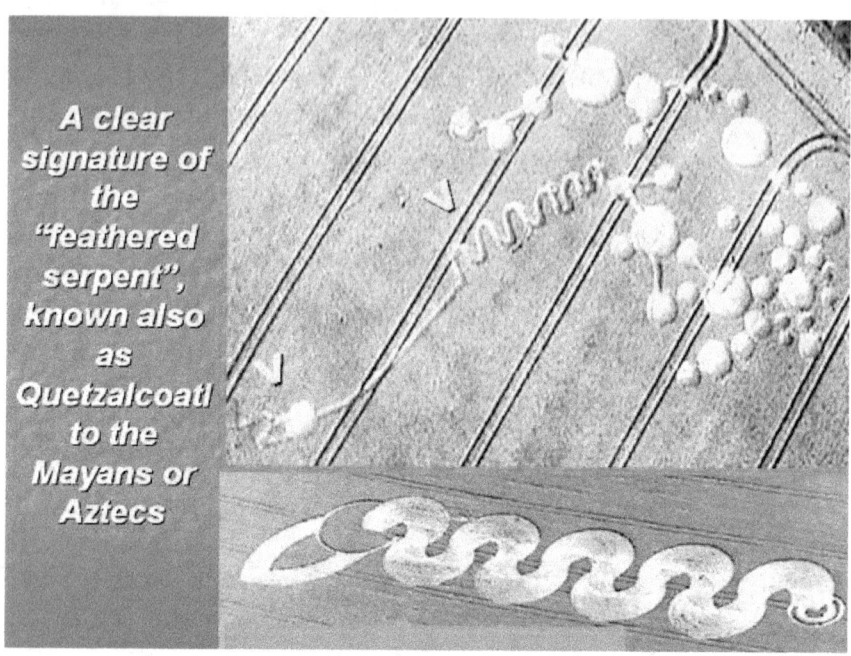

A clear signature of the "feathered serpent", known also as Quetzalcoatl to the Mayans or Aztecs

Then there are the theorists of the 'ancient alien' point of view. They see these Caucasian giants as a set of super-powerful beings that came to Earth from somewhere else. The Mayans of Mesoamerica worshipped a deity named Quetzalcoatl, who is/was tall, pale-skinned, and bearded. Quetzalcoatl was a super-powerful being who also preached a message of love and forgiveness that is very consistent with modern Christianity. Quetzalcoatl was basically a Jesus figure, though he also liked to disguise himself as a serpent or snake. Quetzalcoatl was known to be very tricky and had a keen sense of humor. There are also Bible scholars who insist that Jesus himself was tall and very Caucasian in appearance, which, at risk of blasphemy, suggests that Jesus was one of the Tall Ones. Interestingly, many Native American tribes also have descriptions of a tall, bearded, pale-faced male who went around preaching love and forgiveness. Either Jesus was exceptionally busy and well-traveled, or there were multiple Jesuses: A veritable race of tall, pale-skinned, bearded prophets who tasked themselves with improving the spirituality of the emerging human race.

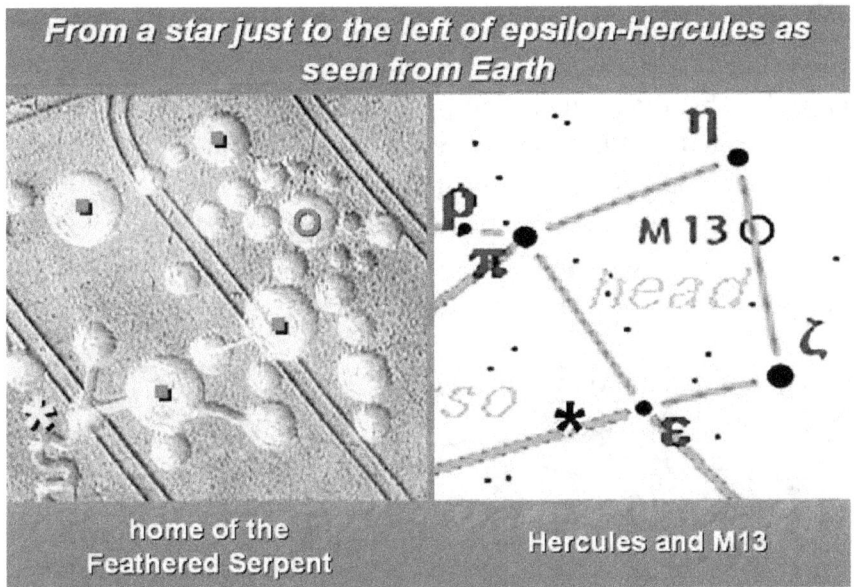

From a star just to the left of epsilon-Hercules as seen from Earth

home of the Feathered Serpent

Hercules and M13

Beyond the simple suggestion that the Tall Ones, including Jesus and/or Quetzalcoatl, came from somewhere off the planet, there is a further suggestion that these benevolent beings may have originated from either M-13 or the star Epsilon-Herculis, both found in the constellation Hercules which also happened to be the target constellation for the Arecibo transmission of 1974 by Carl Sagan and Frank Drake (Chapter 4).

The reader might wish to know from where this suggestion came that the Tall Ones in general, and Quetzalcoatl in particular originate from a star seen from Earth to be in the constellation Hercules? From crop circles, that's where.

A strange crop circle appeared in West Overton, England, on July 28, 2002. It was decoded by Dr. Horace Drew and others to be a bit of a star map featuring the constellation Hercules. Also included in the glyph was a feathered serpent, a very clear reference to the Mayan deity, Quetzalcoatl. Not only is the feathered serpent inserted into the star map, which is quite plainly the constellation Hercules, but the serpent could be construed as pointing to a specific place in the map, and that is a small star just to the left of epsilon-Herculis.

Serpent-like images are among the most common of crop forma-
tions, but rarely are the serpent references as specific as the one
depicting the feathered serpent pointing directly at the specific location in Hercules. This seems too strange to be a mere coincidence.
Interestingly, another star in the next constellation over is Vega, in the
constellation Lyre. It is one of the brightest and the most studied stars
in the sky, after the Sun. While it looks close to M-13 from Earth's
perspective, Vega is actually nowhere near M-13.

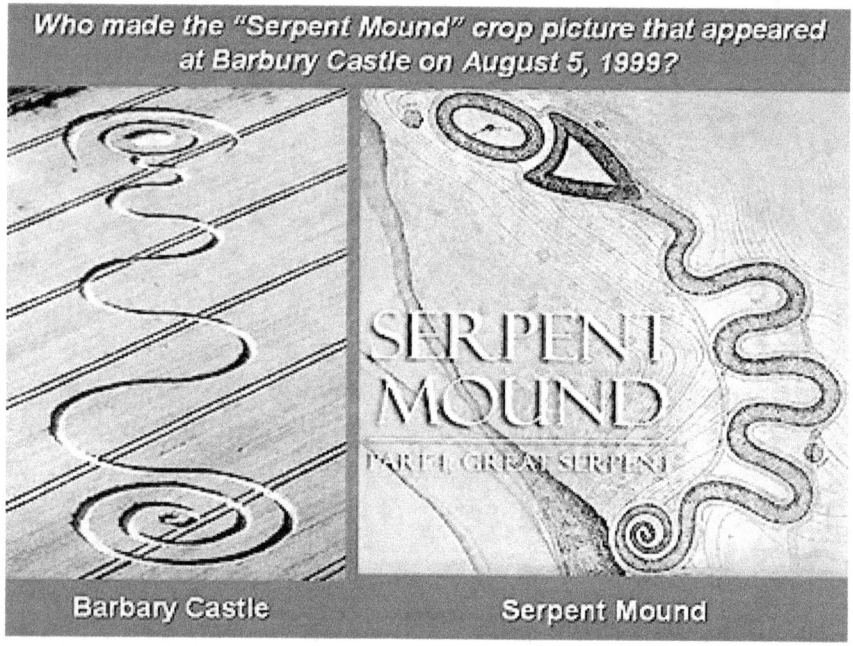

Vega is a star in our own galaxy that is only 27 light years away,
making it one of the closer stars to us. M-13, on the other hand, is an
entirely different galaxy of stars, albeit a small one (known as a star
cluster). It's a whopping 25,000 lightyears away. Despite their vast
differences in distance, they just happen to line up as part of two
neighboring constellations, as seen from Earth. What's interesting is
the fact that Sagan used Vega as a plot element in his book *Contact*,
which was posthumously made into a movie starring Jodie Foster and
Matthew McConaughey. The book and the movie treat the question

40

of how first contact with an alien civilization might unfold. Vega was likely chosen by Sagan because it was one of the first stars ever found to contain either planets or, more likely, protoplanets (planets still forming).

Still, more curiously, other serpent references appear in crop circles, and one in particular is worth noting. A serpent image appeared in the crops in the proximity of Barbury Castle on August 5th of 1997. What is remarkable about this particular glyph is the similarity it bears to an effigy mound in southern Ohio called the Serpent Mound. Effigy mounds are earthen mounds built in the shape of animals or other specific objects. The Sphinx in Egypt is an effigy in that it hearkens to a specific being, albeit sort of a hybrid one. The Serpent Mound, in Adams County, Ohio, near Dayton, is the largest animal effigy mound in the world, measuring over a thousand feet along its serpentine shape. Southern Ohio is rich with mounds of various descriptions, and historically, they have all been attributed to a couple of local tribes, one called the Edena and another called Hopewell.

Native American historians have long disputed this simplistic suggestion, which is often cited as the kind of lazy archeology that has been used to over-simplify historical mysteries like that of the mound builders. Hopewell, after all, was a Civil War sergeant for the Confederacy who resettled in Ohio. His farm had some mounds that produced some artifacts that led to his name being used to describe a purported Indian tribe that was then credited with building half the mounds found in the state of Ohio and beyond. The idea that the Edena and the Hopewell tribes built all the mounds, or even any of them, has been largely discredited. This same conventional archeological thinking dates the mounds of Ohio to about 1200 A.D. for poorly supported reasons. Historians of the Iroquois Nation, who occupied much of Ohio when the first European settlers arrived, dispute this view. Many other revisionist scholars agree with the view that the mounds, as they occur region-wide, are many thousands of years old, and maybe tens of thousands of years.

Skeleton of Mound Builder, 7 ft. in length, Serpent Mound,   Peebles, Ohio.

In any case, the Serpent Mound is one of the most spectacular and the most mysterious of all North American mounds. The alignment of the various segments of the serpent mound points precisely to the location of the Sun and Moon during significant astronomical events like solstices and equinoxes. Consequently, some see the

Serpent Mound as a sort of agricultural calendar used to suggest seasonal planting schedules.

The Serpent Mound does bear complex and precise alignments with the behavior of the Sun and Moon, but I favor the view of those like Vieira and Newman who see mounds not just in terms of their orientation with astronomical objects, but with respect to a more important orientation with the magnetic lines of force that crisscross the Earth's landscape.

Still other oddities surround the Serpent Mound. A giant skeleton (above) was found in one of the three mounds shown in this old illustration of the Serpent Mound (left). Despite the fact that the lower leg bones (tibia and fibula) as well as all carpals, metacarpals, and phalanges (feet bones) were destroyed in the process of exhuming the skeleton, it still measured 7′2″. If all the bones had been recovered, the skeleton would have been two feet taller. This skeleton was probably turned over to the Smithsonian and lost (or destroyed), but it was photographed beforehand, and miraculously, the photo survived the ravages of time and was found by modern researcher Jeffery Wilson. The Serpent Mound skeleton establishes a strong connection between two separate mysteries:

I. The origin of the mounds in general and the Serpent Mound in particular, and,

2. The numerous skeletal remains (mostly concealed or destroyed) that document the race of giants or Tall Ones that is also recognized in Native American lore.

The close association of the skeleton that was photo-documented before it was lost and the mysterious and remarkable Serpent Mound is stirring, but the surprises do not end there. We must also factor in a crop glyph that appeared in a barley field in England on August 5,1997, near Barbury Castle. This crop glyph from the other side of the planet is important because it bears a striking similarity to the Serpent Mound, complete with the coiled tail, serpentine body, and a head that could be seen as devouring an egg. This English crop glyph is today known as the Serpent Mound crop glyph.

A soybean crop picture was seen as "lights in the sky" the night before it appeared on the ground, near Serpent Mound in Ohio on August 23-24, 2003

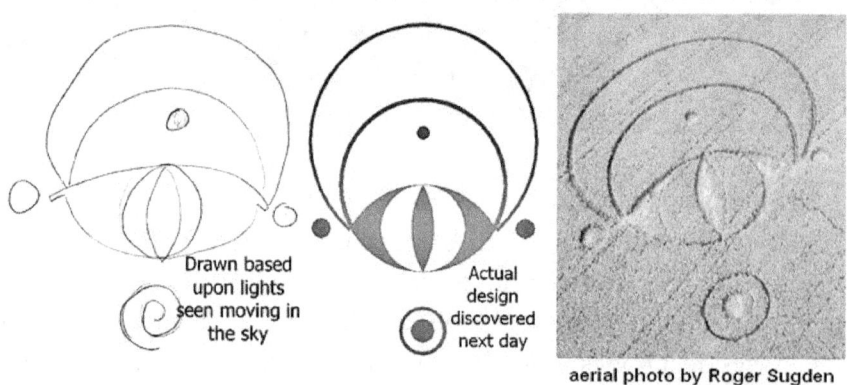

aerial photo by Roger Sugden and Jeffrey Wilson

Why did this important observation not become widely known in 2003? In a private message, Ms. Tree Pruitt explained: "Yes, we really did witness those lights over the field that night, before the design appeared on the ground. I tried to report it at the time, but local news media were not interested."

In the previous chapter, I endorsed the view that crop glyphs are indeed manifestations of off-planeters or possibly subterranean entities. If so, these same off-planeters are using the 1997 Serpent Mound crop glyph in England to direct our attention to the Serpent Mound itself, half a world away, along Brush Creek in Adams County, Ohio. Bear in mind that other serpent motifs appear in crop circles, and at least some of them are probable references to Quetzalcoatl, the Mayan deity and Jesus equivalent. Is it possible that the Serpent Mound is also a reference to the Mayan deity, Quetzalcoatl? I certainly think so, and I will go even further and assert that the crop circle image of 1997 found at Barbury Castle, and the 2003 feathered serpent crop glyph that points to the star in Hercules are all clues in this same mystery, that is, pieces of the same puzzle.

To strengthen this admittedly strange case, another bizarre event needs to be considered: A UFO was seen in the sky over southern Ohio by a Ms. Tree Pruitt, while she was at the Serpent Mound preserve. She drew the object she saw in the sky, which does not resemble any of the traditional UFO shapes like saucers or cigars. She also attempted to report the sighting, but the news media was not interested.

The object Tree Pruitt saw was drawn immediately after the event and is shown below. The center sketch is a generalized view of what she reported. The following day, the identical shape appeared in a soybean field along the opposite bank of Brush Creek, a short distance from the Serpent Mound (see photo below).

It suddenly seems difficult to dismiss all these events as coincidental. What I'm seeing instead is an invitation to draw a connection between crop circles, the Serpent Mound (and maybe mounds in general as they occur worldwide), the UFO phenomenon, the mound-builder giants, and Quetzalcoatl, the feathered serpent and Jesus-like deity of Mayan culture, and his/their potential home star in the constellation Hercules.

Add the geologic fact that Adams County, Ohio, where the Serpent Mound rests, is underlain with limestone bedrock. Limestone bedrock, being water soluble, tends to be riddled with caves. As with the crop circles of England, it seems barely possible that the creators of the crop circle in southern Ohio might not have traveled very far to create it. They could be living much nearer to the Serpent

Mound than a star in Hercules. Given the cave potential of the under-lying bedrock, they could be occupying underground caverns in the immediate vicinity of the place where the crop circle appeared.

Another curious geologic fact is worth considering here. The Serpent Mound sits on the edge of a pretty large asteroid impact crater. Lots of rare elements occur in the landscape in that immediate area as a consequence of this ancient impact that is thought to have happened 320 million years ago. Might these rare elements be of interest to some off-planeters who are comfortably ensconced in the immediate vicinity of the Serpent Mound? Might the Serpent Mound itself be a marker that indicates the approximate location of an underground redoubt, like a street address we put out on the mail box so visitors can find our house? Call me crazy, but that is where I end up. It appears to me that we are following something like a trail of breadcrumbs that leads us to a disturbing but inescapable conclusion: Off-planeters are here, they have been here for a long time, and probably operated openly as the Tall Ones in ancient times. For some reason, they chose to remove themselves from view but not vacate the planet altogether. Perhaps they were busy constructing a set of subterranean enclaves all along, and once they were finally ready, they retreated from the surface and moved into their new digs (literally, digs). They are leaving us clues all over the place, but they're patiently waiting for us to mature and solve the mystery that we have been handed.

3

THE GREAT PYRAMID OF TANSTAAFL

If you repeat a lie often enough and loud enough, people will eventually accept it as truth.

Every dictator knows this well. Hitler made this exact point in his autobiographical manifesto, *Mein Kampf*. But this truism doesn't just apply to politics. It is equally applicable in science, especially archaeology, where modern researchers attempt to explain the actions and intentions of ancient cultures on the basis of scant information.

In fairness, it's not necessarily a lie that is being promulgated; it's just an error, a mistaken conclusion. By virtue of frequent repetition, the mistake becomes an accepted fact. An example of an error that has become accepted 'fact' is the view that the Great Pyramid of Giza, and other smaller pyramids, were built as *burial chambers*.

Aside from the Great Pyramid, also known as the Great Pyramid of Giza or the Pyramid of Khufu, there are about eighty other pyramids in Egypt. Pyramids are also found in other countries on four other continents. There is even a pyramid-shaped mountain in Antarctica that some feel is not natural. This has yet to be fully explored for obvious reasons.

The Great Pyramid of Giza is, however, the largest of all stone pyramids anywhere on Earth. Earthen pyramids may also exist. A cluster of 'flatiron' hills in central Bosnia is alleged by Semir Osmanagic to be earthen pyramids that dwarf the volume of the Great Pyramid. His claims are widely disputed, but the "Monk's Mound' in southern Illinois is a flat-topped earthen structure that is bigger at its base than the Great Pyramid and is quite definitely not a natural feature. No earthen structure, though, comes anywhere close to being the stunning achievement that is the Great Pyramid; the only one of the Seven Wonders of the Ancient World that still stands. Indeed, the Great Pyramid of Khufu (the Greeks called him Cheops) is the largest, most accurately built, and most precisely aligned structure ever built anywhere on Earth. Its base covers thirteen acres. It contains 2.3 million blocks of limestone and granite. The individual stone blocks range from two to seventy tons. The bulk of the pyramid was built with limestone blocks that were quarried only a couple miles across the Nile from Giza. The red granite that makes up the base and the central interior came from a quarry that is a jaw-dropping 500 miles distant.

How was this incredible structure built? Who built it, when was it built, and most importantly, why? These are all open questions. There are generally accepted answers to all of these questions that are probably wrong. Age estimates for the Great Pyramid vary from 73,000 years ago at the outside to 4,800 years ago at the least. Almost all Egyptologists accept the lower number, but there are several reasons to suspect the Great Pyramid is much older. Who built it? We are told it must have been Khufu, the same king who expected to be buried there. Probably not, but this is what I learned in school. What was the labor force? "Slaves," is the time-honored answer. Whether the labor force involved was slaves or hired masons, the construction of the largest pyramids must have taken multiple generations if the materials were extracted, moved, shaped, and placed by primitive means. Using the most modern methods available today, just quarrying and moving that amount of stone would require at least thirty-five years. Since the scope of this project seems so far beyond the capabilities of a bronze-age culture, it is sometimes suggested that the pyramids, especially the biggest ones, were built by alien super beings.

Obviously, mainstream archeologists cringe at such suggestions, instead claiming that the pyramids were either willingly or forcibly built by highly organized Egyptians as burial chambers for their beloved rulers. A troubling fact does remain that has been downplayed for centuries. Excavations in the eighty known pyramids of Egypt have never yielded the remains of an ancient monarch (also known as an 'original burial'). A few were found to contain mummified remains, but not of royalty. None were adorned elaborately. The mummies found also proved to be far too recent to have been put there at the time that the pyramids were built, even if the later 4400 B.C. date is applied. In 1837, sixty sets of mummified remains were discovered under the Step Pyramid near Giza. These remains were traced to the Saite Period (663-525 B.C.) which was at least 4000 years after construction. It is thought that during this time, it was popular to inter remains in pyramids that had been built thousands of years earlier.

When asked, "Why are no kings and queens found in the pyramids?" The archaeologists' answer is always, 'grave robbers.' There *were* mummies of monarchs inside or beneath them once upon a time, we are told, but they were stolen along with the wealth and artworks that accompanied them. Why thieves seeking gold and jewels would take the bodies is not at all clear. Valuable artifacts are an understandable target of thieves, but why mess with human remains that have no market value and might even bring some very bad ju-ju to anyone who possessed them? Even some early archaeologists felt they were cursed for having removed remains from the Valley of the Kings.

The view that the pyramids are tombs was first suggested by

Herodotus in ancient Greece. Yet, not everyone who studied the pyramids was in agreement. Charles Piazzi Smyth, British astronomer, artist, author, and Egyptologist, studied the Great Pyramid in great detail. He made the first photographs of the interior, meticulously measured every detail, and published six books on the subject in his lifetime. Among Egyptologists, he was a maverick for various reasons, including the fact that, as early as 1880, he doubted his colleagues' view that the Great Pyramid was a tomb. "The facts are numerously against them," he famously stated.

Yet the 'pyramids as tombs' view persisted and items in the pyramids, particularly in the Great Pyramid, were cited as supporting evidence. For example, in the King's Chamber, deep in the center of the Great Pyramid, lies a magnificently constructed, one-piece granite box that has been labeled 'The Sarcophagus.' In this massive stone box, we are told, once lay the mummified remains of Khufu, until his remains were stolen in the middle-ages. No evidence supports this speculative assumption, there just are not any other obvious reasons why this empty stone vessel rests deep inside the Great Pyramid. In a bit of circular logic, it is supposed that if the Great Pyramid was a tomb, then the box in its center must be the sarcophagus where the king's remains were placed, and if the pyramid contains a thing called a sarcophagus, then the pyramid, by definition, must be a tomb.

If it befits a king, the tomb should contain not only a mummy but ornate decorations, lots of hieroglyphics, and lots of gold. There are no decorative hieroglyphics, valuables, or decorations in the Great Pyramid. By comparison, hundreds of miles south of Giza lies the Valley of Kings, where many mummified remains of royalty *were* found in highly ornate chambers festooned with fantastic frescos portraying ancient culture and history. Perfectly intact royal mummies like Tutankhamun were discovered and exhumed. Maybe there wasn't as much grave robbing as we were led to believe. Even pyramids that stood completely intact and sealed since antiquity, and there are some, had no mummies, no art, and no valuables inside them.

One modern researcher, Tom Danley, observed that not only are there no decorations in the Great Pyramid, but the interior of the Great Pyramid has an 'all business' interior of austere efficiency that is more reminiscent of a modern production facility. After careful study, Danley and others observed that the Great Pyramid's numerous passageways and chambers were, in many cases, unnecessary. Even early Egyptologists recognized this. It was hilariously suggested by the experts of the time that Khufu just could not make up his mind about where he wanted to spend eternity. New chambers and passageways were built each time he changed his mind! (His building crews must have been very flexible.)

To engineers like Christopher Dunn and others, the passageways and their peculiar orientation suggested a more practical, even technical purpose. They only made sense if the Great Pyramid was built to perform in some sophisticated way. The more carefully they looked, the more the whole structure came to resemble modern power plants. 'Passageways' became conduits for chemicals, liquids, and gasses that were being combined and concentrated in reaction chambers, not burial chambers. These engineers identified numerous features that supported this radical idea. They were left with the inescapable conclusion that the intended purpose of the Great Pyramid was to produce some form of electromagnetic energy. From a purely engineering perspective, the structure's location, orientation, and design were intended to transduce (convert and amplify) vibration energies from the Earth into microwave energy.

To back up a bit, we are told the Earth produces vibrations that we cannot feel or hear. These vibrations are produced by tectonic forces, which are, in turn, produced by motions of the molten interior combined with the pull of the Moon's gravity. The Moon exerts a tidal pull not only on the oceans but also on the Earth's land masses. The land does not move much in response to the Moon's gravity, but it does rise as much as one foot when the Moon is directly overhead. Any structure on that oscillating land mass should also rise and fall slightly under the pull of the Moon's gravity. If that structure were super-massive, then the energy involved in the rising and falling of the structure and the land beneath it would be maximized. While the energy associated with these crustal movements may seem tiny, when it is multiplied by the mass of the continents combined, it is potentially enormous. If a super-massive structure can be added that can also collect, concentrate, and distribute that energy, then we just may be able to produce clean, sustainable energy.

The design and location details of the Great Pyramid do seem to support the view that the structure had such a specific purpose. The dimensions of the Great Pyramid bear a close relationship to the dimensions of the Earth itself. A few fundamental Earth measurements are incorporated into the Great Pyramid's dimensions.

1. The perimeter of the Great Pyramid is equal to half of one minute of equatorial longitude. That means that the perimeter of the Great Pyramid is equal to 1/43,200th of the circumference of the Earth at the equator.
2. The height of the Great Pyramid is equal to 1/43,200th of the polar radius (a line from the center of the Earth to the North Pole.)

Still others are provided in the following graphic (From Dunn's *Giza Power Plant*):

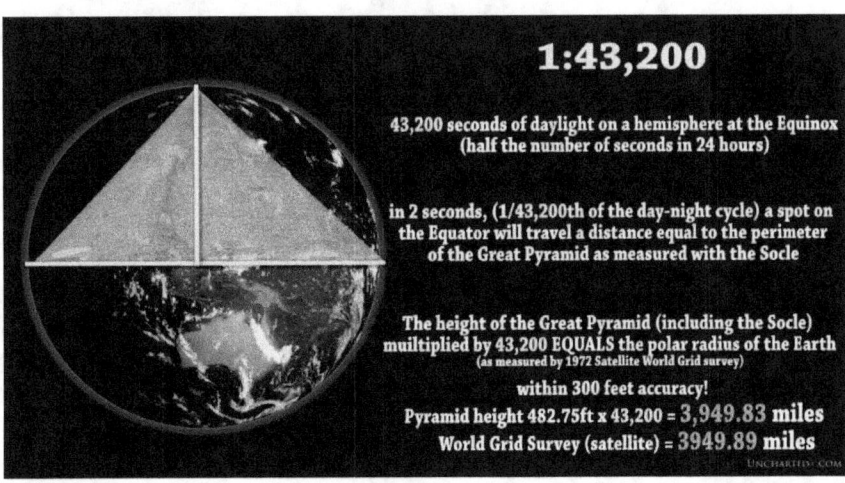

1:43,200

43,200 seconds of daylight on a hemisphere at the Equinox
(half the number of seconds in 24 hours)

in 2 seconds, (1/43,200th of the day-night cycle) a spot on the Equator will travel a distance equal to the perimeter of the Great Pyramid as measured with the Socle

The height of the Great Pyramid (including the Socle) muiltiplied by 43,200 EQUALS the polar radius of the Earth
(as measured by 1972 Satellite World Grid survey)

within 300 feet accuracy!
Pyramid height 482.75ft x 43,200 = 3,949.83 **miles**
World Grid Survey (satellite) = 3949.89 **miles**

UNCHARTED.COM

There are other numerological curiosities, some of them quite complex, involving the mass of the Great Pyramid, the angle of the sloping faces, and more. What is not complex is that the location of the Great Pyramid lies at the exact geographic center of the Earth's combined land masses. The Great Pyramid is also, for some reason, perfectly aligned with what would have been the true north pole of the planet at the approximate time of its construction. (The location of the North Pole shifts slightly over time.)

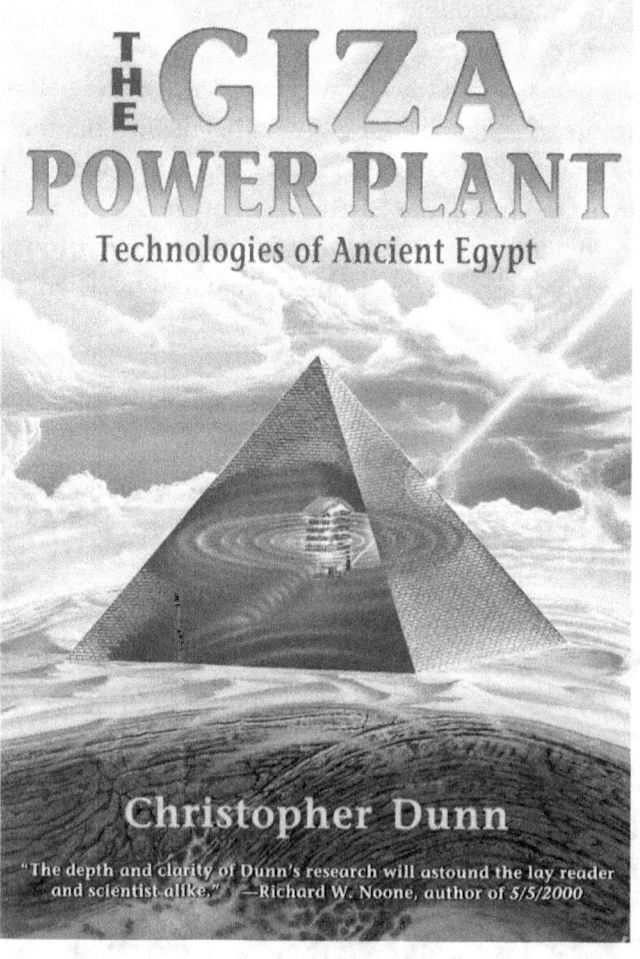

As to why the dimensions and location of the Great Pyramid

correlate so closely with the dimensions of the Earth, it would seem that either the ancient Egyptians were trying to show off their precise understanding of the dimensions of the planet, or they designed and located the Great Pyramid because factoring in the Earth's dimensions and polarity when designing it facilitated the function of that structure. Conversely, if the Great Pyramid were simply a tomb, then the builders went to all this trouble for purely aesthetic reasons. Considering the staggering enormity of the project and the unnecessarily precise and redundant architectural details, the view that it was all done for aesthetic reasons becomes a bit of a stretch. It behooves us to at least search for some more practical and technical 'raison d'etre' than royal burial.

A particularly well-developed theory can be found in Christopher Dunn's book, *The Giza Power Plant*. Dunn, an electrical engineer who has visited the Great Pyramid many times, has a thorough knowledge of all the known passageways and chambers. He speculates that the Great Pyramid was indeed designed and built to tap into Earth's energies and use them as a source of electromagnetic energy. This view is supported by the recent understanding that the Earth is a dynamic body that vibrates with tremendous energy that we cannot see or feel. This energy can, in theory, be accessed, focused, and harnessed. How the ancient Egyptians could have known what modern engineers have come to realize only recently is another open question. Either they were more sophisticated than we're giving them credit for, or they were directed by others who were.

It defies conventional thinking to assert that an ancient culture understood transducing Earth's energies into electricity or microwaves. Modern humans understand how to do it in theory but we've not yet been able to put that theory into practice. Even with outside help, if the Egyptians were in command of such marvels of engineering, why and when was that knowledge lost?

The design of the Great Pyramid suggests that someone back then knew how to build what we now call a coupled oscillator, an object (the Great Pyramid) in harmonic resonance with a much larger object (the Earth). This coupled oscillator would draw energy from the larger source by harmoniously vibrating with it. The fact that the Great Pyramid was built as a mathematic integer of the Earth and centered perfectly on these vibrating continental landmasses does support the radical idea that the pyramid was built to vibrate in harmony with fundamental terrestrial frequencies.

Besides Dunn, two acoustic engineers endorse this view. Tom Danley performed an acoustic analysis of the King's Chamber, which is located in the center of the pyramid's enormous mass. Robert Vawter, another acoustic engineer, is similarly convinced that the King's Chamber was designed specifically to resonate with acoustic frequencies from the Earth. The source of these frequencies is indeed seismic energies that emanate from within the Earth's crust, but the ultimate source of these frequencies traces to the Moon's gravitational field.

The Moon's proper name is Luna, as distinguished from the many other moons in the solar system that circulate around the various planets. Luna is quite unique in its proportions. It is the second largest of all moons (Titan around Saturn is bigger), but no other moon comes close to rivaling the size of the planet it orbits. Consequently, no other planet is as dramatically affected by the pull of its moon as is the Earth.

Another relatively new realization is that the Moon's gravity is thought to be a big driving force behind the tectonic movement of the Earth's crust. Only Earth has this inexorable tectonic movement that pushes whole continents around, perhaps because only the Earth receives so strong a gravitational tug from its moon. Venus has no moons, Mercury has no moons, Mars has two tiny moons, and the outer planets all have lots of tiny moons compared to the size of the parent planets. Only Pluto has a proportionately large moon compared to its size, although it is now thought that Pluto is mostly ice and, therefore, not really a planet at all. Venus and Mars have volcanoes that bleed off heat from within their respective planets, but they do not have large-scale crustal movements as Earth does. Not only can such motions yield energies that can be harnessed, but drawing off this energy would also remove some of the seismic energy that otherwise builds up until destructive earthquakes result.

In this cross-section of the Great Pyramid, we see the center chamber that has long been called the King's Chamber. Here lies the sarcophagus in which it is said Khufu was laid to rest. Beneath the King's Chamber and connected by indirect passageways is the Queen's Chamber. As the name implies, this is ostensibly the resting place of Khufu's wife and queen. (Apparently, early archaeologists did not think it strange that the king and queen would choose to spend eternity in separate bedrooms.) Further, the Queen's Chamber is coated with a chemical residue that defies easy explanation. The earliest explorers of the pyramids noticed strong chemical smells, most notably sulfur, in some of the passages below the Queen's Chamber.

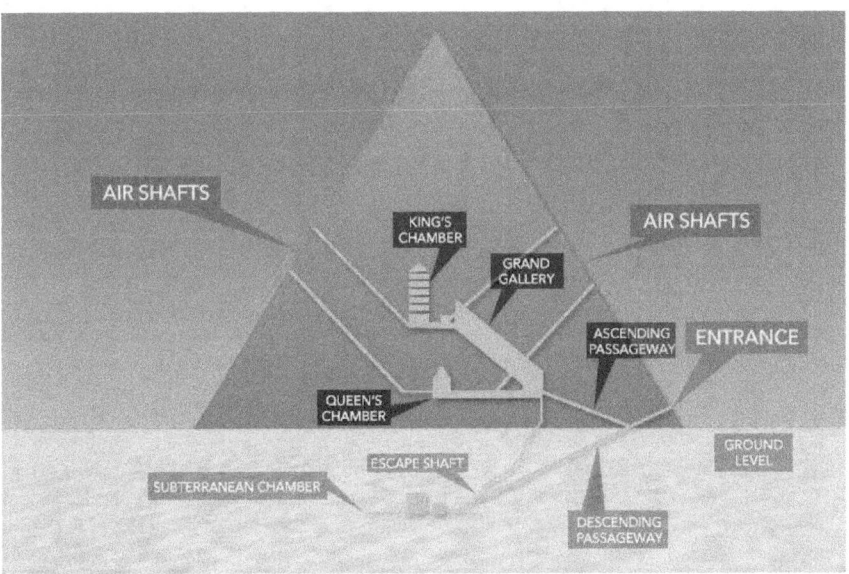

Then there are all the other intersecting passageways and, most curious of all, the Grand Gallery. The Grand Gallery was decided to be a ceremonial chamber and access point for the burial parties. The descending and ascending passageways were 'air vents' even though some of them were dead ends. Again, nothing more than a change in plans.

As with the King's Chamber, one would expect to see lots of decorations in the Grand Gallery if it was indeed the burial party's ceremonial chamber, as most Egyptologists conclude. Instead of decorations, what is found in the Grand Gallery is a steeply inclined, narrow chamber with corbeled walls and a high ceiling. At the base of these walls lie two parallel rows of twenty-seven carefully placed notches. These evenly spaced notches must have had a purpose, but those who view the pyramid as a tomb have no idea what that purpose might have been.

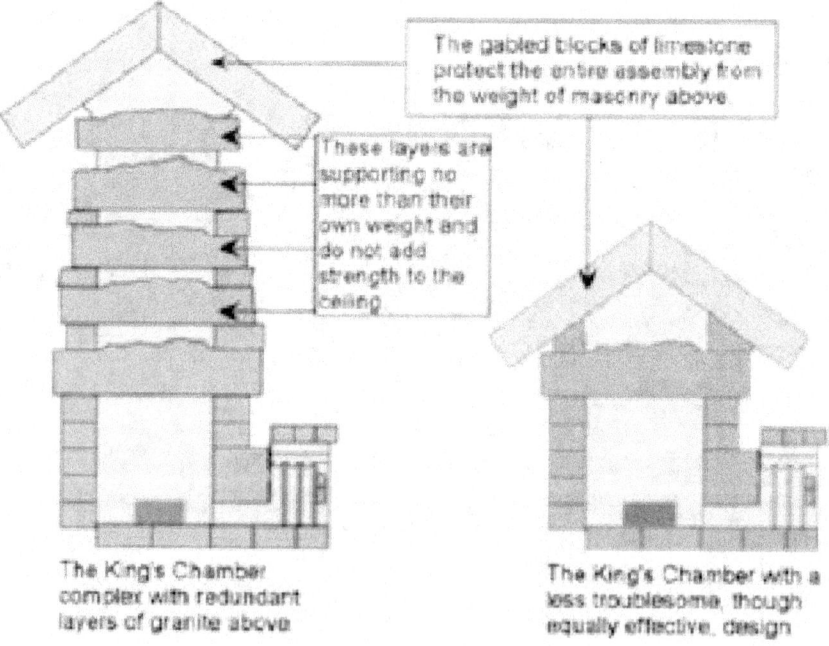

The gabled blocks of limestone protect the entire assembly from the weight of masonry above.

These layers are supporting no more than their own weight and do not add strength to the ceiling.

The King's Chamber complex with redundant layers of granite above

The King's Chamber with a less troublesome, though equally effective, design

What does not show up in diagrams of the interior of the Great Pyramid (GP) is the variety of materials used to construct specific interior chambers. Most of the Great Pyramid, like the other pyramids, was built with limestone blocks that were quarried only a few miles distant. Even quarrying such massive stones from the closest place was no small feat. Over two million of these limestone blocks, each weighing from two to several tons, were somehow transported across the Nile River before they could be put in place.

The King's Chamber in the central interior of the Great Pyramid is different. It is a free-standing room that does not bear any of the load of the overlying pyramid. It is a separately-built and inserted room made entirely of red granite. The walls and ceiling that surround this chamber  consist of forty-three immense granite blocks. Not only were these granite blocks somehow transported hundreds of miles, but the largest five of these granite blocks weigh in at seventy tons each. No boat associated with ancient Egypt has ever been found that could have floated even a fraction of the weight of those seventy-ton stones. Even today, humanity would be hard-pressed to transport such heavy objects so far from their point of origin, and that does not even begin to address the question of how such carefully dimensioned yet enormous stones were extracted from their point of origin and precisely shaped. Once on site, these five biggest stones were somehow raised 125 feet, then placed in a vertical stack with spacers between them to form the five-tiered roof of the King's Chamber. Big limestone blocks were then positioned above these five massive stones, but they were angled (gabled), so that the weight of the millions of overlying pyramid stones was transferred to the surrounding walls, leaving the King's Chamber as an independent, free-standing chamber. Only one of these enormous granite stones would have been needed to support the roof of the King's Chamber and carry the load of the overlying structure to the surrounding walls. But the gabled limestone slabs above the granite stones perform this function, leaving the granite blocks to support only their own weight. Such redundant engineering must have been done for a specific purpose. Limestone slabs would have worked just fine. The red granite was such hard-gotten gains that it must have had a specific purpose.

Red granite does have very different properties than the native limestone that comprises the bulk of the pyramid. For one thing, the granite is much harder. But the thing that makes red granite so hard is the matrix of interlocking quartz, feldspar, and mica crystals. Such crystal formation can only happen if the molten magma from the planet's interior cools very slowly, over thousands of years. The interlocking crystal matrix of the granite also makes the rock heavy and difficult to cut and shape, but it is arguably the strongest and most beautiful dimension stone on Earth.

In modern times, quartz crystals have been found to possess very useful piezoelectric properties. Quartz is used in timepieces because it naturally regulates current flow at precisely sixty cycles per second, making it the perfect basis for timekeeping devices. Quartz crystals have other very useful piezoelectric properties, namely the ability to store electronically configured data. When these facts are considered, a possible use of red granite emerges. It had a lot to do with electricity. Of course, ancient Egyptians are not normally thought of as having an understanding of electricity, especially an understanding that rivals our own.

As to why the King's Chamber was built to stand independently of the surrounding structure, it doesn't take an acoustic engineer to see that this chamber was intended to move, perhaps vibrate, independently of the building that encased it. Such vibrations might resonate with the frequencies encoded in the quartz and feldspar crystals of the granite, in which case there is another reason why scarce granite was chosen for the King's Chamber, especially the five immense stones that form its roof.

Inside the King's Chamber lays the chocolate-brown granite sarcophagus, which is too large to fit through the one and only egress. The Great Pyramid must have been built around this object. There's no other way it could have been installed in such a restrictive location. If it were a crypt, the mummified remains of King Khufu would have been brought in much later. Curiously, the sarcophagus has no lid, and one corner of the sarcophagus is seriously broken. Most assume early tourists carted off the lid in chunks and broke off pieces of the corner as souvenirs. To Dunn and others, the corner shows signs of having been melted, not just broken.

Returning to the Grand Gallery, we encounter a steeply sloping chamber leading diagonally upward to the antechamber, then the King's Chamber. The stones that comprise the two long walls of the Grand Gallery are staggered inward to form a twenty-six-foot high ceiling. Egyptologists see it as a ceremonial chamber where a funeral party gathered, despite the inclined floor being awkwardly steep and the whole room being narrow. The twenty-seven opposing sets of notches were built into the base of the walls at regular intervals and seem to suggest some very specific purpose again.

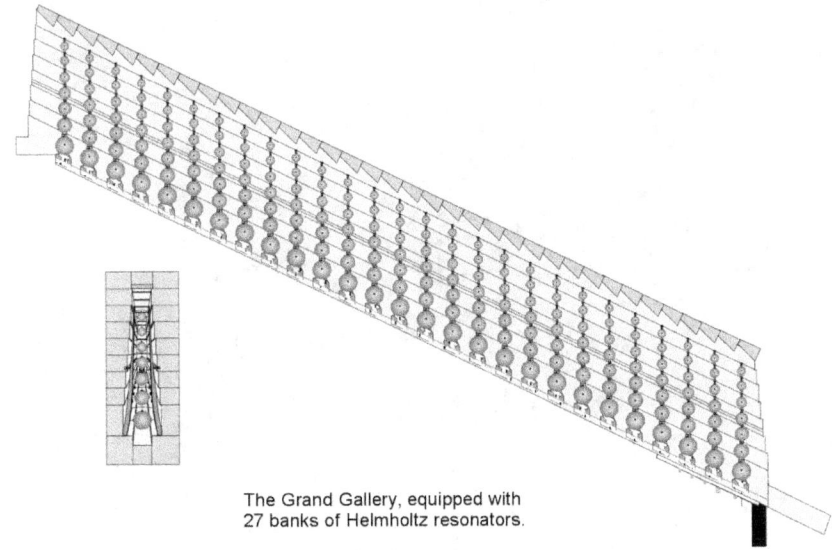

The Grand Gallery, equipped with 27 banks of Helmholtz resonators.

Figure 42. Grand Gallery Resonators

Dunn has concluded that the Grand Gallery was built to house an array of resonators that were an essential element of the power plant system. He describes devices called Helmholtz generators that would have been arrayed in banks along the entirety of the Grand Gallery. The twenty-seven sets of notches in the floor correspond to the twenty-seven arrays of resonators that Dunn envisions as occupying the corbelled walls of the Grand Gallery.

A Helmholtz resonator is a device that concentrates energy from an outside source of vibration like a tuning fork. We may have encountered resonators in modern life without fully realizing what they were. Guitars with a circular metal plate on the soundboard (National Guitars, Dobros, and Mule Guitars) are resonator guitars. Such guitars produce unique and beautiful sounds that boom with natural volume. The National Guitar seen above is worth six thousand dollars. Resonators are also applied to the exhaust system on cars, usually by *twenty-something* males who want their engine to growl with a low, throaty roar.

Probable Helmholz generators discovered in Egypt.

In the case of the Great Pyramid, resonators would concentrate and raise the vibrating frequencies from within the Earth. Dunn explains that the high ceiling of the Grand Gallery would have accommodated resonators that were stacked in vertical arrays. Dunn has even found metal spheres in Egyptian museums that show signs of being very carefully engineered and having no known purpose. Carefully constructed metal spheres are indeed an element of Helmholtz resonators (right).

And finally, the 'Queen's Chamber,' ostensibly the resting place of Khufu's wife and queen, also contains peculiarities that defy simple explanations. Sloping corridors, again too small for people, connect this chamber to other installations in the pyramid. Chemical residues coat the walls. As usual, no sign of decorative art or hieroglyphs is found anywhere. All in all, it is a very sterile chamber that would never befit the tomb of a beloved queen. The southern shaft (as it is called) extends upward and outward from the Queen's chamber and ends abruptly just before it meets the outside surface of the pyramid. It was mechanically probed in 1993 by Rudolph Gantenbrink, who found what he called a door at the terminus. Protruding from the surface of this door are fitted two rods that look a lot like electrical terminals.

The oddities do not end there. Christopher Dunn enumerates numerous purposely installed peculiarities in the Great Pyramid that are consistent with power production. In Dunn's view, the reaction began with the production of elemental hydrogen atoms in the Queen's Chamber. This was done by feeding zinc chloride down one of the so-called air shafts that emptied into the Queen's Chamber. Dilute hydrochloric acid would be fed down the other. The reaction of the two chemicals would produce hydrogen gas. Because of its super low density, the hydrogen flowed naturally upward and into the Grand Gallery. There, the energy level of the Hydrogen atoms would be raised by applying the transduced energy from the resonator arrays in the Grand Gallery. It all came together in the King's Chamber. The King's Chamber appears to be a resonant cavity where the transduced sound energy generated in the Grand Gallery was used to elevate the energy level of the hydrogen atoms that flowed upward from the Queen's Chamber.

The electrons in the hydrogen atoms would be energized to a higher orbital (quantum level) before falling back to a resting state, at which point a small burst of electromagnetic energy would be emitted in the microwave region of the EM spectrum. This reaction, the same reaction that occurs in stars, happens over and over again in the King's Chamber. It takes place millions of times per second, generating a steady stream of microwaves. As this energy passes through the King's Chamber, it is focused on the so-called sarcophagus. Dunn noticed that the ends of the sarcophagus both curve inward (concave), making it possible that its true purpose may have been to refract the energy beam, spreading the beam out at one end of the sarcophagus and then refocusing it at the other end, after which the beam was trained up and out of the system through the southern (air) shaft.

Sphinx and Great Pyramid with insert showing the two copper 'electrodes' that were investigated by Rudolph Gantenbrink in 1993.

Residual energy from the original Big Bang still reverberates in space. This low-level radiation, known as background radiation, would then be introduced into the system by way of the north air shaft, where it was focused and concentrated by the crystalline granite vessel called the sarcophagus. It too was amplified by the massive granite stones of the King's Chamber ceiling to produce intense microwave radiation that exited the pyramid through the southern air shaft.

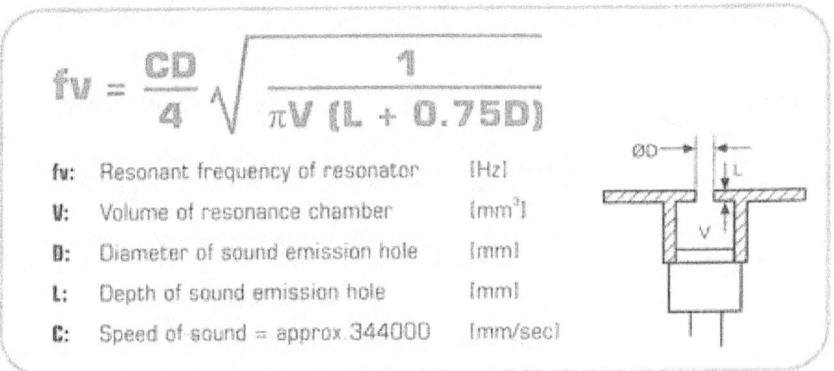

$$fv = \frac{CD}{4} \sqrt{\frac{1}{\pi V (L + 0.75D)}}$$

fv:	Resonant frequency of resonator	[Hz]
V:	Volume of resonance chamber	[mm³]
D:	Diameter of sound emission hole	[mm]
L:	Depth of sound emission hole	[mm]
C:	Speed of sound = approx. 344000	[mm/sec]

Where and how this energy was used is less clear, for again we know of no use that the ancient Egyptians would have had for electrical, much less microwave energy. There are hieroglyphs that depict people holding oblong objects that are glowing like bulbs. Such depictions are given a bit more validity because they are reminiscent of tricks that Nikola Tesla used to do, concentrating electrical energies to illuminate light bulbs that he held in his hand. Indeed, Tesla also conducted very large experiments with energy generation at a Wardenclyffe, New Jersey facility. The tower he built there bore many similarities to the energy propagation scheme that Dunn suspects to have been the true intended purpose of the Great Pyramid. Could the ancient Egyptians have not only used Earth's energies to produce power but also distributed it in some sort of wireless power grid? To be sure, no sober Egyptologist is going to take that possibility very seriously. There are competing views even among alternatively-minded researchers. One researcher sees the Great

Pyramid as a type of nuclear reactor although no residual radiation is detectable today.

Interestingly, the pyramids of Incan and Aztec cultures of Mexico and Central America appear to bear strong similarities to the Great Pyramid of Egypt, suggesting that the Egyptians were not alone in their efforts to harness Earth's energies. Pyramids are found at widely dispersed locations on five continents. All pyramid-like structures in North America, outside of Mexico, are earthen, while pyramids in Mexico, Cambodia, Central America, and Turkey are made of stone. They bear such strong similarities to the construction of the Egyptian pyramids that many now see them as clear evidence that there was once a global culture that shared knowledge and technological capabilities. This, of course, begs the question of not only how the ancients managed to traverse the vast distances between continents, but what happened to cause such an apparently sophisticated world-wide culture to disappear.

These unanswered questions are so troubling that most academically oriented archeologists reject these suggestions altogether. Still, conventional paradigms are challenged as new evidence and new archeological sites are discovered and studied. Two lines of evidence that are fairly new, compelling, and still not totally explained are the worldwide distribution of very similar pyramids and the worldwide occurrence of polygon rock walls that are also of extremely similar construction. These walls are found in Japan, South America, North America, Asia and Africa.

Sonic frequencies can be very powerful. They can be concentrated and applied to other uses but lifting heavy boulders is not something we know how to do today. It's a circular logic, but Christopher Dunn speculates that the energies that were captured and concentrated by the pyramids could have been used to build the pyramids themselves. If the polarity of the crystals in the quarried stones could be aligned and made to match the polarity of the ground beneath them, then the big stones would repel the earth beneath it, and the multi-ton rocks would hover weightlessly above the ground, making the movement of the heavy blocks vastly easier.

Even if Earth's energies could be focused and applied so impressively, one rightly wonders how a pyramid could be made to perform this function even while it was still under construction. Perhaps smaller pyramids were built first and their power was used to facilitate the construction of larger ones. There are eighty or so pyramids in Egypt. Perhaps the pyramids could function as arrays. Again, it is true that we cannot duplicate such feats of electrical engineering in our modern times, so no one can be blamed for doubting this. If such feats were able to be performed in ancient Egypt, then it could *only* happen if one of the following scenarios were true:

1. The ancients had help from highly advanced off-planeters
2. The ancients who built them were divinely inspired but they did the building themselves
3. The pyramids were put in place fully assembled and intact

Regardless of which of these possibilities, if any, have merit, we are forced to revise our thinking about the level of sophistication that ancient cultures had available to them. Not only must we salute them for their sophistication, but we ought to figure out how to reinvent this long-lost technology. Maybe scientists and engineers can figure out how to reactivate one of the existing pyramids. On the other hand, world energy needs today must be vastly greater than anything in the ancient past. The total world population in 5000 B.C. would have been in the tens of millions at most, as opposed to the 7.9 billion as of 2022. I should think that the free energy produced by a pyramid power plant would be a neat trick, but it would not come anywhere close to satisfying the energy appetite of the modern world. The question becomes whether a renewed understanding of this energy source, not to mention the cost of bringing it on line, would make a meaningful difference.

If such leaps in human ingenuity are to happen, then geniuses like Nikola Tesla would be the ones to make them. Tesla's tower at Wardenclyffe, New Jersey, bore strong similarities to the function of the pyramids that Dunn and others suspect, but they are not identical. At the time he was building his device, his principal financial backer, J. P. Morgan, went to visit the Great Pyramid and is said to have sent Tesla telegrams with specific measurements of the Great Pyramid. This would suggest that Tesla was aware of pyramid power as it pertained to his project.

The Wardenclyffe Tower was not designed to capture and concentrate Earth's sonic energies but to distribute electrical energy wirelessly throughout the Earth. Toward this end, Tesla had pipes beneath his tower that penetrated deep into the earth, tapping into the subterranean aquifers. His intent was to pump longitudinal (back and forth) electromagnetic waves into the earth. Like the builders of the Great Pyramid, Tesla wanted to find the resonant frequency of the Earth itself so that the waves he pumped into the Earth would resonate back and forth, building up more and more power in the Earth. One could then plug into the Earth anywhere and access this power.

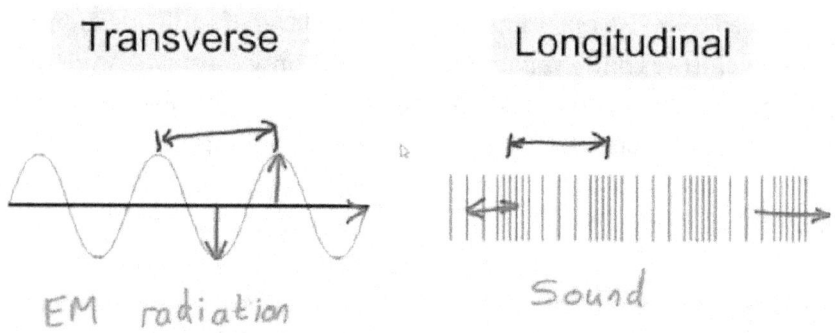

Electricity flow through wires is often likened to water flowing in a pipe but there is a problem with this analogy. Sound waves and other energy forms can be transmitted through water and solid ground in waves that travel longitudinally (back and forth) as well as transversely (side to side). The problem Tesla ran into is that, unlike water and sound waves, electromagnetic waves always travel transversely, never longitudinally. Tesla either didn't believe or didn't want to believe this. It is possible that Tesla, being a genius, had devised a scheme for bypassing this natural law.

In any event, J.P. Morgan pulled the plug (pun intended) on Tesla's work for selfish reasons. Copper is the best electrical conductor for the money so most wiring is made of copper. Morgan was heavily invested in copper and copper futures so wireless transmission of energy was not in his best financial interest.

As we posthumously try to reconstruct what Tesla had figured out, we do not have Tesla's own notes to help us. In his later years, Tesla often held back details of his inventions when submitting patent applications. He did not want rivals (like Thomas Edison) finding out all details of what he was doing and then ripping him off, which was constantly happening. Tesla did keep his private notes, but all those notes disappeared from the hotel room in which he died. Several sources report that John G. Trump, distinguished MIT engineer and uncle of Donald Trump, was asked to review Tesla's papers after his death. There was a concern that some of Tesla's work could be weaponized, specifically a so-called 'death ray.' We are told Professor Trump declared that idea to be impractical. Still, Tesla's papers were never made public. We can only hope that other geniuses of electrical engineering will eventually come along and that their discoveries do not get squelched the way Tesla's were.

As interesting as it is to consider that the Great Pyramid represents a sustainable source of clean energy, it should be noted that the whole project may not have ended well for the ancient Egyptians. Christopher Dunn's keen eye has noted damage in the King's Chamber and the Grand Gallery that is consistent with a kind of meltdown of the system. Something exploded within the King's Chamber and the whole power plant was severely damaged. The independently standing red granite walls of the King's Chamber, despite their enormous mass, are all pushed outward about one inch in all directions, indicating some sort of violent energy release. Also, the five huge granite blocks that form the ceiling of the King's Chamber are deeply cracked. They don't support the weight of the overlying structure, so they are in no danger of collapsing, but they, like the walls, show damage that is consistent with an explosion. The black granite of the sarcophagus may have been the same red granite as the rest of the chamber before the explosion. It was scorched to black by the energy of that explosion. The damage to the corner of the sarcophagus may have been caused by melting and or fracturing due to explosive energy and high heat, rather than thoughtless tourists.

Beyond the King's Chamber, the limestone walls of the Grand Gallery walls also show evidence of being cooked by extreme heat. Dunn's considered conclusion is that power production of the Great Pyramid ended in a sudden, uncontrolled release of enormous energy. Interestingly, some of the pyramids of Mexico's Teotihuacan complex also show signs of similar high heat damage. The old saying that applies to technology in general seems to be relevant here: 'Anything that can go wrong, eventually will.' The pyramids may have worked wondrously for a while, maybe for a great while, but like nuclear power plants and even windmills, something eventually goes wrong, and maybe even horribly wrong. As appealing as the idea of free and sustainable energy is, it may be a bit of a fool's errand.

Nothing is free, we are told. Free to you, perhaps, but always at some cost to someone else. Energy production invariably bears hidden costs. Those hidden costs are paid by someone else in the near term or by everyone down the road. Pyramid energy, nuclear energy, wind energy or hydropower always seems to entail a Faustian bargain. Put another way, all energy production boils down to 'robbing Peter to pay Paul.' For the Egyptians, a sustainable energy source, wirelessly transmitted, seemed to be the ultimate goal, as it is today. Toward that end, it bears remembering that simpler living, with less consumption of resources, will always be part of the equation.

The Second Law of Thermodynamics tells us that in any energy transfer, ninety percent of the energy is lost due to heat and friction. Being a scientific law, it is, by definition, always true. There are no shortcuts.

Pyramid-based energy production is quite attractive if it is true, but it will not solve the problems of humanity and, as with every Faustian bargain, it might end up making things worse. The Second Law of Thermodynamics is a mathematical equation but it can also be summarized in an aphorism that may be the most broadly applicable aphorism of all. That aphorism can be further reduced to an acronym, and that acronym is TANSTAAFL. It sounds like the name of another Egyptian king, but it's short for: **There Ain't No Such Thing As A Free Lunch.**

The Chilbolton Radio Telescope and crop circle that appeared on August 14, 2000.

4

SPILLING THE BEANS

R adio telescopes were developed as an instrument of the Cold War. Their original purpose was to intercept Soviet satellite communications. Scientific applications quickly became apparent. Arnaud Penzias and his colleague Robert Wilson earned a Nobel Prize for using an early radio telescope to detect three-degree background radiation, the so-called 'echo of the Big Bang.'

Even as early as 1959, radio telescopes had gotten so sensitive that they could, at least theoretically, be used to detect faint radio signals from distant civilizations. The pioneer in this field was Frank Drake, then director of the National Radio Astronomy Laboratory in Green Bank, West Virginia. Drake was the first 'radio astronomer' to take up the challenge of searching for intelligent radio signals from space. He used the Green Bank receiver to conduct a systematic search for radio signals from two nearby stars. Drake focused on these two stars over a four-month period, recording any and all signals for six hours each day. He detected absolutely nothing. Soon after this preliminary effort, Drake hosted a meeting of several other scientists who shared his interest in detecting the presence of alien civilizations. One of these fellow scientists was the eminent astrophysicist Carl Sagan. At the meeting, Drake planned to discuss the various factors that must be factored in when trying to detect intelligent signals from space. As he made a list of the possible factors, he spontaneously devised a formula that would combine the effects of the various factors. This formula, a simple multiplication of combined factors, later became known as the 'Drake equation.' Each factor became a multiplier that would be combined to produce an estimated number (N) of inhabited planets, galaxy-wide. Drake's equation, a simple multiplication of seven factors, is shown here: $N = R^* \times f(p) \times n(e) \times f(\text{l}) \times f(i) \times f(c) \times L$

The seven factors, or multipliers, combine to produce a number (N), that being the number of civilizations in the galaxy that are theoretically capable of communicating with us. The seven multipliers are as follows:

R^*= rate of star formation
$F(p)$= the fraction of those stars that have planets
$N(c)$= the fraction of those planets that can support life
$F(\text{l})$= the fraction of those planets that actually have life
$F(i)$= the fraction of those planets that develop intelligent life
$F(c)$= the fraction of those planets that develop communication technology (like radio signals)
L= the length of time that they send out those radio signals

Notice that five of the seven factors are fractions, expressed as decimals, each of which will reduce the value of the whole number (L), the number of years that a civilization sends out detectable signals. Some of these factors, particularly the last four, are beyond current scientific knowledge, so assigning any decimal number to these multipliers would require pretty large amounts of guesswork. Any value produced from such guesswork would be quite variable and, therefore, pretty debatable. As Drake himself stressed, the idea of the equation was not to produce an undisputable answer but to initiate a dialogue as to what would constitute reasonable estimates for each factor. When the equation was first applied, low and high estimates were applied to each factor, and results were produced which ranged from twenty other planets in the galaxy on the low end to fifty million on the high end. Talk about variability!

At the first official meeting, the attendees arrived at the unanimous conclusion that whatever number was used for L (the length of time the civilization transmitted signals), after it was multiplied by a bunch of decimal fractions, would be roughly equal to (N), the number of planets with communication ability. Of all the numbers that were estimated back then, the one that has changed  the most in recent times is F(p), the fraction of stars that have planetary systems. In Drake's day, it was thought that one star in a thousand had planets. Now, with the advent of satellite observatories that are used in a concerted search for exoplanets, astronomers feel that virtually ALL stars have planets. This realization tremendously increases the chances that other solar systems host life, whether it is intelligent or not.

At the meetings, Carl Sagan also observed that the only whole number factor, (L), is key for another reason. (L) is tied to the survivability of a civilization. In other words, the ability of a civilization to avoid destroying itself is of critical importance if the civilization is ever going to be detected. In later years, Sagan used this thought to advocate for more awareness of our own vulnerabilities from such threats to humanity as nuclear war and the ensuing, years-long nuclear winter. After Sagan's death, Stephen J. Gould and others identified still other threats to civilization from things like comets and asteroids that could inflict the same nuclear winter that would follow nuclear exchange. Over time, it has come to light that the threat from collision with comets or asteroids is even greater than was first supposed. More evidence of past impacts is being found with time, so the more recent the estimate, the more grim it seems to be. Based on the abundance of historical impacts, the most recent estimates put the major impact interval at 15,000 years. The last known big impact on the Earth is thought to have been the so-called Younger-Dryas event that happened 12,800 years ago. Randall Carlson and Graham Hancock persuasively argue that the Clovis culture in North America, and maybe even Atlantis, were wiped out by this ancient set of closely-spaced impacts that spanned a century.

The Arecibo radio telescope in Puerto Rico.

It became clear in 1961, after this first meeting of The Order of the Dolphin (as Drake's group named themselves) that, even though making contact with an alien civilization was possible, it was a very remote possibility. Listening for signals from space has been happening off and on for fifty years. While some mysterious and promising data has been collected, nothing definitive has ever been made public. Rapid radio bursts, short high-energy radio signals with no known source, are a mystery. The "Wow signal" collected by an Ohio State radio telescope in August of 1977 is another mystery. This seventy-two second signal came from the direction of the constellation Sagittarius and was noticed by researcher Jerry Ehman while reviewing data collected by the Ohio State "big ear" antenna in Delaware, Ohio. When Ehman saw the signal on computer printout 6EQUJ5, he circled it and wrote "Wow" in the margin, hence the name used to refer to the event. The signal was never repeated and the signal contained no modulation. (Modulating is how information is sent in radio waves.) The "Wow" signal is said to be the best candidate for an alien signal to date, but it is not seen as definitive, either. There are a few other possible explanations for it.

Meanwhile, Drake got busy on a more proactive approach to alien contact than just passive listening. His next idea was to advertise; that is, send a signal out into space to solicit alien contact. After all, why stand against the wall, waiting for an invitation? Why not get out there and ask someone else to dance?

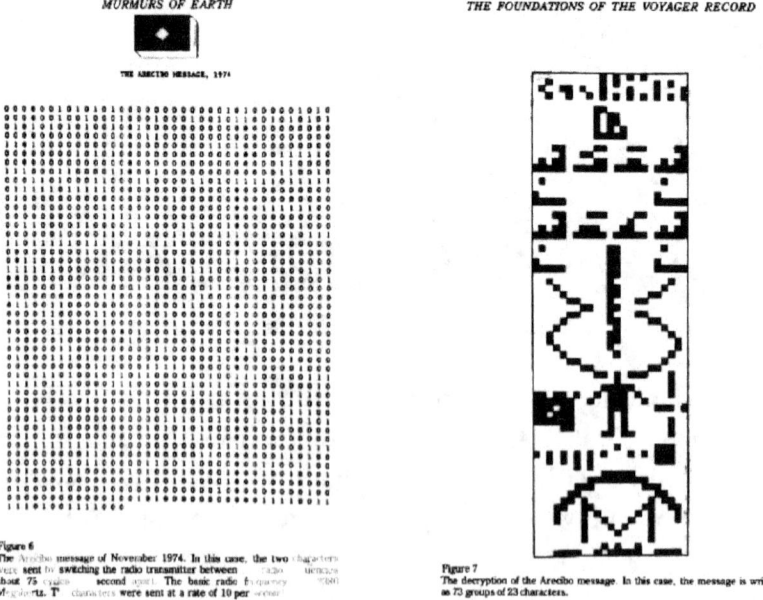

MURMURS OF EARTH

THE ARECIBO MESSAGE, 1974

Figure 6
The Arecibo message of November 1974. In this case, the two characters were sent by switching the radio transmitter between radio frequencies about 75 cycles second apart. The basic radio frequency 2380 Megahertz. The characters were sent at a rate of 10 per second.

THE FOUNDATIONS OF THE VOYAGER RECORD

Figure 7
The decryption of the Arecibo message. In this case, the message is written as 73 groups of 23 characters.

Drake was in the perfect position to do this because, by then, he had been promoted to director of the Arecibo transmitter, the world's largest transmitting radio telescope. This 1,000-foot diameter dish is so big and heavy that it is built into a bowl-shaped limestone valley in Puerto Rico. Since it is built in, the dish cannot be moved, but the transceiver that hangs from overhead cables can be moved some fifteen degrees from side to side, allowing for aiming of the focus to a small degree. Beyond this small variability, the Arecibo dish points in one general direction and relies on the fact that, as the earth rotates, the stars and galaxies pass overhead and into the range of the radio wave receiver.

In 1974, this powerful instrument had just been resurfaced and 'souped up.' The surface of the dish was recoated and the power output was upgraded to 20 terawatts (20 trillion watts). For publicity purposes, Drake and Sagan were eager to publicly demonstrate the instrument's new, stronger capability. Their idea was to send a message into space that might someday be received by an alien world. Drake, Sagan, and a few others got busy and devised a picture-based message that was relatively free of language barriers, and that could be quickly and cheaply sent out into space.

Not everyone thought this was a good idea. Some folks, even a few scientists, who had probably once read H.G. Wells' *War of the Worlds*, raised the objection that it might not be so smart to give away our cherished position in the galaxy. After all, if the message were received by aliens with hostile intent, invasion would ensue, as in the plot from *War of the Worlds*. Other astronomers, most notably Carl Sagan, reassured nay-sayers that the Earth positively shrieks radio signals of all kinds, so our existence cannot possibly be a secret at this point.

As it was being prepared, Drake shared a draft of the message with Sagan. Over lunch, Sagan critiqued the message from an alien's point of view. Sagan made a few suggestions, and Drake put the finishing touches on the message. The intent was to send a narrowly focused beam of energy out in the direction of M-13, a globular cluster of 300,000 stars in the constellation Hercules. On November

16th, at 12:30 in the afternoon, M-13 would pass within the fifteen-degree window directly above the Arecibo antenna, so that would be the date and time of the ceremonial unveiling of the new and improved Arecibo radio telescope in 1974. Champagne was served, Sagan gave a short speech, and audible 'beeps' and 'boops' were played for the benefit of the assembled dignitaries as the message was sent. A hush fell over the crowd. Those who were there at the time later described the event as a somber, even moving experience.

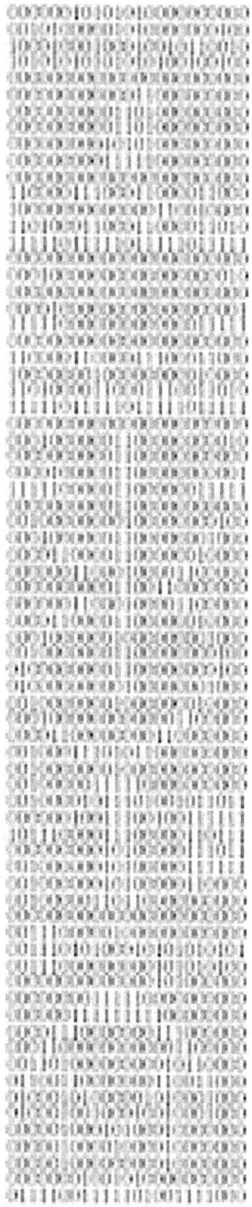

Arecibo transmission in its raw form and in 23 by 73 format

The message was a three-minute burst of radio energy consisting of 1679 bits (210 bytes) that were transmitted at a frequency of 2380 MHz. The message was frequency shifted (modulated) at the rate of ten bits per second to produce a series of ones and zeroes. The 1,679 binary digits were intended to be arranged into a rectangle that was twenty-three columns of seventy-three digits each. These numbers were chosen because they are unique prime numbers multiples of 1679, the number of digits in the entire message. Any mathematically intelligent alien species that stumbled upon Drake's message ought

Fig.2

to be able to figure out how to configure it to get the intended picture.

When correctly displayed, the message can then be broken down into seven sections, the top one being a kind of key to binary coding. The numbers one through ten are translated into binary code. This presumably enables the receiving party to decode the numbering system used in other parts of the message. Below that appear binary-coded atomic numbers for five elements (hydrogen, carbon, nitrogen, oxygen, and phosphorus) that are essential for life as we know it. These same five elements are arranged in the next line to represent the molecular formula of the key nucleotides in the DNA molecule: deoxyribose, adenine, thymine, phosphate, cytosine, and guanine. Below that, a DNA molecule is depicted twisting down the sides in the center of the pictograph. A bar in the center of the double helix gives a binary-coded number for total number of nucleotides in the DNA molecule, which was, according to textbooks of the time, thought to be about one billion base pairs. Curiously, the number shown in the message is 4.2 billion. This is either a mistake by Sagan or a deliberate move for some unknown reason. This oddity has an important bearing on the Arecibo reply that will be discussed later on.

Below the DNA double helix is a stick figure human, with human height of 5'10" in binary code, and a human population estimate of 4.3

billion (1974 figure). Toward the bottom is a representation of the solar system, with the third planet highlighted, because that is where we live. Toward the bottom is a representation of the radio telescope used to send the message, with its dimensions, 1000', given in binary code.

The globular cluster that the message was directed toward is 25,000 light-years away so, at the speed of light, a reply is not to be expected for twice that long (50,000 years), and that is assuming they get busy and send a reply right away.

Here is where things get strange. On the morning of August 19, 2001, a "crop circle" (more of a crop rectangle, really) appeared in the wheat field adjacent to the Chilbolton radio telescope, owned and operated by the British military. On first inspection, it looked like an 'Oriental rug' in its shape and design, so the first crop circle enthusiasts to happen upon it called it the Persian carpet. Weirder still, another crop glyph of a face appeared in the same field only five days prior, on August 14th. Still another crop formation had appeared exactly one year earlier, on August 14th of 2000 (see below). A day or two after the Persian carpet appeared, Paul Vigay, a crop circle researcher of some repute, was inspecting it from the air. Being fully aware of recent strides in astronomy, Paul Vigay immediately recognized the striking similarities between this brand-new crop glyph and the famous Arecibo transmission that was sent into space in 1974. Photographs were taken and inspected, only to find stunning similarities, right down to the 23 by 73 pixel grid that Sagan and Drake used in the original Arecibo transmission. Many other elements of the original transmission were faithfully reproduced, but other elements of the original message were distinctly different.

The one through ten binary numbering systems were identical. The seven elements that were identified as essential for life were depicted, but with an addition: silicon, atomic number 14, had been added. The most obvious change was that the stick figure human had been replaced with the classic big-headed grey alien that we are used to seeing in depictions of Roswell-style aliens. The height of this stereotypical alien form, binary-coded into flattened wheat, was three and a half feet. The population estimate for humanity (4.3 billion) was changed to 12 billion. Silicon, as previously stated, was added to the list of basic elements for life. The planets in the revised solar system were only eight, and the highlighted planets (that support life) was revised as well. (See the diagram, below.)

This crop glyph, which mimics the Arecibo transmission, is often called the 'Arecibo answer hoax,' the assumption being that the crop glyph was some kind of prank. It might seem fair to suppose that this crop glyph found near an English radio telescope is someone's idea of a joke, since a reply was not expected for fifty thousand years, and the alien being in the glyph seems like a corny caricature. Yet, for many other reasons, the view that the 'Arecibo reply' is indeed a hoax or a prank does not stand up to careful scrutiny.

Published photos of the Arecibo reply crop glyph are often dismissively stamped bold "hoax," but the more one studies this mysterious glyph in all detail, the harder it becomes to dismiss it as a hoax. The first problem with dismissing the 'Arecibo reply' is that it appeared so suddenly and in the shadow of a sensitive military installation with a security force. The glyph lay within two hundred feet of the fence that encloses the Chilbolton Radio Observatory in Hampshire, England. Once a World War II airfield, the site now houses a radio telescope that was built by MoD, the British Ministry of Defence. They claim the radio telescope is now used for weather research, and that may be true some of the time, but the highly technical device was built during the Cold War, like most radio telescopes, to eavesdrop on Soviet satellite communications. The Chilbolton Radio Observatory has a security force and security cameras all around. Other crop circles had appeared in the same field right outside the fence, so you better believe the security force was keeping their eyes open. As recently as five days prior, a huge and complexly pixelated face appeared in the same field. That was August 14, 2001, just five days prior to the appearance of the crop glyph that I will rightly or wrongly call the Arecibo Reply. One year prior, on August 14, 2000, the fractile pattern appeared that is seen in the photograph at the beginning of the chapter. The wheat field in Hampshire, next to the radio telescope, definitely had a history.

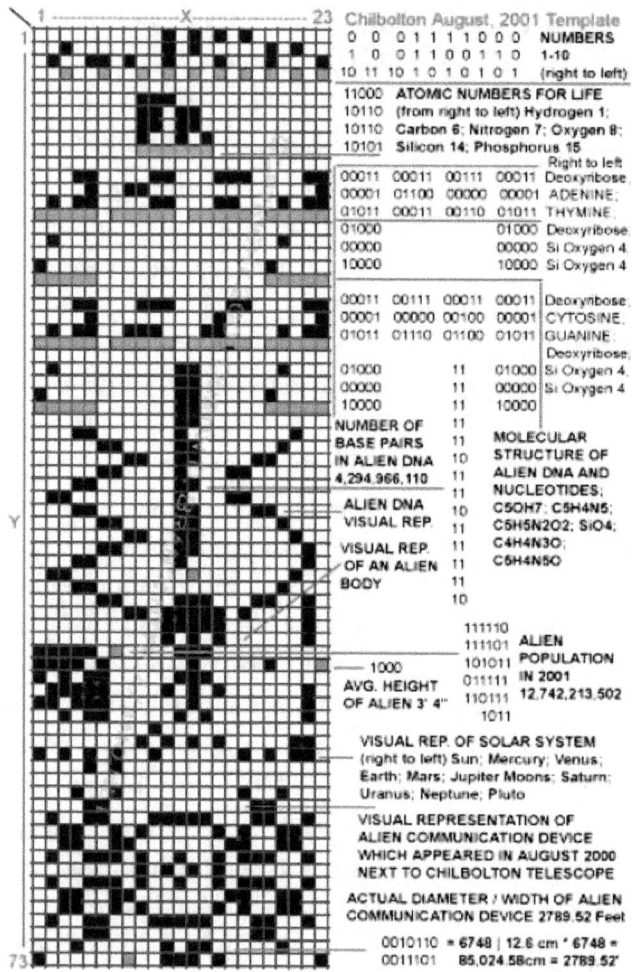

Did a group of hoaxers create this crop glyph right under the noses of the base security? For starters, veteran crop circle researcher Colin Andrews sat down with Darcy Ladd, manager of the Chilbolton Radio Observatory, and asked him point-blank if their security team had seen any activity in the field in the days prior to the appearance of the Arecibo reply glyph. The answer was a definite "No." This point alone seems to dismantle the view that the Arecibo reply is a hoax. Certainly, it would have taken hours, if not days, for a group of people using conventional methods to construct such a detailed and elaborate crop circle. The observatory manager offered that they also had security cameras and at least one was trained in the direction of the wheat field. Mr. Ladd offered that the camera captured 'nothing unusual.' The cameras were not equipped with night sight, but if any lighting was used in the construction of the glyph, it would have been detected by the cameras.

Could such a detailed and precise set of impressions have been created in a single night, in total darkness? The observatory manager assured Colin Andrews that the glyph appeared overnight. Of that, there is no dispute. The glyph appeared in one night, perfectly encoded, without any apparent mistakes. It is simply not possible for even the most highly organized team to have executed the task of constructing such a detailed and precise glyph in the dark, two hundred feet from a sensitive military installation, under the nose of their security team, in the undisputed time frame of a single night.

Not only would the degree of precision that the glyph manifests not be possible to achieve in total darkness but there was no trace of pedestrian or vehicle entry or exit to the wheat field. Whoever made the glyph certainly didn't park at the radio telescope facility. The perimeter of the radio telescope facility is surrounded, of course, by a tall fence with barbed wire on top, like all sensitive government facilities. Some kind of staging area would have been needed for lights, tools, food and water, maybe a generator, and so on. Anyone who thinks that particular glyph was constructed in a single night by people with hand tools and string has never tried to do such a thing. In my view, creating accurate binary coding in a crop on the first try is all but impossible. James Deardorf, Senior Scientist at the National Center for Atmospheric Research in Boulder, Colorado, noted that there are over 800 right angles in the crop glyph known as the 'Arecibo Reply.' Under the best of conditions, right angles are the toughest thing to get right and bear in mind that every single right angle was done correctly. There are no second chances when one is mashing down wheat stalks. It has to be done perfectly the first time and it has to be done within a very limited time window. The glyph could only be done by laying out a very complex grid of twenty-three by seventy-three intersecting strings stretched from 192 wooden stakes arranged around the perimeter of the glyph. Either stake holes would remain after the stakes were removed, or someone would have to fill in the stake holes once the job was finished. This was the first thing crop circle researchers looked for when they investigated the site. None were found. Crop circle researcher James Deardorff calculated that a team of at least six people would have been needed and working constantly, it could not be done in less than thirty-one hours. At the latitude of southern England, there are only five and a half hours of total darkness in mid-August.

Further, how could anyone on the ground position themselves accurately enough to make all the highly detailed impressions. An aerial viewpoint and communication would be indispensable. The whole glyph is just too expansive to work solely from the ground. Even a camera on a tall mast would not provide a helpful view of the entire image as it was being created. A hovering aircraft, lots of lights, and walkie-talkie communication would be indispensable, yet total silence would have also been necessary to avoid alerting the base security.

No individual or group has ever come forward and taken credit for this glyph, nor has anyone ever demonstrated their ability to do such precise work, even in broad daylight. The only way to succeed at such a task would be to practice constructing it, repeatedly. Where was that done? No practice locations were ever found, and even if the practice sites were obliterated after they were used, the crop damage would be difficult to fully conceal. Researchers have gotten good at identifying genuine versus fake crop circles. A key item is the way the crop is flattened. In 'real' crop circles, the wheat is interwoven and bent over at a ninety-degree angle, but the plants are otherwise undamaged and still growing. In fake crop circles, the plants are mashed by impact, the stalks are all broken, and the plants are irreparably damaged. The undamaged wheat plants in the Arecibo Reply bore all the features of a genuine crop glyph.

What is just as puzzling as how the glyph was constructed are the numerous subtle changes to the original message that was sent into space in 1974. For example, the crop glyph offered 3.2 billion as the number of base pairs in the human genome. The Human Genome Project was not even finished until 2003 yet the number first published in 2003 appeared in wheat in 2001. Silicon was left off the original Arecibo message and silicon was added to the crop glyph. The fact that silicon was left out of the original Arecibo message is now seen as a bit of an oversight.

Of course, the classic big-headed, small-bodied alien was inserted in the 'Arecibo reply' crop glyph. A consistent body height of three and a half feet was included, again in binary code that was, again, perfectly etched in the still-growing grain. The glyph seems to describe a body type quite similar, if not identical, to the Roswell-style alien. Next to the alien body is a population number, which is also corrected. It lists twenty billion, as opposed to 4.3 billion which was Earth's population in 1974. Below the alien body on the Arecibo reply glyph is a solar system that also has some changes made. Perhaps the most curious of all changes is the highlighting of not just one planet in the solar system representation, but three. What is the message here? Is it representing 'their' solar system elsewhere in the galaxy, or is it a revision of our own?

It bears such strong similarities to our solar system that it begins to look like they are correcting our numbers, in which case the message seems to be that life, or at least visitation, has happened on other planets besides the Earth. If it is our solar system, then our next-door neighbor, Mars, and something just beyond Mars has something to do with life. Next to the Mars object is a configuration of four smaller objects. Could they be the moons of Jupiter? But the two big twin planets beyond that seem to suggest the Jupiter and Saturn pairing, in which case the four smaller bits would have to be the asteroid belt. If so, then they are saying the asteroid belt is or was once inhabited. Curiously, Zecharia Sitchin stated that the Sumerian clay tablets had tales of a destroyed planet Tiamet, between present-day Mars and Jupiter. Phaeton is another name for the hypothetical destroyed planet that formed the asteroid belt. If Jupiter and Saturn are the two big twins depicted in the outer solar system, then Nepture is the last planet, meaning Pluto was omitted from the Arecibo reply glyph. As we all know, Pluto was deemed by the International Astronomical Union to not be a planet in 2006, five years after the Arecibo reply happened. How could pranksters have known in 2001 that Pluto did not belong?

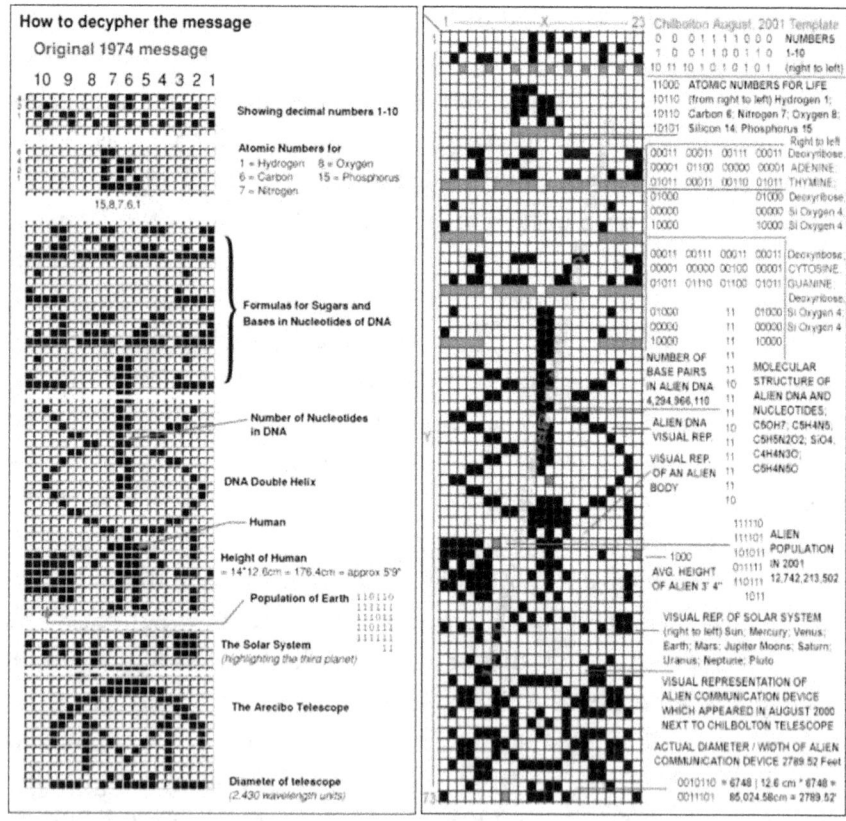

Finally, it is easy to see that a different contraption is represented in the place of the radio telescope that Drake included in the original Arecibo message. Interestingly, that same object was etched into that very same wheat field exactly one year prior. We can safely assume that this object is the device used to create crop glyphs, which may be some hyperdimensional technology or something else that is 'their' version of a radio telescope. One crop circle researcher argued that if the Arecibo reply is a hoax, it was created by a cabal of scientists who possess very advanced knowledge.

The most remarkable interview I have yet seen on the subject of the Arecibo Reply was an interview with Frank Drake, the designer of the original Arecibo transmission. In 2010, a German interviewer sat down with an aging Frank Drake, armed with a few glossy photographs of the original Arecibo transmission and a photo of the purported Arecibo reply. As he was preparing to show Drake the photo of the Arecibo reply glyph, the interviewer explained the image he was about to present to Drake. At first, the corners of Drake's mouth came up, followed by a bigger smile. By the time Drake had been handed the photograph, he was flat-out laughing. It is not at all clear whether Drake was previously aware of the so-called Arecibo answer. It seems unlikely that something so relevant to Drake's own work could have gone unnoticed by him for almost a decade. Still, I am willing to give Drake the benefit of the doubt and assume he was completely unaware of the appearance of the Arecibo reply glyph. I use the phrase 'benefit of the doubt' because Drake's reaction to the photo and his verbal responses to the interviewer's subsequent questions display an astounding degree of ignorance, so much so that I am willing to assume that the words of this otherwise intelligent scientist were the words of a person who was simply unin-formed on the matter.

"There's no chance whatsoever that this is legitimate," Drake confidently declared almost at the same instant that he set his eyes on the photograph he was handed. The interviewer patiently asked him to explain. "For two reasons," Drake continued. "First of all, the message structure is wrong. The DNA structure is clearly wrong. Other parts of the message are chemically impossible. They make no sense at all."

"Second, if you traveled all that way, you wouldn't go out in a cornfield and spend a great deal of effort cutting down stalks of corn. You would go up to the radio telescope, knock on the door, and hand them one of your books, or something."

In light of all that has been written about this glyph and the situation that surrounds its appearance, the degree of ignorance on Drake's part to these same widely publicized details is quite shocking. To begin with, the crop in the field next to the radio telescope was wheat, not corn. Let's give Drake a pass on that one, since English farmers often refer to their crops as "corn" no matter what species of grain is being cultivated. Perhaps more stunning is the view Drake expresses that the corn was cut (with great effort) to create the glyph. In fact, not a single stalk of wheat was cut, or even broken. As previously stated, the plants in genuine crop circles are bent but otherwise undamaged, in contrast to the fake crop glyphs in which the plants are damaged or destroyed by the trauma of being smashed down by a board. Drake clearly knows nothing about the formation or study of crop glyphs as it has been conducted since the first modern crop circles were documented in England in 1972. The fact that Drake is displaying a degree of ignorance is, in itself, understandable enough. One cannot be an expert in everything. What IS shocking is how strong his convictions and opinions are, despite a near-total lack of knowledge about the details of the subject.

By comparison, Drake's former colleague, Carl Sagan, might have been equally dismissive of the Arecibo Reply glyph if it had occurred while he was still alive (he died in 1998), but he always spoke with a guarded precision that would not have included the kind of dismissive blanket statements that Drake uses in this interview. One of the most salient points for me is that it is universally assumed that the Arecibo transmission of 1974 would be received by a distant alien civilization, who then might travel 'all that way,' as Drake said, to offer a response.

The message was indeed sent in a narrowly focused beam that was directed at the M-13 globular cluster 25,000 light-years away in the direction of the constellation Orion. Several astronomers have commented that it is unlikely that the beam could be intercepted by another, much closer alien civilization that happened to get in the way of the beam. If this were true, then we should not expect a response from a civilization in the target galaxy for 50,000 years. Why weren't closer stars in our own galaxy chosen as targets for the message?

The answer, of course, is that in 1974, when the Arecibo transmission was sent, no other planetary systems had yet been discovered. The first exoplanet was not discovered until 1992 by Wolszczan and Frail orbiting the pulsar PSR1257+12. Amazingly, current thinking about exoplanets has changed so much that astrophysicists now agree that, based on the statistics, most or even all stars have planets. This fact suddenly forces us to revise upward the estimates of alien civilizations produced by Drake's now-famous equation. It also increases greatly the chances that the Arecibo transmission was intercepted before it left our galaxy, which it still has not. But another thought seems to be uniformly overlooked by almost everyone who tries to explain away the validity of the Arecibo reply. That is the possibility, indeed the likelihood that the message was intercepted alright, but not somewhere else in the cosmos. The message was intercepted before it ever left Earth because 'they' were already here. Further, 'they' didn't intercept the focused radio signal that was sent into space on that November day in 1974. My guess is that they picked the message out of newspaper and magazine articles that appeared after the event, if not Sagan's own book, Cosmos, which presented a version of the Arecibo transmission on page 290. I say a 'version' of the message because the graphic Sagan used in his book was not an exact reproduction of the Arecibo message sent into space. Almost all published versions of the original message are the technically incorrect mirror image of the message that was sent into space. It is a little-known fact that Sagan probably misrepresented the message on purpose whenever he published it. He also misstated (probably deliberately) a few key details of the message, most notably the number of base pairs in the human genome.

This becomes much more important than it might first seem because the Arecibo reply, regardless of who generated it, used the mirror image that appeared in Sagan's book, not the actual transmission that was sent into space, as the basis for the reply. The Arecibo reply used a template corresponding to the published-on-Earth message, not the message sent into space!

Additionally, Sagan used a binary-encoded precise number in the range of 3.2 billion to describe the number of base pairs in the human genome. When asked where they arrived at that number, Drake explained that they got it from off-the-shelf textbooks of the time. In 1974, the best estimate for the number of base pairs in the human genome, produced by Watson and Crick themselves (the discoverers of DNA), was one billion base pairs. Much more recently, as in the mid-2000s, the estimate has been upwardly revised into the neighborhood of 3.2 billion, and counting. But Sagan was using this number (repeatedly) when he published explanations of the Arecibo message. How could he have known something that no other molecular biologist of the time seems to have known?

Richard Hoagland, a contemporary of Sagan's and one of the most prolific researchers of crop glyphs in general and of the Arecibo reply in particular, has suggested that Sagan had a bit of a double life, and that his area of professional expertise was very highly valued in military and intelligence circles. Hoagland has gone so far as to suggest that Sagan got his super-accurate estimate for the number of base pairs in the human genome from the only place he could have gotten it: the super-secret work that was done on the alien cadavers recovered from the Roswell crash. Naturally, such suggestions are a real 'eye-roller' to those who do not take the Roswell story seriously. It would require another chapter, maybe even an entire book to resolve that complicated issue, but regardless of how one feels about that infamous event, the fact remains, as Richard Hoagland convincingly explains, somehow, Carl Sagan had information about the human genome that no one else had, and he repeated that inside knowledge several times, so it was no typographical error. Hoagland speculates that Sagan may have even been attempting to convey some knowledge that he had but that the rest of us would not come to realize until some time in the future.

But how could information about the human genome be gleaned from a presumed secret study of alien DNA obtained at the Roswell crash site? Sagan never offered an answer, so we can only turn again to Richard Hoagland, who knew Sagan, although they never discussed this particular issue. In a lengthy article he published on the Enterprise Mission website, Hoagland suggests that, as a consequence of his involvement with the analysis of the DNA tissue gathered at the Roswell crash site, Sagan was in possession of another piece of very closely-guarded information, namely that alien DNA bore certain unmistakable similarities to our own DNA, and maybe even identical in certain respects. Was Sagan, then, leaking classified top secret information to the public in a way that was 'under the radar?' Hoagland feels that if this is true, it wasn't the first time Sagan did such a thing. Hoagland points out that Sagan was such a highly valued asset that he was uniquely positioned to get away with it. Sagan was, after all, an advisor to scientists, military men, academians, and presidents. Within limits, Sagan could say whatever he wanted.

Tellingly, Hoagland even points to Carl Sagan's statement in print: "In the deepest sense, the search for extraterrestrial intelligence is a search for ourselves." Hoagland feels, and I agree, that Sagan was being both cryptic and literal about what he knew to be true, but could not discuss openly. I heard Carl Sagan speak when he came through Portland, I've read most of his books and watched his Cosmos videos countless times with students in my science classroom. Sagan was always very measured and very precise when expressing himself. He never overstated his knowledge, in fact, he tended to understate it. He never spoke with certainty about matters that were speculative. He qualified his remarks when he was speculating and acknowledged the degree of uncertainty whenever it existed. Compare that to the exaggerated certainty that Frank Drake displays when he declares with absolute confidence something that he could not possibly know: how extraterrestrials would behave if and when they would arrive. The German interviewer respectfully challenges Drake, "How do you know?" that aliens would not have "spent a great deal of effort cutting down stalks of corn." Drake doubles down. "What I do know is that they are intelligent, because they somehow got to Earth, if this is really from an alien (he's holding a photograph of the Arecibo reply), and they will know better than to try and communicate with humans in this ridiculous way."

This is the kind of blanket statement that Sagan would never have made. To be sure, Drake has his supporters among mainstream scientists such as Seth Shostak, Sagan's successor as head of the SETI project. Still, such statements cannot help but portray guys like Drake in an unfavorable light. It puts a certain closed-mindedness on public display. The interview that is being referenced here can be easily found by entering "Arecibo Message-Chilbolton Reply HOAX" on YouTube. Many people submitted their reaction in the Comments section. One comment seemed to summarize my impression of the video without being too snarky. "If you are smart with numbers, you give something up, like being curious or open-minded."

Make no mistake. As a career astronomy teacher, I have a great deal of respect for the numerous contributions that Frank Drake made to the field. I am also fully aware of the possibility that his low opinion of the Arecibo reply is totally justified. I do, however, see an arrogance in the way he claims to understand all alien species and their presumed motivation. "They will know better than to try and communicate with humans in this ridiculous way."

Interestingly, it didn't seem like a ridiculous way to communicate when Drake and Sagan originally devised the code to send their message out into space. Why is it ridiculous that the very same code they devised was employed to respond? Perhaps he means just the crop glyph is ridiculous. I think that, too, is ingenious, especially the bit about locating the reply in the shadow of an operating radio telescope.

I can think of a few very good reasons why the aliens would leave the message in the field outside instead of knocking on the door of the radio telescope. First, there is the fence and locked gate. Then, there is the chance of getting shot for trespassing on an off-limits facility. Is Drake really suggesting that the aliens would be well received if they presented themselves at the door of an off-limits facility that is owned and operated by the British Ministry of Defense? Might such a move provoke a military response?

It is speculative but I do feel that, at some time in the history of UFO encounters and investigations, there have already been government or military interactions with extraterrestrials. Roswell is but one possibility. And one thing we now know for sure about Roswell and other incidents like it: We were, and still are, being lied to about the events that transpired. There was also an alleged meeting between Eisenhower and 'The Greys' at Edwards Air Force Base in January of 1954. The Greys were objecting to the testing of the first thermonuclear (hydrogen) bombs. That meeting was kept secret by mutual agreement of both parties, but can be referenced by searching 'Greada Treaty.'

The military, especially the American military, is in no way forthcoming about their putative contact with UFOs and the putative extraterrestrials that operate them. If the crop circle phenomenon is real, and I obviously think it is, then it is the chosen means of communication simply because it cannot be easily hidden from public view the way direct alien contact with government and military authorities always is. The aliens may want the messages seen and studied by open-minded, curious individuals, and southern England is the perfect place to make that happen.

There may be other reasons why the majority of crop circles occur in southern England. It is thought that there is something unique about the interaction of groundwater, chalk deposits, and clay soils that characterize the region. Or maybe it's because the English are smarter than the rest of us. I say that half in jest, but there is no denying that there are some brilliant, dedicated souls in that area, including Lucy Pringle, Paul Vigay, Colin Andrews, Freddy Silva, and many others who have dedicated a large portion of their lives to the cause of comprehending the crop circle phenomenon in all its dimensions. And among these dedicated thinkers, there is indeed a consensus that the crop circle phenomenon is extra-terrestrial in origin. Almost all other possibilities for the origin of *real* crop circles have been ruled out for one reason or another. The only alternative that has maintained some slight viability is that crop circles are manifestations of a secret technology called Hyper-dimensional (HD) technology, which is currently in the hands of the military. What does not make perfect sense is why the technology, which presumably uses super-high speed rotational motion to cast images into cereal crops, is being put on public display. If it is such a valuable top secret, why show it off? And, displaying it within two hundred feet of a government installation does not seem to be consistent with the kind of discretion we have come to expect from military planners who are in possession of top-secret technologies.

To conclude my repudiation of Frank Drake's blanket dismissal of the Arecibo reply, two final points must be explored. The first one is Drake's declaration that if they came "all that way" they would choose a more persuasive means of conveying their presence. The flaw in this is the logical assumption that they came all that way to use a form of communication that is not even intelligent. But whoever is doing crop circles is in possession of this hyperdimensional technology. How can such a capability, which may or may not even be in human hands, be seen as unintelligent? Beyond that lies a fundamental and potentially flawed assumption that they journeyed from anywhere farther than southern England to create crop circles in southern England. In this view, off-planeters, the real crop circle makers, reside here on Earth, maybe even somewhere in southern England, and elsewhere.

Where, exactly? In plain sight? Obviously not. In another mystical dimension? Maybe. Remember, we're talking about hyper*dimensional* technology. If the simplest explanation is always the favored explanation, as Occam's Razor suggests, then my answer to this question is favorable because it is only one word long: underground. They may come and go using flying saucers or other dimensions, but when they're here and they want to stay out of sight, they do so by operating out of subterranean installations that were built a long time ago. In a manner of speaking, subterranean hideouts can be thought of as alternate dimensions. Humans essentially inhabit a two-dimensional

world (give or take) that is the planet's surface. Aside from the occasional mine or subterranean government installation like the one
near Dulce, New Mexico, and numerous other places, we really do
not inhabit the subterranean world that could be viewed as a third
physical dimension of terra firma. This realm could be accessed via
subterranean passageways of sub-aquatic egress, and assuredly, UFO
activity has been witnessed in both of these realms. This idea will be
discussed in more detail in subsequent chapters.

But the final flaw in Frank Drake's logic-challenged argument
against the validity of the Arecibo reply is that he speaks with
complete conviction about matters that are well outside his area of
expertise as an eminent astrophysicist. Specifically, he confidently
declares that the DNA structure that is displayed in the Arecibo reply
is "clearly wrong" and that other elements of the Arecibo reply are
"chemically impossible." Since there are only a few references to
chemistry and nucleotides in the Arecibo reply, it should be pretty
easy to focus on the parts of the glyph Drake is referring to. And
when one does, we see that Drake is absolutely wrong.

The only reference to chemistry is the set of binary codes below
the one-through-ten numbering system at the very top of the glyph.
The binary codes refer to the five elements, Hydrogen, Carbon, Nitrogen, Oxygen, and Phosphorus, that were seen in 1974 as the ones that
are most essential for life on our planet. The Arecibo reply made one
simple change to that statement of fundamental biochemistry: the
element silicon (atomic number 14) was added right between Oxygen
(8) and Phosphorus (15).

Could this mean that the beings that sent the message are a silicon, rather than the carbon-based life form that we are. Perhaps so.
Anyone who wishes to argue that a silicon-based life form is chemically impossible is overstepping their academic competence by a
good bit. The universe is a mighty big place. No one knows what
other life forms could exist and how they might be chemically based.
If, on the other hand, the Arecibo reply is viewed as more of a correction of the original Arecibo transmission, this view ends up having a
certain validity because, in the years since the Arecibo transmission

was sent, some new strides have been made in the field of biology, and one of them is the fact that silicon is more important to life on Earth than was realized in 1974 when the Arecibo transmission was sent.

Three researchers from the Scripps Institute of Oceanography, Ben Volcani, Charles Mehard, and Neal Sullivan have shown that silicon is much more essential to carbon-based life forms than was previously realized. Sagan and Drake were probably unaware of the fact that silicon plays a critical role in binding other minerals to bones and cartilage. Without silicon in the mix, our bones would be so rubbery that we would not be able to stand upright in Earth's gravity. It's no particular shame for Drake that he did not know this in 1974. Even much later, Seth Shostak, successor to the directorship of the SETI program, dismissed the Arecibo reply in a debate he did with Richard Hoagland on an episode of the late-night radio program, "Coast to Coast." Shostak declared that the reference to silicon in the Arecibo reply was "science fiction." Not only is he wrong about the absence of silicon in bone structure, but Neal Sullivan's work shows that silicon is essential to the production of critical enzymes required for DNA synthesis in diatoms. Not only do diatoms form the base of virtually all aquatic food chains, but other researchers, like Hildebrand, have shown that Sullivan's work also applies to mammals, including humans.

The fact that the Arecibo reply is serving to correct elements of scientific knowledge is humbling. To suggest that such perceptive additions to the Arecibo reply are being stuck in there by pranksters or hoaxers is patently absurd. Whoever fashioned the Arecibo reply is on the cutting edge, or even ahead of the cutting edge of human knowledge. As further affirmation of this claim, we must now turn to the representation of the DNA molecule in the Arecibo reply, as it differs from the double helix that is represented in the original Arecibo transmission. The Arecibo reply seems to show a three-strand DNA molecule, one strand on the one side of the human stick figure, and a double strand on the other. Again, our so-called experts like Drake and Shostak are tempted to dismiss this change as yet another work of fiction. In 1974, perhaps this had validity but it doesn't anymore.

Maybe the glyph depicts a different DNA structure to our alien counterparts. But again, recent advances in DNA knowledge suggest that our understanding of DNA was being corrected in 2001 when the Chilbolton glyph appeared. The tireless research of Richard Hoagland has turned up a company that has figured out a way to modify DNA by temporarily adding a third strand. Enzo Biochem, Inc. applied for a patent for this new process, which joins this third strand of DNA to precise places in the usual double helix of the DNA molecule, allowing for an opportunity to insert new chemical patterns, thus altering the original DNA molecule. What Hoagland suggests is that the triple helix shown in the Arecibo reply could be a suggestion that this process, which is brand new to us, is not new to the creators of the Arecibo reply. They may be telling us that human DNA was genetically engineered in the past. Not only is this something that Sagan may have been hinting at when he poignantly stated that "the search for extraterrestrial intelligence is the search for ourselves." If that is what Sagan was getting at, he was not alone.

Recall that, in the previous chapter, Zecharia Sitchin stressed that the account he gleaned from the Sumerian clay tablets described the Enki, the son of Anu, was in such need of indigenous labor that he created the worker species he needed by combining the genetics of indigenous bipeds, specifically Homo erectus with their own 'alien' DNA. The stories gleaned from Sumerian tablets thousands of years old can easily be discounted as the stuff of myth and legend to be sure, but it is a curious coincidence that these myths and legends suddenly gain traction from multiple sources, the Arecibo reply and new advances in gene-splicing technology. Conversely, Sitchin's translations and these new advances in DNA technology seem to support the view that the Arecibo reply hints at the process by which human DNA was recombined with DNA from other sources. Regardless, Enzo Biochem's new technique for recombining DNA potentially invalidates Frank Drake's blanket statement that the DNA structure represented in the Arecibo reply is "clearly wrong." It may just be showing us that there is a process for manipulating DNA that Frank Drake knew nothing about when he and Sagan crafted the original Arecibo message. This is because the chemical information depicted in the Arecibo reply is not "chemically impossible," as Drake so confidently states. "I do know this, they are smart..." Drake intoned. Might the Arecibo reply be evidence that they are smarter than Frank Drake is giving them credit for? I certainly think so, and there are still other secrets hidden in the Arecibo reply that support this fact.

The first is yet another correction to our thinking. Recall that Sagan almost surreptitiously stuck a number in the original message that was unknown to science at the time. Instead of one billion, the textbook number of base pairs in the human genome, as it was understood at the time, Sagan used the precise number 4,294,441,822, which is approximately 4.3 billion. When the Arecibo reply was decoded by Richard Hoagland, he came up with the number 4,294,966,524,288. That is an increase of 524,288 base pairs over Sagan's estimate, which was seen as way too high back in 1974. The exact number of base pairs is still not precisely known, but no one is laughing at Sagan's seemingly wild estimate, and adding a mere 500 thousand base pairs onto an estimate that ranges around 4.3 billion is stunningly specific. So specific, in fact, and so insightful, that I cannot understand how anyone who bothers to carefully dissect the Arecibo reply can conclude that the message was made by pranksters. If it wasn't highly advanced off-planeters, the only possibility I can even consider is that the Arecibo reply was devised by a secret cabal of college professors. Imagining those same college professors sneaking around in a wheat field at night, in their tweed sport coats with patches on the elbows, is again more of a stretch than the extraterrestrial-origin scenario.

The final deviation from the original Arecibo transmission that I will consider here is the replacement of the radio telescope with some other curious device, which is presumably the alien equivalent of a radio telescope. If the reader will allow me to again suggest that the message was created locally and not sent across the void of space, then the contraption being represented is just the device used to create the message in the wheat, and not necessarily a long-distance communication device.

Curiously, this same device had been seen once before by crop circle researchers under circumstances that give me a chill. On August 14, 2000, almost exactly a year before the appearance of the Arecibo reply, the same exact shape appeared in the wheat in precisely the same place, a couple hundred feet from the Chilbolton radio telescope! Not only are we being shown a device that bears some connection to the radio telescope at Chilbolton, but the occurrence of the same pattern one year prior to the Arecibo reply suggests quite plainly that, whoever did the Arecibo reply had conceived at least part of it, maybe the whole thing, a year before it was delivered. Hoagland points to the work of physicist Bruce DePalma, when he speculates that the contraption being portrayed is an instrument of hyperdimensional (HD) physics that utilizes high-speed rotational force to create impressions in wheat or grass. DePalma conducted experiments as far back as the 1980s that showed how gyroscopes and rotating masses could have an effect on living systems, particularly grasses.

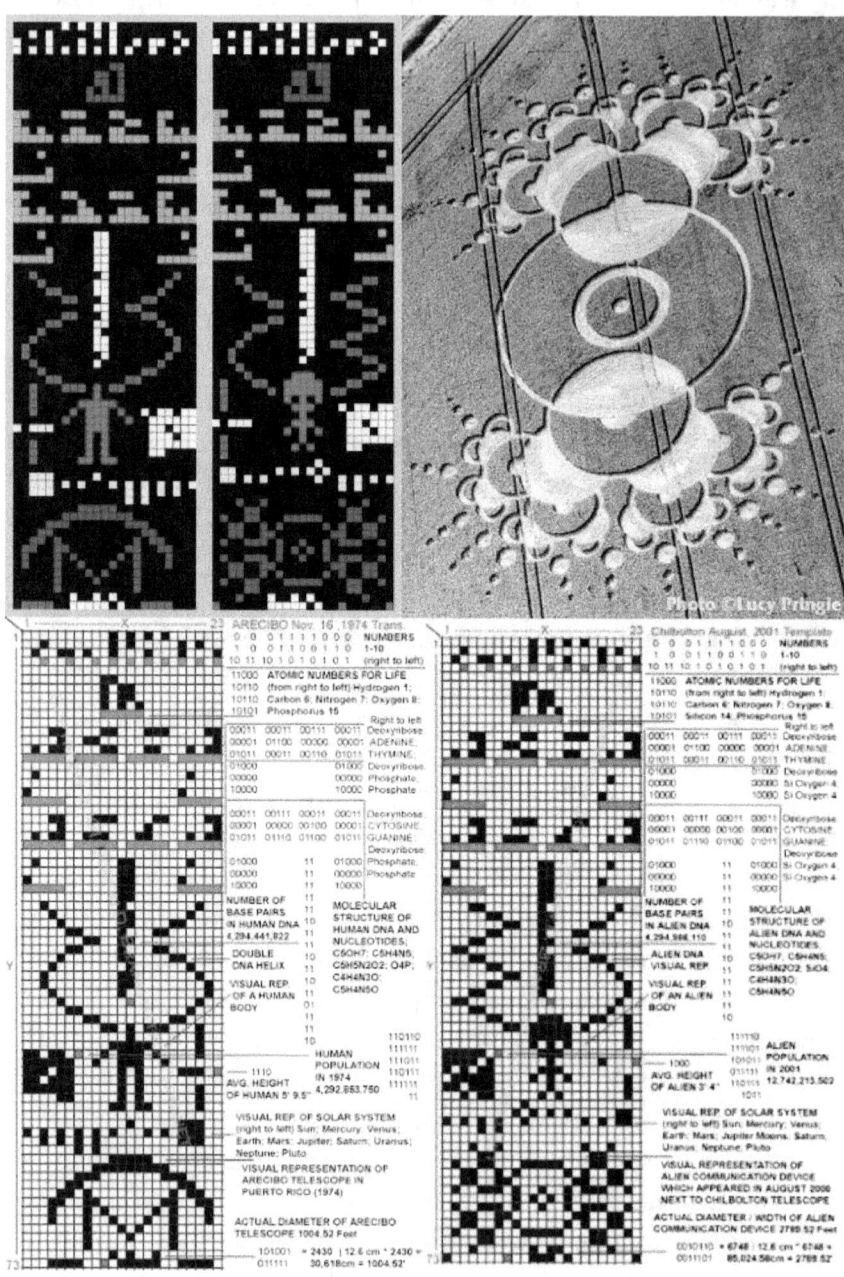

Using rotational forces, DePalma was able to create energies that flowed into plants. Crop circles are nothing if not members of the grass family that are rotated and woven with some unknown energy. Hoagland speculates that the appearance of this particular shape, in the shadow of a radio telescope, is no coincidence. We are being shown someone else's equivalent of an electromagnetic radiation device. A smaller version of the same device, appearing in place of the Arecibo antenna is no coincidence. We are being shown that this is the equivalent device in someone else's technology, and the repeated presentation of this image cannot be easily explained away as the work of pranksters. It references a concept with scientific validity, as the work of Bruce DePalma has shown, rather than being another one of the elements of the Chilbolton crop glyph that Frank Drake blithely dismisses as "chemically impossible" or "clearly wrong."

A final coincidence has happened to Richard Hoagland that is probably more of a manifestation of premeditation than coincidence. As previously stated, Hoagland was a colleague and contemporary of Carl Sagan. As such, Hoagland was aware that, in 1972, Sagan was involved in the construction of a probe, Pioneer 10, that was going to be sent on a one-way trip into deep space after doing a fly-by of Jupiter. Richard Hoagland and another colleague, Eric Burgess got with Sagan and suggested that this would be a great opportunity to send a message into space. Sagan liked the idea, and he spearheaded the preparation of a gold plaque that was attached to the outside of the spacecraft. It portrayed a male and female human with the spacecraft behind them for scale, along with a couple of different representations of our solar system and Earth's place in it. The Pioneer 10 probe, with the message plaque attached, was launched in the spring of 1972. Hoagland says that he and Burgess were just in the right place at the right time to suggest it to Sagan. But it is the keen mind of Richard Hoagland who also noticed that the very first crop circles to appear in modern times, in fields all across the British Isles, appeared only a few months later, the very first growing season after the launch of Pioneer 10. I have to agree with Richard Hoagland that this juxtaposition of events is too suspicious to dismiss as coincidence. In November of 1974, the Arecibo transmission was sent into space. Twenty-seven years later, we received a purported reply. (27 is three to the third power. Tesla was big on numerology and he revered numbers that were multiples of three. He lived and died in apartment #303).

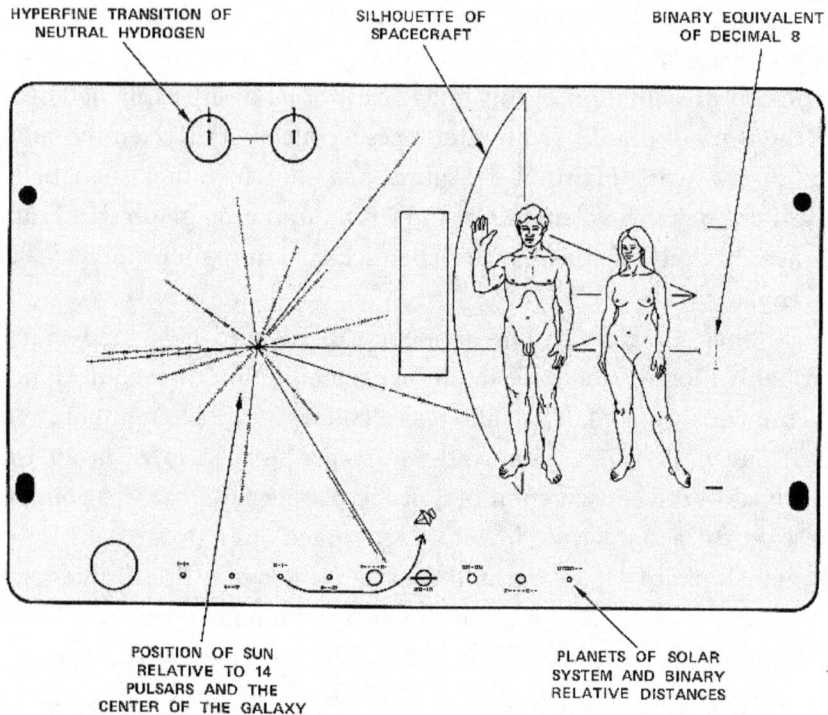

HYPERFINE TRANSITION OF NEUTRAL HYDROGEN

SILHOUETTE OF SPACECRAFT

BINARY EQUIVALENT OF DECIMAL 8

POSITION OF SUN RELATIVE TO 14 PULSARS AND THE CENTER OF THE GALAXY

PLANETS OF SOLAR SYSTEM AND BINARY RELATIVE DISTANCES

The groundbreaking work of Richard Hoagland opened my eyes to the ingenious messages so cleverly encoded into the Chilbolton glyph, also known as the Arecibo Reply. When it was first discovered, it was called the Persian carpet before Paul Vigay realized its unmistakable similarities to the Arecibo transmission twenty-seven years earlier. After all the analysis was said and done, Richard Hoagland concluded that the Arecibo reply was not the work of extraterrestrials or off-planeters, as I like to say. Rather, it was his considered opinion that it is the work of an extremely sophisticated intelligence agency operation that is employing hyperdimensional physics. This is about the only place where I disagree with Richard Hoagland. He thinks they are trying to convey a very important message concerning the gradual disclosure of extraterrestrial intelligence. I think he gives the intelligence agencies too much credit. There have been so many opportunities for them to open their files to the public that have been bypassed that I cannot see them suddenly deciding it is time to be more honest and forthcoming to the public they are supposed to serve. But if Richard is correct, it is only because their hand is being forced from the outside. I think the off-planeters began formulating their reply to the Arecibo transmission on November 16, 1974, the very day it was sent.

Suppose Hoagland is right, and government spooks decided to use their secret HD physics capability to share some previously secret knowledge about the existence of off-planeters who live under our noses. In that case, it's only because the off-planeters themselves decided it was high time that they themselves let the cat out of the bag.

5

THE MUTES

There are several lines of evidence that combine to prove the point that 'aliens' or off-planeters, as I prefer to call them, do indeed reside with us, right here on Earth. Perhaps the strongest line of evidence comes to us from the unlikely subject of cattle mutilations. Before we get too far, it helps to know that every subject has its favorite abbreviations and acronyms, and this subject has a lot of them. The first one to know is that 'mutes' is the one-syllable version of the multi-syllabic phrase, 'cattle mutilations.'

And, as with a lot of paranormal subjects, mutes have been happening for a longer time than most people realize. Also, like other paranormal subjects, mutes occur in clusters that are of key importance. There are a few prominent researchers and many less-informed rubes like me. In my view, the biggest dog in the whole mute kennel is Chris O'Brien, whose book, *Stalking the Herd*, is an absolute marvel of both field research and the critically important academic research behind it. He has at least two other books, Secrets of the *Mysterious Valley* and *Enter the Valley*, both of which focus on the strangeness of the San Luis Valley in northern New Mexico.

I was lucky enough to meet Chris in 2017 at the Mile High Mystery Conference in Denver, Colorado. The conference was sponsored by author David Paulides, who has penned numerous books on the grim subject of missing people. I was there to speak on the Sasquatch subject and Chris was, of course, the expert on mutes, which he definitely is.

I was only vaguely familiar with cattle mutilations before I met Chris. Certainly, I came to the conference pretty convinced that cattle mutilations were attributable to a combination of predator activity and cultists who were dismembering cattle as part of some weird Satanic ritual. After all, that is the story I had always heard in the media. While some mutes may be attributable to predation or Satanic ritual, Chris emphatically stated that such factors do not even come close to explaining all mutes. He also emphasized another important point that I was completely unaware of before hearing his presentation: In the forty or so year history of the cattle mutilation epidemic, not a single person, cultist or otherwise, has ever been caught or charged with this crime. As soon as he finished speaking, I purposefully strode over to his vendor table and bought his book.

While presentations may not prove anything, Chris persuasively suggested that whoever is doing the mutilating is at least very clever and, at the most, may not be human at all. In truth, there are a few very good reasons to suppose that the perpetrators of this grotesque crime aren't human, but they aren't just animal predators, either. To illustrate this point, let's examine a case that happened very recently in my home state of Oregon.

In July 2019, five valuable breeding-quality bulls were found killed and mutilated in a remote part of the Silvies Valley Ranch in the arid rangeland south of Burns, Oregon. The crime scene was in many ways typical of the countless cattle mute scenes that Chris O'Brien has investigated over the years in northern New Mexico, southern Colorado, and beyond. The first curious fact in the Silvies Ranch case is that no tracks, animal, human, or automotive, could be found at the scene. Indeed, there were none of the usual indications that predators, presumably mountain lions or wolves, were the culprit. No sign of a struggle, no torn flesh, scattered bones, or, most importantly, the mandatory animal tracks that must be present. This naturally led both the sheriff's office and the ranch owner to conclude that it was the work of "some sort of cult." Yet, there were numerous other oddities: all the blood was gone without a trace. None was spilled on the ground. Also gone were specific soft tissue organs such as the anus, the tongue, and the reproductive organs. As is also typical, the missing organs were removed with a certain surgical precision that would be difficult, even impossible, to achieve under field conditions anywhere, not to mention in the middle of nowhere and maybe even after dark. No definite cause of death could be determined in any of the bulls. No bullet holes, no blood, no sign of struggle or violence, except for the surgically removed body parts which, given the lack of blood, could only have occurred post-mortem.

Still, the Harney County Sheriff's Office needed to attribute the killings to some group of evil people, so it was decided that a tranquilizer dart must have been used to incapacitate the bulls, and a syringe was then used to remove all the bulls' blood via the tongue, after which the tongue was also removed to conceal all evidence of what could only have been one tedious procedure. Am I the only one who thinks such forced conclusions are preposterous? A bull's blood is measured in gallons, and cow blood is easily obtained at slaughterhouses if anyone really wanted it. Why journey so far and go to so much trouble for something that is so readily available? Ranch country is not 'cult country' but even if there are rural cults, how and why would they spend hours extracting blood (and it would take hours) without being detected or leaving any footprints or tire tracks. Not a single ounce of meat was removed from the ample carcasses; only certain organs that have no real value to butchers. The bulls were of breeding quality, which are the best. They were healthy, young, but full grown. They were the least likely victims in the entire herd of predation by wolves, cougars, or bears, but even that was moot because there was none of the trauma to the torso that invariably accompanies wildlife predation.

The sheriff's office issued the usual rewards for information or suspects. I sent the sheriff's office a copy of Chris O'Brien's book and even highlighted a few pages that offered some cogent conclusions from his exhaustive research. I never heard back, nor did I expect to. I did see in one newspaper treatment of the story that the sheriff's office admitted that 'aliens' were suggested as the perpetrators by some members of the public, although, not surprisingly, the sheriff's office did not take these suggestions seriously. One article mentioned that someone advised the investigators to look for a dent in the ground beneath the bulls, suggesting that they had been dropped to the ground from some height. According to advocates of the extraterrestrial hypothesis (ETH for short), this would indicate high strangeness, presumably of the extraterrestrial sort.

While no one piece of evidence can be cited as being present in all mute cases, Chris O'Brien would be the first to agree that, in many cases, the carcass of the mutilated beast does indeed lie in a considerable dent in the earth that bears the same shape as the deceased cow. O'Brien cites even stranger cases in which the mute was found in a tree or even tangled in power lines a dozen feet above the ground.

Hundreds of similar cases surfaced in the 1970s and Chris O'Brien visited everyone that came to his attention. While Chris stressed the fact that no one characteristic was common to every case, there were certain recurring traits: no blood, no obvious cause of death, no tracks, missing organs like the tongue, eyes, anus, and sex organs. No sign of predation, extremely clean surgical cuts, even laser-like, which delineated the area where those organs were removed. A veterinary surgeon at Oregon State University and a surgeon in Denver both arrived at the same conclusion that the incisions they inspected in the mutilated cattle showed definite signs of high-heat incisions, of the kind that would be made by laser surgery. Somehow, this does not sound like the work of "cultists." Maybe I'm crazy, but I would expect cultists working in remote ranch country to be using something closer to a chainsaw than laser surgery.

David Perkins, another researcher of high strangeness, found an interesting connection between some cattle mutilation sites, suspected UFO landing sites, and crop circle locations. They all bore the same high concentrations of the mineral magnetite. Tiny beads of magnetite were concentrated around a dead cow in the San Luis Valley that was investigated by our guy, Christopher O'Brien. The concentrations were estimated to be five hundred times greater than that which could be called normal. This suggested that there was some common thread that joined the seemingly separate phenomena of crop circles, UFO activity, and mute sites.

Granted, this is the kind of eye-roller stuff that mainstream science, the media, and law enforcement just don't want to hear. Aliens are a topic that has been dismissed and even ridiculed for so long that it may be asking way too much to expect such conventional thinkers to wrap their heads around such a kooky idea. Serious consideration of any hypothesis as unconventional as the ETH seems too crazy to consider. Why is this? Personally, I look at an unwillingness to entertain ALL potential hypotheses as decidedly unscientific. 'Bias' is a dirty word in scientific circles. Again, recall the words of the founding father of paranormal research, Charles Fort:

> "People with a psychological need to believe in marvels are no more prejudiced and gullible than people with a psychological need NOT to believe in marvels."

In modern time, it might be more accurate to frame this as a reluctance to 'entertain unconventional hypotheses' instead of '[believing] in marvels' but the idea is the same: if conventional science and conventional thinking fails to deliver suitable explanations for mysterious events, then it behooves us to give at least some consideration to the unconventional explanations. Or, in the words of Arthur Conan Doyle's famous detective character Sherlock Holmes, "When you have excluded the impossible, whatever remains, however improbable, must be the truth."

Unlike the sheriff's office in Harney County Oregon, Chris O'Brien is at least willing to entertain the possibility that the extraterrestrial hypothesis (ETH) is a worthy option. While he was understandably reluctant to 'go there,' Chris remains open to this possibility, although Chris is quick to point out that every explanation for cattle mutes, from the most outlandish to the most ordinary, has problems. Contradictory evidence abounds, regardless of the paradigm that is being entertained. In the final paragraph of his magnum opus, *Stalking the Herd*, Chris acknowledges the aspects of this grim subject that seem to be almost deliberately confusing:

> "The cattle mutilation mystery is like a monochromatic 1,000 piece jigsaw puzzle with several extra misshapen pieces thrown in for good measure."

Having personally experienced similar contradiction and confusion in my investigation of the Sasquatch and other high-strangeness subjects, I have formulated a suspicion, perhaps even a hypothesis, to explain why this is so. It is because, quite simply, we are being deliberately misled. Whoever or whatever is behind these mysterious phenomena and their contradictory evidences,

a.) Knows we are trying to understand them
b.) Does not want us to totally and easily understand it
c.) Is a little bit, or even a lot, smarter than we are.

These suggestions then force us to the next logical step, which is to try and understand why we aren't supposed to know everything that is going on 'behind the veil.' Even more necessary, we would like to understand, if we are going to consider the ETH, why would off-planeters kill and mutilate cattle in the first place? Fortunately, we can revert to Chris O'Brien's seminal volume for a compelling answer. While it is definitely compelling, it is not a simple idea, in fact, it is quite complicated, but let's not let that stop us from trying to understand it.

The following paragraph, while technically factual, will serve to highlight the need for a glossary to help sort out and remember the acronyms and technical terms.

NIDS, or National Institute for Discovery Science, attempted to get to the bottom of mutes. NIDS issued a summary report in 2003 that was authored by Colm Kelleher. In the report, Kelleher and others concluded that animal mutilations were part of long-standing, covert disease sampling operations by intelligent perpetrators who were aware of and monitoring the spread of a prion-based family of fatal infections, which are variously called CWD (in deer and elk) and BSE(in cattle), and either CJD or Kuru (in humans), all of which are variants of a prion-based set of diseases that are collectively known as TSE.

Let's just back up and offer a glossary of key terms and acronyms for future reference:

NIDS: National Institute for Discovery Science

CDC: Center for Disease Control, Atlanta, GA

NIH: National Institute of Health

Prions: (not an acronym) The tiniest proteins known by science that are able to insert themselves into living cells and distort them. Much smaller than viruses, highly transmissible, attacking nerve and brain tissue, very hard to detect, almost impossible to kill, long incubation period but always fatal to the host mammal, whether it be cattle, sheep , deer, monkey, or human.

TSE: Transmissible spongiform encephalopathy; this acronym refers to a whole family of prion-based diseases (of which mad cow is one) that attack nerve and brain tissue of any animal, eventually killing it.

BSE: Bovine spongiform encephalopathy, also known as 'mad cow disease.' This is the variant of the prion-based TSE that infects bovines (cows).

CWD: The variant of the prion-based transmissible spongiform encephalopathy (TSE) that attacks wild cervids (deer, elk, and moose).

CJD: Cruetzfeldt-Jakob Disease; the human variant of the prion-based disease, TSE.

Kuru: The first prion-based disease ever discovered in

humans. First detected in the Fore tribe of Papua New Guinea in 1953.

Scrapie: The prion-based disease that infects sheep and goats, which first surfaced in England in the 1730s.

To start at the beginning, prions are the tiniest protein molecules ever discovered. They are a thousand times smaller than viruses. They are extremely difficult to test for, and until recently, could only be tested for by biopsy of brain or nerve tissue of animals, but only after the animals are already dead. They are almost impossible to completely kill, they are highly transmissible, and they cause an abnormal folding of cellular proteins in the brain that leads to brain damage that slowly kills the host organism. As the human variant, CJD gradually kills its human host. The victim manifests symptoms that so closely resemble Alzheimer's or dementia that it is now thought that some people who are diagnosed with dementia or Alzheimer's may actually have Cruetzfeldt-Jakob Disease (pronounced KRUTZ-feld-YOK-ob). Frighteningly, the only way to tell the difference is by post-mortem brain biopsy, which almost never happens AND, still worse, Alzheimer's and dementia diagnoses have greatly increased in recent years. Hidden in the dementia statistics may be a much bigger outbreak of CJD.

The first of these insidious prion-based diseases to be discovered was scrapie (pronounced SKRAPE-ee), which appeared in certain sheep herds in England in 1732. As the nerve damage intensifies, the sheep tend to scrape against fences, trees, etc. to assuage their discomfort, hence the name. Where scrapie came from is not known. Chris O'Brien suspects that it may have been brought to England from New Guinea by the earliest English explorers of the South Pacific, which took place in that same decade as that first scrapie outbreak in England.

Other scientists speculate that prions might spontaneously generate in a tiny fraction of animal populations and then spread from there, especially when livestock are kept too close together. Overcrowding of livestock facilitates the spread of virulent pathogens like scrapie. The same is true for disease transmission in humans. Recall how quickly Covid-19 viruses spread in airports and on passenger planes.

Since there was no known cure for scrapie and it was always fatal, the whole sheep industry, which was a very important element of the English economy at the time, did what they could to eliminate all infected animals. Some researchers think that not only was scrapie not fully eliminated, but it may have even been accidentally transmitted to the U.S by way of sheep parts that were sold in the U.S. as feed for mink ranches, particularly in Wisconsin.

Whoops.

Again, an attempt was made to eliminate all the infected animals. They were supposedly destroyed. Remember that prions are insidious, difficult to destroy, and virulent, even to the point of being able to cross species barriers between one kind of animal and the next.

To this day, scrapie still occasionally shows up in sheep. It always kills the sheep, and until very recently, it defied all attempts to test for it before it killed the host organism. Finally, in 1998, a test of sheep's nictitating membrane (a transparent eyelid) was found to reliably indicate the presence of scrapie, not that you could do anything to stop it from killing the animal once it was infected. Later, another diagnostic test was developed that sampled mucus tissue from a sheep's rectal area. This was the second stride in the attempt to at least monitor the spread of the disease without killing the livestock, just to find out. Another promising step, to be sure, but still nothing close to a cure for the disease.

This is where it gets interesting. Chris O'Brien observes that, from his vast experience with mute investigations, the eyes and rear ends are the specific body parts that are most often surgically removed! (Coincidence? Hold that thought.)

Again, so little was known about the transmissibility of these highly virulent prion-based diseases that samples may have been horribly mishandled. No one is sure, but next thing anyone knew, a variant of the disease, CWD, showed up in deer and elk herds in Wyoming, not far from the very lab where scrapie-infected sheep were being housed and studied. Then, in 1997, a much bigger outbreak was detected in deer herds around Ft. Collins' where scrapie was also being studied. It quickly spread through deer and elk herds in most of the central and eastern United States. By 2013, CWD had been detected in deer and elk herds in 18 states.

Now, let's move on to prion-based disease in humans. In the mid-1950s, a disease that the natives called kuru killed hundreds of members of the Fore' Tribe in the highlands of Papua New Guinea. It was also called "laughing sickness" because the degraded nerve tissue caused the face to freeze in a facial grimace of sorts. First, Australian medical researchers, then Americans, descended on the South Pacific island nation. It was found that one important vector that greatly expedited the spread of this fatal disease was the ritual cannibalism that had been taking place in this tribe for centuries. The flesh, and even the brain tissue of deceased relatives, was being 'recycled,' even among members of the deceased person's own family. Still worse, the kuru disease was familiar to the tribe, yet they understood so little about how it was transmitted that human flesh was prized for its fatty texture and pork-like taste. The brains of kuru victims were even considered to be a bit of a delicacy. Yikes! If a tribesperson didn't get the disease from eating infected flesh or nerve tissue, there was also a vector for contracting the disease simply by being involved in dismembering and handling of the deceased relative's tissue, particularly if one had an open sore on, say, the hands.

The disease was not fully nailed down until 1976 by Daniel Gajdusek, who not only defined the disease and won the Nobel Prize for doing so, but also injected the disease into the brains of monkeys, thereby showing that kuru could cross the species barrier. Meanwhile, samples of kuru-infected tissue were being sent to U.S. laboratories in Maryland and maybe elsewhere, for some ten years before Gajdusek finally came to understand any of the key elements of this insidious disease.

Did the kuru prions escape the research laboratories? When Colm Kelleher was doing his research on mutilated cattle in 2004, he discovered that kuru brains were being sent to the U.S. by researchers as early as 1957. Even worse, large-scale inoculations were happening to several species of animal in the middle of a wildlife refuge in Maryland in the late 1960s. Meanwhile, scrapie-infected sheep were being kept at wildlife research centers in Wyoming and Colorado. Next thing you know, prion diseases like CWD show up in mule deer around Ft. Collins and in mule deer near the wildlife research lab near Laramie, Wyoming. While the connection cannot be proven, it is a curious coincidence that these two locations were the beginning point of CWD infections that spread throughout the deer population of other states.

So, what it appears that we now face is some sort of potential contamination of the food supply, not only in the wild deer and elk herds, but in the cattle that comprise our enormously valuable beef industry. I eat as much beef as anyone so I certainly am not presenting these alarming facts as an argument in favor of a vegetarian diet. I am presenting this information simply because it may offer a suitable explanation for some, maybe even most, cattle mutilation cases that occurred from 1970 until at least 2003, as unlikely as this may seem on first consideration. In order to grasp this concept, one must first understand all that has been explained up to this point. The overarching theory seems admittedly absurd if the facts that underpin it are not adequately understood.

"It is a capital mistake to theorize in advance of the facts. Insensibly, one begins to twist facts to suit theories, instead of theories to suit facts."

— ARTHUR CONAN DOYLE'S SHERLOCK HOLMES
CHARACTER.

This statement embodies the approach that is generally taken by the media, as well as law enforcement personnel when trying to grasp the undeniably unlikely explanation that the ETH factors into the mutes phenomenon. Despite the fact that it provides a possible explanation for most, if not all, of the facts of the mute phenomenon, the ETH has not been given its due by law enforcement or the media. What is it about the ETH that so prevents it from serious consideration?

"The world is full of obvious things which nobody by any chance ever observes."

— SHERLOCK HOLMES

Fortunately for us, there are a few individuals who see what so many others have missed. One such person is Colm Kelleher, the researcher for NIDS who headed a team that may have done the best job of objectively investigating cattle mutilations. There were certainly other attempts to get to the bottom of the mystery. Mutilations were happening on a regular basis when the FBI finally got involved in 1979 and commissioned a study that was headed by FBI agent and bank-robbing expert Kenneth Rommel. In light of the above quotation by Arthur Conan Doyle's fictional detective, it is interesting to note that Kenneth Rommel was quoted in an interview for Taos Magazine that "[He] had reached [his] conclusion almost immediately after accepting the job."

Rommel's prosaic conclusion was that the 10,000 or so mutilations that had occurred up to that point were almost completely attributable to natural predation. Rommel acknowledged that some mutilation sites bore anomalies, but these too were dismissed in his 1980 report in which he concluded that "most credible sources have attributed this damage to normal predator and scavenger activity."

Gabe Valdez was a New Mexico state patrolman who had investigated dozens of cattle mutes by the time Kenneth Rommel was commissioned to head up his study in 1979. He told Chris O'Brien that, "During the six to eight months when Rommel was actively investigating the mutilations in New Mexico, the state became strangely quiet, with very few if any true mutilations being reported to officials."

Valdez speculated that the phenomenon shifted to other parts of the West during the short time when Rommel was actively investigating. So, Rommel never saw any of the more bizarre aspects like the high strangeness cases that Valdez and Chris O'Brien were so used to seeing. Interestingly, western Canada experienced quite a spate of cattle mutilations during the same time that the trail went cold in New Mexico.

This does not surprise me. If the mutes phenomenon *is* intelligently directed, efforts would be made to confuse and obscure the true nature of the phenomenon. If they are intelligent, there is every reason to suppose that the perpetrators behind the mutes are going to, literally and figuratively, cover their tracks. In any case, it didn't take much to throw Rommel off the scent. His heart may not have been in it from the outset. According to Valdez, Rommel didn't have much of a stomach for viewing the mutilations that he encountered. In the short period of time that he actually investigated in the field, Rommel tended to stay in the car and leave the actual documenting to others.

Meanwhile, during the same several months when Rommel was active in New Mexico, Canadian law enforcement experienced a big up-tick in exactly the kind of high-strangeness cases that were suddenly NOT happening in New Mexico. No matter. Rommel issued his summary findings in 1980, just eight months after he began his supposedly definitive probe. Rommel attributed the vast majority of cattle mutilation cases to natural predators like mountain lions, bears, and wolves. Not surprisingly, Rommel's summary finding came across as a bit of a whitewash, especially to RCMP investigator Lyn Lauber, who headed the Canadian investigation in Calgary. "I'd like to see Rommel write off our confirmed cases as due to predators," Lauber objected.

Indeed, the official investigation of the cattle mutilation matter bears a strong similarity to the official whitewash that summarized the Project Blue Book investigation into the UFO phenomenon: No UFOs here. Just misidentified clouds and planets. Nothing to see here, folks. Let's just all move along...

Despite their best effort to sweep the whole matter under the rug, it was not the last word on the matter of mutes. Colm Kelleher headed a more insightful and objective NIDS investigation into the cattle mutilation epidemic between 1970 and 2003. The NIDS report was issued in 2003 and it offered the stunningly courageous conclusion that,

"The animal mutilation epidemic of 1970-2003 was and is a monitoring operation for an infectious agent that is spreading through the human food chain (cattle, sheep, and wild and farmed deer and elk). In North America (Canada and the United States), the infection comprises a full-blown CWD epidemic in deer and elk, and a subclinical BSE infection in cattle."

The report went on to reveal that kuru-infected brains had indeed been mailed from New Guinea to NIH labs in Maryland as early as the late 1950s, and scrapie research was being conducted in labs in Colorado and Wyoming in the immediate vicinity of future outbreaks of CWS. But, the report continued, the ability to test for prion-based pathogens by utilizing tissue in the eyes and rectum of sheep had been known to science only since the 1980s, yet these very same tissues were being removed in mutilation cases that predated this scientific understanding by as much as twenty years!

This is a huge deal because it basically removes the government, military, or covert scientific programs from consideration as culprits in the majority of mutilation cases. Whoever was doing the mutilating had advanced knowledge of prion testing protocols. These same protocols were apparently being used some twenty years before they were even known to science.

If this information is correct, and I believe it is, then that leaves us with a certain Sherlock Holmes-like piece of logic:

"If we eliminate the impossible, then whatever remains, however improbable, must be the answer."

Of course, it must be said that things that were once seen as impossible are not any more. Humanity did not have the knowledge to test eyes and rectal secretions for prions at a time when, by all outward appearances, it was in fact, happening. Therefore, early cattle mutilations and the food-supply monitoring that is implied *were not being done by humans.*

One might choose to deflect this troubling conclusion by insisting that cattle mutilations and the environmental monitoring it represent was really a covert government program, and they just knew how to do the advanced prion-testing procedure much earlier than anyone realized. As always, Chris O'Brien provides a bullet-proof line of reasoning to refute this suggestion.

If the government or just the military were behind the testing, why wouldn't they use their own herds or even utilize the enormous sampling opportunity that is available at slaughterhouses in virtually every state? There would be no need to sneak around in the dead of night and risk getting caught in the act of killing and dismembering the cattle, which represents some ranchers' livelihood. Also, one would expect that, at the very least, government agents would be more discrete about how they disposed of the remains. Surely, they would conceal the evidence of wrongdoing by hauling away the live-stock of interest, testing them in a secure location, and then disposing of them in the same or some other secure location where they never would be found.

For this reason, Chris leans heavily toward rejecting the view that covert government research is responsible for the totality of cattle mutilation, though he accepts the possibility that they may be responsible for some part of it.

But, shouldn't the same logical question be applied to the view that off-planeters are behind some, maybe most, of the mutes? Why would super-sophisticated off-planeters return the carcasses where they would be discovered and investigated? Why not keep the dead cows or somehow destroy them (with their presumptive advanced technology) so we never have evidence of the rather ruthless testing?

First of all, as Chris O'Brien suggests, if the valuable cattle are stolen, then a crime is committed that would necessitate a criminal investigation. If the cows are returned, dead or alive, with all the valuable meat completely untouched, then it obfuscates the whole view that there was even a crime that was committed in the first place. Also, back off on the sampling (mutilating) while shallow thinkers like Kenneth Rommel are active so that they are more inclined to conclude that natural predation is responsible for all, or even most of the cattle mutes. If it's a natural process of predation, as Rommel concluded, then there is no crime to investigate. As Chris O'Brien would say, "No harm, no foul."

Even if the news media, or the cops, attribute part of the phenomenon to 'cultists', then we leave the investigators and the public chasing their tails. That is, they go off looking for a group that doesn't even exist. Mind you, no person has ever been caught or charged with mutilating cattle. Ever.

If 'cultists' were responsible for all or even some of the forty-year history of the mute phenomenon, then it becomes highly unlikely that at least one of them would not have made a mistake that would have led to their arrest. Cops are not perfect but they aren't stupid, either. Crooks might get away some time, but sooner or later, they make a mistake and get caught. Yet, in the history of the phenomenon, it has never happened. Really? It seems that the law of averages would catch up with cultist criminals, if they existed, over the course of forty years and tens of thousands of mute cases.

But our resident expert, Chris O'Brien, raises one more cogent point that bears articulation, for I don't think most people, myself included, would have thought of it all on our own. Why would off-planeters return the mutilated carcasses? Simple. The cattle carcasses are being conspicuously dumped for a reason: it is a warning, a heads up, an indication that our food supply is threatened. We are being given an overt indication that our food supply is compromised. It's a wake-up call. We are given a warning that there is a problem that may have been created by some careless scientists, but that society at large needs to fix.

Scientists meant well when they naively mishandled prion-infected tissue and accidentally (or purposely) infected livestock and wildlife with virulent prion-based pathogens. Regardless of past tragedies, science has to now get busy and find a workable solution, even if it means abandoning our long-standing fondness for a meat-based diet. It would not be a choice I am eager to make. I like steak. But, we do face a potential human health crisis in the near future, if not already.

There is a line of thinking that states that the best and smartest solution to any serious problem is not the one that solves only one problem at a time. The smartest and most enduring solutions are the ones that solve multiple issues at once by employing the most ingenious, most multi-faceted solution possible. The ability to devise such multifaceted solutions, I should think, is the hallmark of a truly intelligent species.

As much as I like my cheeseburger, transitioning to a planet-wide, plant-based diet is the kind of multi-pronged solution that befits an advanced species that is thinking about their long-term survival. The benefits of a plant-based diet include reduced greenhouse gases (specifically methane), improved health, longer lifespans, reduced cancer rates, and elimination of the prion-based family of pathogens that threaten humanity. Further, Chris O'Brien observes that we could feed an additional two billion people on Earth if the grain we currently feed to livestock is diverted to human consumption.

As important as this issue is to humanity, it has not yet fully addressed the thesis of this book. How does this whole discourse support the view that off-planeters have already arrived on the planet and why do the off-planeters care so damn much about the terrestrial food supply? As always, the most cogent answer to this key question is as obvious as it is easy to overlook.

The fictional Sherlock Holmes character is credited with saying, "The world is full of obvious things which nobody by any chance ever observes."

Nobody except, maybe Chris O'Brien. In *Stalking the Herd*, Chris suggests in his summary remarks that they, the off-planeters, care about the earth's food supply because *our* food supply is also *their* food supply. That implies that at least part of the time and maybe even all of the time, they live right here with us!

Where exactly do they reside on or in planet Earth? That subject will be addressed in future chapters. Meanwhile, the fundamental conclusion that can be logically derived from careful examination of the cattle mutilation phenomenon is that we share the planet. The food supply that sustains us may be sustaining someone else, as well. They are more advanced, staying out of sight, and concealing their activities from us, but they are very concerned about the long-term viability of both our and their food supply. They are the ones who have been conducting this mysterious, ruthless, and systematic monitoring of the Earth's food supply that we call 'the mutes.'

6

_____

PLAIN SIGHT

The Moon is an enigma. It shouldn't even be there. It shouldn't be so close and it shouldn't be so big. Our closest neighbor in the solar system is also the solar system's biggest mystery.

We all know that the Moon's gravity causes tides in the oceans but the Moon does a whole lot more. Without the stabilizing effect of its gravitational pull, Earth would wobble as it rotated by as much as ninety degrees. The Sun's rays would strike the Earth very differently. Climatic fluctuations could force animal life to pick up and migrate as different parts of the Earth become too hot, then too cold. Intelligent life might still be possible, but it would be a much greater struggle, and our lives would be focused on simple survival to a much greater degree as the planet's tilt changed. But because of the Moon, we have a mild, stable climate that allows for liquid water pretty much everywhere on Earth. Ours is the only planet in our solar system where this occurs, and it makes food production and finding shelter much simpler. Human civilization might not exist without the stabilizing influence of the Moon's gravity.

The fossil record tells us all that Earth's original life forms were all aquatic. First, plant life found fertile soil, and then animal life followed the food source out of the water. Evolutionary biologists speculate that terrestrial animal species may have evolved first in tide pools. The fluctuating interface between water and land created opportunities for evolutionary changes in locomotion and respiration. Tide pools are still seen as nature's best evolutionary nursery, all thanks to the Moon. The Moon's gravity is also thought to drive tectonic changes in the Earth's crust. We do not see evidence of tectonic changes on other planets, and the reason we have so much of it on Earth is probably because we have such a huge moon. Without these tectonic motions, continents would not move, and minerals that crystallize from the planet's molten interior magma would not be brought to the surface where plants and animals can use them.

In a sense, we owe our lives to the Moon, but it is still very mysterious. We've been studying the Moon for a long time, but there is still a lot we do not know. We don't know how it got there, why it is so big, what is in its interior, how old it is, why it behaves the way it does, and so much more.

It's not the biggest Moon in the solar system but no other planet has a moon that is so similar in size. Our Moon is one-fourth of the diameter of the Earth, and one-sixth of the volume. Our moon is so big that it almost qualifies as a sister planet. The Moon doesn't really orbit the Earth. Owing to its size and proximity, the pull of the Moon also slows down Earth's rotation. Without the Moon, our Earth days would be about six hours instead of twenty-four. Without a Moon, our planet might still be livable, but it probably would not be a climatically stable oasis with liquid water everywhere except the poles. Everything about the Moon: its size, its distance from the Earth, the speed at which it travels, its density, and the circular perfection of its orbit combine to make our earthly existence easier. One must wonder what happy accident gave us such a useful orbital partner.

At least four theories try to explain how such a small planet ended up with such a huge moon. The oldest of these theories is the 'fission theory.' First proposed by Charles Darwin's son George in

1878, it held that the pull of the Sun's gravity tore loose a big chunk of the still-molten and rapidly spinning Earth. The chunk of matter coalesced and cooled to form our moon. In the 1920s, Harold Jeffries refuted that theory and a new theory gained favor that had the moon coalescing from either the same cloud of matter from which the Earth formed, or from a Saturn-like ring of matter that surrounded the Earth. This became known as the 'co-acretion theory', and it was also refuted for reasons concerning the angular momentum of the Earth-Moon system.

Thirty years later, the co-acretion theory was in turn replaced with the 'intact capture theory' that held that the Moon formed somewhere else and got caught by the Earth's gravity as it happened by. Later, it became clear that the physics of the situation would not allow for such an unlikely event. For one thing, the Moon would have to be traveling very slowly as it happened by, which objects in space don't tend to do. More likely, the Moon would have either smashed headlong into the Earth, or it would have skipped off the Earth's grav-itational field and kept right on going. The planetary physics of the capture theory didn't pencil out and as recently as the 1970's, there still was no generally accepted theory for the Moon's origin.

Once we visited the Moon and brought back samples, it became clear that the Moon and the Earth had some identical rocks. Oxygen isotope signatures from moon rocks indicate that the Moon and Earth are not just of similar origins, but that they are virtual twins. Not all Moon rocks matched Earth rocks, but there were enough similarities to revise the theory of the Moon's origin. Two scientists, Hartmann and Davies, suggested that a rogue planet about the size of Mars whacked into the Earth, and a big chunk of the Earth was knocked free and later coalesced into an orbiting body. Called the 'Big Whack,' this is the favored theory at present, and the moon rocks collected by Apollo astronauts are a big reason why it is widely accepted.

While computer models seem to support this theory, there is one big problem. As a consequence of the big whack, the Earth should be spinning terrifically fast; much faster than it does. To solve this problem, Dr. Robin Canup came up with a most unlikely coincidence. She suggested that the Earth was whacked a second time, this time from the exact opposite direction. That second impact, called the 'Big Whack 2,' slowed the Earth's rate of rotation to that which we now experience. But striking similarities between Moon rocks and Earth rocks seem to rule out the possibility that the rogue planet came from somewhere far away. The size of the rogue planet would also have to be much bigger than Mars-sized in order to give the Earth the 23 ½ degree tilt we have today. Matter ejected from the Earth in such a big collision would scatter too widely to contribute to the formation of a moon. It is, therefore, argued that our moon is both too big and too close to have been the product of such an enormous collision.

Our moon orbits 1/400th of the way to the Sun, and whether or not it was acreted, it assumed a diameter of 2160 miles. That ends up being one-fourth of the Earth's diameter and exactly 1/400th of the Sun's diameter. Are we expected to believe that, somehow, a random collision created an object that is both 1/400th of the Sun's diameter and also 1/400th of the distance to that Sun? This highly improbable coincidence makes us Earthlings sole witnesses to perfect solar eclipses. No other known planet gets perfect solar eclipses in which their moon perfectly obscures the whole face of the sun with nothing to spare. If the diameter of the moon were even one mile different, the eclipses we see would not be as precise as they are. Not only is the size and distance orientation perfect, but the perfectly circular orbit of the Moon makes it unique in the solar system. Author Isaac Asimov calls this "the most unlikely coincidence imaginable."

Most astrophysicists agree that the Big Whack theory is the favored theory not so much because the facts support it, but because the other theories are so much worse. The Moon has so many other peculiarities that a new, very wacky theory for the Moon's origin has been seriously suggested. That theory alleges that the Moon is an artificial satellite that was deliberately inserted into Earth orbit by intelligent beings. As improbable as it may seem, this is actually the only Moon-origin theory that explains all of the Moon's puzzling mysteries. There are no mysteries to the Moon's composition or behavior that are unresolved and no data of any kind refutes this theory, far-fetched as it may seem.

One curiosity of Moon behavior that defies easy explanation is why Luna is gravitationally locked to the Earth. It is thought that uneven weight distribution inside the Moon causes this. Gravitational studies of the Moon indicate that its center of mass is offset by some six thousand feet in the direction of Earth. This offset should give the Moon a wobble as it spins, but the Moon also has a sizable bulge on the back side that counterbalances the offset to its core. The crust on the back side of the Moon is nine miles thicker than the crust that faces us. This helps balance the internal imbalance, enabling the Moon to rotate smoothly. Since it rotates on its axis at the same rate that it revolves around the Earth, once every 29.53 days (about a month), we always see the same side of our moon. There is no dark side of the Moon, Pink Floyd's famous album notwithstanding, but there is a *back* side of the moon that we never get to see from Earth. It is not dark. It gets lit by the sun just as often as the side we see, but we never see it from our vantage point on Earth.

In preparation for the planned missions to land on the Moon, a lunar orbiter was sent to the Moon to map the surface and get detailed measurements of the Moon's gravitational field. When the lunar orbiter arrived, we got our first surprising look at the never-before-seen backside. The back side of the Moon was much more rugged than the side we always see. It is much more pock-marked than the front side, where large dark areas (marias) form the jack-o-lantern face we see on the side facing Earth. Gravitational studies conducted by the lunar orbiter raised other curious anomalies, like the Moon's low density and surprisingly small, offset core.

Our Moon is one-fourth of the diameter of the Earth. It is so big that it could be considered a sister planet. They are so similar in size that the Earth and Moon mutually orbit each other. The center of revolution of the two masses (called the barycenter) lies inside the Earth, though not at the Earth's center. Despite their size similarities, the Earth's and Moon's densities are very different.

The Moon is less dense than the Earth by quite a bit. If the moon was formed from the same material as the Earth, the density of the two orbiting bodies should be the same, which they are not. The Moon's density is calculated to be 3.34 times the density of water. The Earth's density is 5.5 times the density of water, making the Earth twice as dense as the moon. The Moon is so much lighter than the Earth that it must have a wholly different interior. Since the first probes were sent to the Moon in the early sixties, the data being generated has convinced many scientists that the Moon is at least partially hollow. Planetary geologist Sean Solomon believes that gravitational studies of the Moon do indicate hollow places in its interior. He stated that the lunar orbiter studies "indicat[ed] the frightening possibility that the Moon may be hollow."

NASA scientist Gordon MacDonald summarized the lunar orbiter studies in an article he published in 1962. In the article, he observed that, "If the astronomical data are reduced, it is found that the data require that the interior of the Moon is more like a hollow than a homogenous sphere."

Nobel laureate and chemist Harold Urey discovered deuterium, worked on the Manhattan Project, and studied the rocks brought back by Apollo 11. He observed that, "There is a large area inside the Moon that is simply a cavity." Carl Sagan, the greatest of all planetary scientists, stated in 1966 that, "A natural satellite cannot be hollow." So, if the Moon is at least partially hollow, then it must not be a natural satellite. "So if the Moon is a hollow construct as the facts lead us to understand," says J. P. Robinson, a UFO researcher, "who built the Moon, how did they get it into its present orbit and why did they put it there?"

Besides the gravitational studies, seismic experiments were also conducted on the Moon as part of the Apollo program. Seismometers were placed on the Moon between 1969 and 1972 and operated until 1977. During that time, many moonquakes were recorded, the biggest being magnitude 5.5. Three kinds of quakes were noted. Deep quakes are thought to be caused by meteor impacts. Thermal quakes are said to be caused by the Sun's uneven heating of the surface. The strangest ones are shallow moonquakes which ring throughout the Moon for up to ten minutes. All this activity is taking place on a celestial object that is said to have no geologic activity. If tidal forces from the Earth's gravity were causing those quakes, they should affect the whole Moon, but the shallow quakes are localized.

After installing the first seismometer, Apollo 12 engineers planned to calibrate it by deliberately crashing the two-ton lunar ascent stage into the surface of the Moon after the astronauts got safely back into Moon's orbit. On November 11, 1969, the ascent stage crashed into the Moon's surface forty miles from the seismometer. The shock wave built to a peak in eight minutes and the seismometer continued to record reverberations for over an hour. By comparison, quakes here on Earth last for a few minutes. Years later, NASA scientists explained away this disparity in quake duration. The groundwater in the Earth, we were told, dampens earthquakes. The Moon has no groundwater, so the quakes ring a lot longer. Yet, more recent probes like the Lunar Prospector in 1999, and Strategic Observatory For Infrared Astronomy (SOFIA) in 2020 detected water on the moon. The Lunar Prospector detected hydrogen ions that imply water near the poles. SOFIA collected data indicating that water existed in the regolith (soil) of the sunlit Clavius Crater. Apollo 14's ALSEP (Apollo Lunar Surface Experiment Package) included a spectrometer that detected a cloud of water vapor that hung around for several minutes. At the time, NASA dismissed it as water that was somehow spilled from water tanks on the lunar module. Water was also found in the chemical structure of some of the moon rocks that were brought back, but this was not acknowledged for decades. China's Chang'e 5 probe was the first to detect on-site evidence of water in 2021. The Moon does have water, on the surface and in its interior. A lack of water on the Moon cannot be cited as the reason some lunar quakes last so long.

The seismic data produced by Apollo 12's deliberate impact was so intriguing that the experiment was repeated by Apollo 13. After an accidental explosion in a cryogenic oxygen tank, their Moon landing was canceled, but they proceeded to the Moon and orbited it just to get turned around and head home. As they orbited the Moon, they still carried their third-stage booster rocket, which weighed fifteen tons. Far heavier than the lunar ascent stage that Apollo 12 slammed into the Moon's surface, Apollo 13's third stage would impact the Moon with the force of a thirteen-ton TNT explosion. The rocket motor crashed into the Moon eighty-five miles west of Apollo 12's seismometer. When it hit, the Moon again rang like a bell. The moonquake reverberated for a whopping three hours and twenty minutes, yet the quake only penetrated twenty-five miles into the Moon. The protracted reverberations and the lack of deep quaking both pointed to the same unmistakable conclusion: the Moon has no core or at most, a very small one. Based on all the available seismic data, the Moon is not the solid object it appears to be.

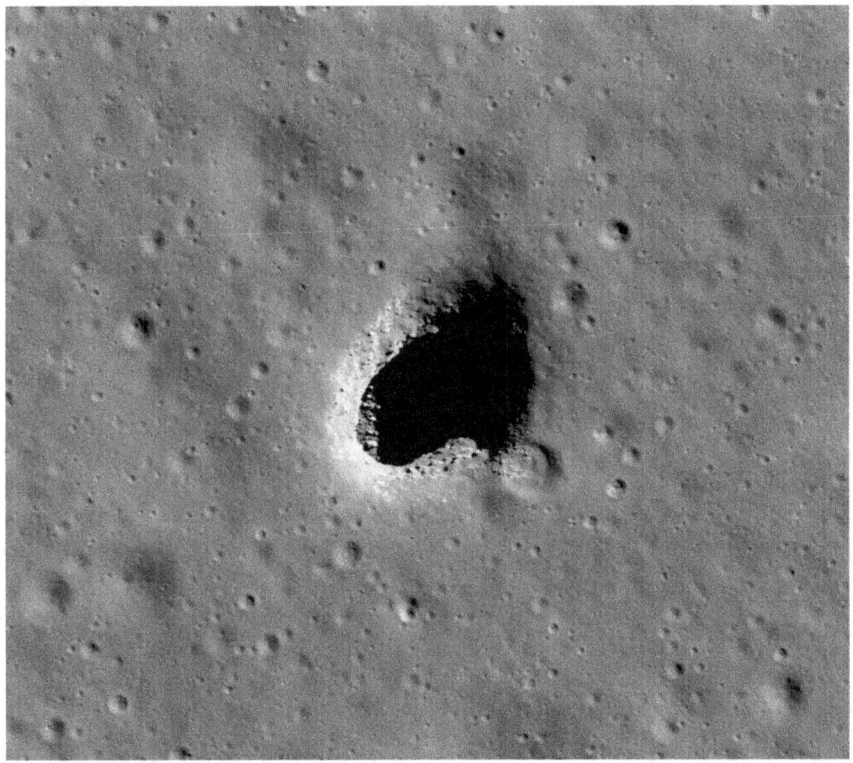

The examination of surface features by recent probes supports this. Amateurs and professional astronomers alike love to pore over photos of the Moon's surface and look for things that shouldn't be there. Pyramids, bridges, buildings, obelisks and more have been claimed, although I do not find the images to be very convincing. Richard Hoagland pointed out an object he called 'the shard', which he felt was over a mile high. The back side gets studied a lot more now that we have more and better photos. In 2021, the same Chinese Chang'e 5 mission (*Chang'e* is the Chinese Moon goddess) previously mentioned rolled out a robotic vehicle, YUTU-2 onto the back side of the Moon. It produced one intriguing photo of a distant object that looked vaguely cube-shaped. It took a couple months for the probe to move closer. Meanwhile, there was quite a bit of excitement and speculation, but when the probe closed in on what was being called 'the cube' and 'the hut,' it began to appear that the rock on the crater rim looked more like a rabbit than a cube. The feature is now being called the jade rabbit.

Since the Moon was first studied with telescopes in the 1600s, people have been reporting lights and flashes on the surface. Over the centuries, over 800 examples of blinking lights and flashes on the Moon have been reported, often by scientists. Seemingly geometric structures almost always dissolve into explainable combinations of rock and shadow, but not always. The Lunar Reconnaissance Orbiter in 2009 photographed two sizable holes in the Moon's surface that do not appear to be craters. In the Mare Ingenii, a 426-foot diameter hole that lunar geologists called a 'skylight' was photographed. Here on Earth, the roof of subterranean lava tubes sometimes collapses to form an opening called a skylight. This process is being used to explain it, even though it is in an area of the Moon's surface showing very little volcanic activity. Elsewhere on the moon, sinuous channel-like structures that resemble river channels have been photographed. These, too, are being called collapsed lava tubes. Lava tubes seem to be a bit of a 'go-to' when having to explain mysterious features. It does suggest that such scientists are pretty OK with the view that there are many empty spaces and caves beneath the Moon's surface. Even NASA recognizes their potential value as shelters or bases. Subterranean redoubts provide some protection from dangerous rays, definite protection from surface heat, and maybe even cavities that could be filled with air if they could be adequately sealed. I have read of an extreme-terrain vehicle that NASA is working on as part of a future mission that could lower itself into holes or caves so as to determine their size and integrity.

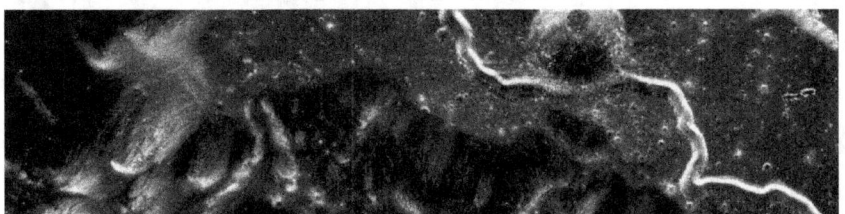

Sinuous channels are being called collapsed lava tubes.

The back side is said to be a busier place than the side we see because, until very recently, it could not be scrutinized from Earth. It does make perfect sense that, until such time as we began sending probes and spacecraft to the Moon, the back side of the Moon afforded a certain measure of privacy, if that is desired. Since we started going there, UFO researchers claim that virtually all Apollo spacecraft are said to have been followed at a distance, and sometimes at close range. Any discussions of strange objects that were observed in orbit are explained away as pieces of the spacecraft, pieces of ice, and so on. Space shuttle missions captured video of quite a few mysterious objects in motion. No astronaut has ever come forward and unequivocally stated that they saw UFOs in orbit or on the way to the Moon. They're a tight-lipped bunch, as we would expect from guys and gals with military backgrounds. Michael Collins did admit to seeing a UFO, but it was while flying over Germany in the early 1950s.

Authors of UFO books contend that many strange lights were seen, especially as the Apollo spacecraft orbited high over the previously unseen backside, but the astronauts would never admit it. Amusingly, it has even been contended that enough observations and encounters took place that the astronauts began using code phrases like 'Santa Claus' to refer to encounters with unexplained objects.

Walter Schirra, the only astronaut to fly Mercury, Gemini, and Apollo missions, commanded Apollo 7 in 1968. He was the first to use the term Santa Claus in reference to an intelligently guided object that was following his spacecraft. The next flight, Apollo 8, was not planned to land but it was the first to orbit the Moon and see the backside. Their mission was to test the process of firing the thrusters to first enter, then exit the Moon's orbit. This had never been previously tried. After a three-day trip to the Moon, it was Christmas Day of 1968 when Apollo 8 passed behind the Moon and into radio silence. The three astronauts were the first humans to personally witness the backside of the Moon. As they passed behind it and into radio silence, they also had to fire the rocket motor at just the right moment, or they would never get back home. As they emerged out the other side of the Moon's orbit, Lovell broke radio silence with the statement, "Please be informed, there is a Santa Claus." Most assume he was expressing relief because the maneuver went as planned, but some suspected there was a double meaning.

One item of folklore that is often cited by UFO researchers is the unsettling information that NASA obtained by the first crew to set foot on the Moon. Neil Armstrong allegedly made a statement to the effect that he was being watched from a crater rim as he exited the spacecraft for his historic "one small step." During his extravehicular activity, there is a period of radio silence in which we are told he switched to a medical channel to describe some alien activity in his vicinity. There was indeed a private ASA radio frequency that was used for medical issues. Ham radio operators here on Earth periodically intercepted transmissions on that private channel. It was used on Apollo 8 when Frank Borman got sick with vomiting and diarrhea. Neil Armstrong was famously tight-lipped in his later years. He said very little in public and wrote even less about his place in history. He said he wanted the other members of his crew to have the publicity. Buzz Aldrin was often asked about aliens and such. He denied all reports of sightings or encounters.

They are not known for speaking off the record, but we do know that the astronauts did encounter some unexpected anomalies. Some of the Moon rocks they brought back were much older than the rest. It is assumed that they are meteorites and asteroid fragments. Some Moon rocks are almost a billion years older than the oldest known Earth rocks. Moon rocks as old as 5.3 billion and Moondust as old as six billion were collected. Titanium is abundant in the regolith, or lunar soil, especially in the marias that are thought to be lava flows. Marias, the smooth dark areas we see on the front side, have been found to contain dense 'refractory elements' that should be found closer to the core. Potassium, cerium, dysprosium, erbium, europium, and phosphorus are curiously abundant in marias, presumably as a consequence of historic volcanism. Large amounts of uranium 238 and thorium are also associated with marias on the side we see, yet not yet detected on the back side. Don Wilson, author of *Secrets of Our Spaceship Moon* concludes that they were brought to the surface by some unknown process. NASA has been trying to explain it for years. Another bigger question that needs answering is why there are many marias on the front side and none on the back. Very recently, NASA scientists suggested that the high percentage of refractory and radioactive elements in the marias explains their existence. Rocks containing these elements are thought to melt more readily, explaining why so much rock in the marias was once melted. This bit of circular logic illustrates a tendency to use one mystery to explain another, even by empirically-minded scientists.

As well as in the marias, a great deal of radioactivity was detected in the upper eight miles of the Moon's surface. The surface, especially the back side, is also scorched, and a lot of it is coated with a glass-like material. The surface is very hot, yet the inside of the moon is thought to be much cooler. The marias were natural landing sites for the earlier Apollo missions, and astronauts can be seen having a great deal of difficulty drilling into the surface of the marias. Gravitational and seismic studies indicate that the Moon has three distinct layers, with the outermost layer being the most dense. This is the opposite of what is normal for planets. The dense exterior of the Moon seems to limit the depth of craters, even the biggest ones. The bigger the crater, the deeper it ought to be. They are not. The Moon's craters are of uniform depth throughout the Moon's surface, some even curve upward in the center. Scientists say that is because molten material filled the hole after it was made. Outside-the-box thinkers like Wilson, Knight, and Butler see it as representing the tough exterior hull of a well-travelled spacecraft, and the relatively empty interior is the domain of advanced beings who like their privacy.

Note central highland. Close up at right.

In the books that discuss this theory and the evidence that supports it, it is agreed that excavations by intelligent beings have brought material to the surface that normally would exist at depth. There are peculiar piles of material in some craters, such as King Crater. Astrophysicists counter that crater formation is a messy process. Impacts will eject stuff widely, but usually, it all settles outside the crater. Mounds of material inside the crater are a puzzle. Gashes and track-like marks on the surface are explained by Spaceship Moon theorists as remnants of the mechanical processes that were employed while excavating the interior. Moonquakes are indications of on-going subsurface construction or the vibrations from the collapse of historical construction.

King Crater as photographed by Apollo 16.

Since the Apollo program, no one has yet returned to the Moon but probes have been sent by U.S., Russia, India, and China. They have verified the existence of water, as well as Hydrogen-3 (tritium), a Hydrogen isotope that would be very useful in generating fusion reactions. NASA also conducted a classified test on the last manned lunar mission, Apollo 17, the results of which still remain classified to this day. Public records indicate that an experiment called Chapel Bell was conducted, but even fifty years later, the experimental data has not been published. We can only assume that is because it got some unexpected results. The name of the experiment certainly hearkens to acoustical research.

John Podesta, Chief of Staff for President Clinton and counselor to President Obama, once stated, "I'm skeptical about many things, including the notion that government always knows best and that people can't be trusted with the truth. The time to pull the curtain back on alien presence on the Moon is long overdue."

Aside from conventional wisdom, outside-the-box thinkers cannot be blamed for connecting the dots and forming unconventional, alternatively-minded conclusions. The history of science is full of unconventional conclusions that were roundly ridiculed and later accepted. Galileo's planetary motions, Wegner's plate tectonics, and Bretz cataclysmic floods are but a few examples. The Moon does have big empty places in its interior. Of that there is little doubt. The big question is whether those empty places are inhabited by beings, either temporarily or all the time.

Subterranean redoubts are the safest, best place to colonize another planet or moon. Plans for subsequent missions to the Moon and Mars do include identifying and utilizing subsurface cavities. Whether it was constructed somewhere far away, then transported to our solar system and inserted into Earth's orbit is an intriguing question that bears consideration, given the mass of confusing and contradictory information about the Moon's composition and location. We don't understand how to build or move such an enormous object. Of course, we don't know how the enormous mass of the pyramids was moved and built either. My view is that when we figure out how something as immense as the Great Pyramid was built, we have a pretty good idea how to move enough material to hollow out a moon.

The final question that always comes to mind is, why? The most obvious answer is that someone has a strong interest in Earth resources or human activities, or both. Authors who write on the Spaceship Moon theory suggest that the Earth is a laboratory or experiment. As far back as the 1930s, author and outside-the-box thinker Charles Fort wrote that, "The Earth is a farm, and we are the crop." Fort, by the way, was the earliest writer to assert that the unexplained aerial lights and objects people sometimes see in the sky are from other worlds.

It is inviting to speculate that the Moon is the vessel used to transport human ancestors to this planet. Of the many books that consider this idea seriously, my favorite is *Who Built The Moon?* by Knight and Butler. What I enjoy most is the originality of their ultimate conclusion. They surmise that the Moon was built not by aliens but by time-traveling humans, who, using advanced technology, journeyed far back in time to create a moon that would stabilize and improve Earth's life-sustaining qualities.

The study of ancient writings, not to mention oral traditions, does not prove anything, but there are some interesting tidbits to be found in a survey of myths and legends. As it happens, cultures on both sides of the Atlantic have legends that tell of a time when the Earth had no moon. Indians that reside in the Bogota Highlands of Colombia have an oral tradition that tells of "the earliest of times when the moon was not yet in the heavens." The ancient calendar of Tianaca is a set of symbols on a wall of a courtyard in Keynesia, and it even offers a date. It says the Moon arrived between 11,000 and 13,000 years ago.

In ancient Greece, both Democritus and Anaxagoras wrote of a time when the Earth had no moon. Aristotle wrote of a region in Greece known as Arcadia, which was inhabited in his time by people called Hellenes, but the original inhabitants, called Pelasgians had inhabited this land "before there was a moon." There are two Scriptural references to a moonless Earth, one in Job 25:5, "before there was a Moon and it did not shine," and Psalms 72:5, "Thou was feared since the time of the Sun and before there was a Moon a generation of generations ago" (in other words a very long time ago).

Perhaps the most interesting and specific of legends comes from the Zulu tribe that has long inhabited the country we now call South Africa. Their oral tradition instructs that the Moon was put in place by two brothers, Wowane and Mpanku. The brothers, who had scaly, fish-like skin, stole the Moon from a fire-breathing dragon. They then emptied out the egg-like satellite of its yolk before placing it in Earth's orbit. Before the Moon was placed, the Earth was shrouded in water mist, and after the Moon was placed, that mist came raining down.

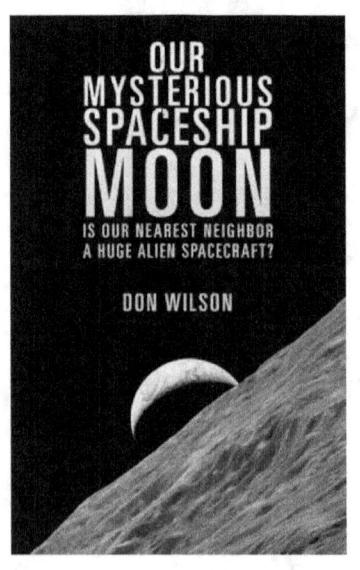

This legend is fascinating in that it bears curious similarities to the Sumerian cuneiform tablets that also describe two brothers, Enki and Enlil, who installed humanity on the Earth, and who are also depicted as wearing fish-like attire. Recall from chapter one that the two Anunnaki brothers from the Sumerian account originated from a planet known as Niburu, the twelfth planet, which traveled the solar system in a highly eccentric elliptical orbit. Rather than journeying from Niburu, perhaps they brought Niburu with them and parked it in orbit around Earth. The Moon is almost large enough to qualify as a planet, or at least a dwarf planet, but it does not orbit a star. The timing of the Moon's arrival in the Bolivian highlands calendar is also quite interesting. The Zulu legend seems to credit the moon's arrival with causing a major climatic event that bears an uncanny similarity to the great flood that Randall Carlson and Graham Hancock estimated to have happened 12,800 years ago (see Chapter 1).

The accounts in the Sumerian clay tablets, as translated by Zechariah Sitchin and others, do provide another missing piece of the human origins puzzle. They attempt to offer an answer to the question of why we were put here. Sitchin, and later Michael Tellinger would have it that we humans were genetically engineered as a 'slave species of the gods,' as described in Tellinger's book, *Slave Species of the Gods*. If Tellinger's view has any merit, and if the spaceship moon theory also has

merit, then we have the potential answer to one big question. The current occupants of the spaceship Moon may include the Niburu-ans, also known as the Reptilians in extraterrestrial lore.

Conclusions based on legends and ancient lore are a long way from scientific fact, but it is always amusing when multiple accounts overlap and align with each other. In *Who Built the Moon?* Butler and Knight raise another possible purpose for the moon. Their convoluted conclusion stems from the question of why, if there are other beings that inhabit planets elsewhere in the cosmos, have they not presented themselves to us? Is it because we just aren't listening? The search for extraterrestrial intelligence is trying to do just that, and SETI scientists have not yet detected any intelligent signals. Butler and Knight submit that such efforts are futile because the signals we hope to detect are too brief and ephemeral to allow for detection. Instead, they speculate that intelligent beings have devised another way of making their presence known, but only when the time is right.

By way of allegory, they reference a scene in Stanley Kubrick's 1968 film, *2001: A Space Odyssey.* In that scene, astronauts on the Moon (no less) unearthed (un-mooned?) the black monolith. One of the astronauts touches it and the monolith suddenly activates. It then sends a signal out into space, and it is received by beings who reside on a moon of Jupiter. The purpose of the monolith, then, is to be intentionally discovered but only when humanity has progressed sufficiently to become space-faring. The monolith is a mechanism for notifying the alien civilization that installed it that humanity has finally become cosmically relevant. They don't need to send us signals or watch for ours. When the monolith was activated by human touch, the alien civilization automatically received a kind of text message.

Butler and Knight speculate that the Moon, in black monolith fashion, is a clue; a really big clue. And when we finally become astute enough to realize that the Moon cannot be a natural object, we will recognize that clue for what it is. Then we will have the answer to the question we have been asking for so long. It's the same question that the SETI scientists are trying to get answered: Is anybody out there? And if there is, who and where are they? The answer may not be obtained by sending messages or listening for somebody else's. Once we have figured out what the Moon really is, perhaps we will have the answer. They're right in front of our faces, *hiding in plain sight.*

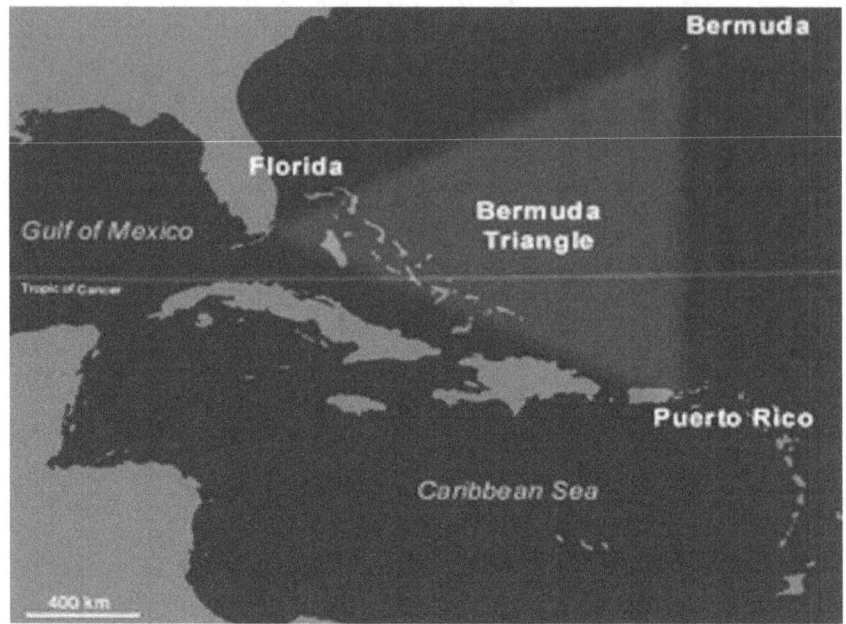

7

THE WORLD'S GREATEST MYSTERY

I must confess that I, like a lot of other folks, never took the whole Bermuda Triangle thing seriously. Documentary TV shows, magazine articles, books, and fictional movies all portrayed a mysterious triangular-shaped area in the North Atlantic. The troublesome waters are bound by three vertices: Miami, Florida; San Juan, Puerto Rico; and the Bermuda. It is a place where mysterious and sometimes deadly events befall the unlucky occupants of planes and ships. But it is also a very busy patch of ocean and since so many people traverse this Texas-sized area without incident, it has led many to doubt that there is anything paranormal going on. Indeed, most televised documentaries and magazine articles, especially the earlier ones, advocated the view that any crafts that went missing could be explained by stormy weather, human error, rogue waves or other natural occurrences.

There is no total agreement on how many ships and planes have gone missing over the years. One source I saw said 300 ships and 100 planes have gone missing in the past century. Another source estimated that fifty ships and one hundred planes have vanished there over the last 100 years. Either way, the Bermuda Triangle has a long history of being a navigational hazard, dating back to the time of Christopher Columbus, whose logbook detailed strange lights, compass malfunction, and flaming streaks crossing the sky and entering the water. When it comes to missing ships, there are many cases in which the crashed plane or sunken vessel is finally located on the sea bottom years after its disappearance, often in very shallow water. More commonly, no trace of the missing ship, plane, or its occupants is ever found. Perhaps the most famous case, which put the Bermuda Triangle 'on the map,' so to speak, was the disappearance of Flight 19.

In December of 1945, shortly after the end of World War II, a squadron of five Avenger torpedo bombers, with a combined crew of fourteen, went missing within the general confines of the Bermuda Triangle. They were the nineteenth training flight to leave the Fort Lauderdale air base that day, hence the name Flight 19, and they successfully launched their torpedoes before becoming disoriented in clouds. By 6 p.m., all five planes had lost radio contact with their base, and by 7 p.m., five PBM Mariners and two ships were dispatched to search for the missing aviators. One of the PBM Mariner search planes, with another thirteen airmen, also went missing.

Other well-known disappearances include a six-hundred-foot military vessel called the Cyclops, which disappeared in 1918 with a crew and passenger manifest totaling 306 people. In 1961 another military flight, a K B Hayes bomber, went missing, but not before reporting  engine trouble. In 1963, two jet-powered strato-tankers disappeared. Between 1945 and 1950, in addition to the Flight 19 tragedy, three other aircraft and one cargo ship disappeared. In 1969, two small light-houses on Great Isaac Cay disappeared. In 1881, a military vessel known as Ellen Austin happened upon a 'ghost ship' that was adrift with absolutely no crew on board. The Austin boarded the vessel and installed a crew to sail the vessel to port. The two ships became separated in bad weather and when the ships eventually reunited, the ghost ship was again devoid of any and all crewmen. While there are many, many more maritime and aviation tragedies associated with this patch of ocean, the books, articles, and TV shows that treat this mystery more often use ordinary explanations to discount the allegedly paranormal goings-on.

In the case of Columbus, his compass problems may have been nothing more than changes in declination owing to his changes in location with respect to Earth's magnetic north pole. The streaking lights Columbus reported are dismissed as a probable meteor shower, although one might expect that any experienced mariners would know about meteor showers. The Caribbean has a history of bad storms, including hurricanes and tropical storms. Anna is often cited as the probable reason for the disappearance of the two lighthouses on Great Isaac Cay. As far as the disappearance of the Cyclops, it was indeed a very large vessel for the time, and it was loaded (maybe overloaded) with a cargo of magnesium ore. When last seen leaving Bermuda, it was not only riding low in the water, but it was listing slightly, and one of its two engines was not working. It is thought that the vessel may have gotten sideways to a swell, had the heavy cargo of ore shift, causing the ship to swamp and sink suddenly. Still, one would expect to find lifeboats, lifejackets or some other buoyant debris, though no such debris was ever found.

In the case of Flight 19, a great deal of scrutiny has been put on this mystery because it was such a tragic and high-profile event. There is also a log of the communication between the individual planes and their home airfield in Fort Lauderdale and there is a lot there that suggests the pilots became disoriented and then ran out of fuel and had to ditch in open ocean. Four of the pilots were trainees. Only the lead pilot was experienced. While Commander Charles Taylor was indeed experienced, all of his recent training missions were conducted over the Florida Keys, south of Miami. The less-experienced pilots had also trained over the Florida Keys. They had just been transferred to Fort Lauderdale and Flight 19 was their first training mission out over the Bahamas. Radio communications, as recorded in the flight log, suggest that some of the pilots and even the commander were so used to flying over the Keys, and the Keys look so similar to the Bahamas, that they forgot which archipelago they were flying over. At one point, one of the planes got separated from the group and the rest of the flight doubled back, making a complex series of turns that further disoriented them. At another point in the flight log, Commander Taylor uses his old call sign from the Miami airfield rather than his correct call sign from Fort Lauderdale. Further radio communications indicate that both of Taylor's compasses were malfunctioning and that the Commander had become very disoriented. He even acknowledged over his radio at one point that he was lost, but he made multiple comments that suggest he thought he was over the Keys, not Bermuda. The fact that both of Taylor's onboard compasses were malfunctioning may be the toughest thing to explain away.

In the ensuing decades, a lot of time and energy has gone into trying to find the wreckage of this infamous event. Some think a few pilots made it back to dry land before running out of gas and crash-landing in a remote part of the Florida Everglades. Avenger wreckage has also been found off-shore in recent years owing to concerted search efforts sponsored by TV productions. As far as the PBM search plane that also disappeared, it was one of five search planes dispatched five hours after Flight 19 failed to return on December 5th, 1945. Among the search ships, one of the crews observed a bright flash in the dark December sky 20 minutes after the ill-fated search plane took to the air. It is supposed that the PBM had an onboard fire or explosion, which was something that the PBM had a previous history of. Among the pilots of the time, the PBM was known to be an aircraft that was difficult, even dangerous, to fly owing to frequent engine failures and onboard fires.

When books and TV shows attempt to explain away all the anomalies that seem to occur in the Bermuda Triangle, they tend to apply some faulty logic: If one can show that some of the disappearances have ordinary explanations, then all the other ones do, too. It's the same logic that is often applied to UFO sightings: if some can be explained away, they all can. This fails to address the potential complexities of the subject. In reading multiple books on the subject, I noticed a recurring idea: one cannot get to the bottom of such a multi-layered mystery in a short, simple treatment of the subject. A short article or a twenty-minute TV segment doesn't have time to address all the details or all the disappearances. No understanding of the subject can be achieved by a limited investigation of some of the events. When things get complicated, it is often because more than one thing is going on. Instead of a single underlying explanation, there may be several, and a lazy attempt to penetrate only the surface appearances will not generate any meaningful understanding. Most, maybe all, televised treatments of mysteries like the Bermuda Triangle can only give between twenty and forty-five minutes of air time to their investigation, which is not enough time to address the subject's complexities, patterns, and subtleties. There are so many disappearances and so many complexities that one must read a book, if not several books, before it becomes possible to understand the topic in all detail.

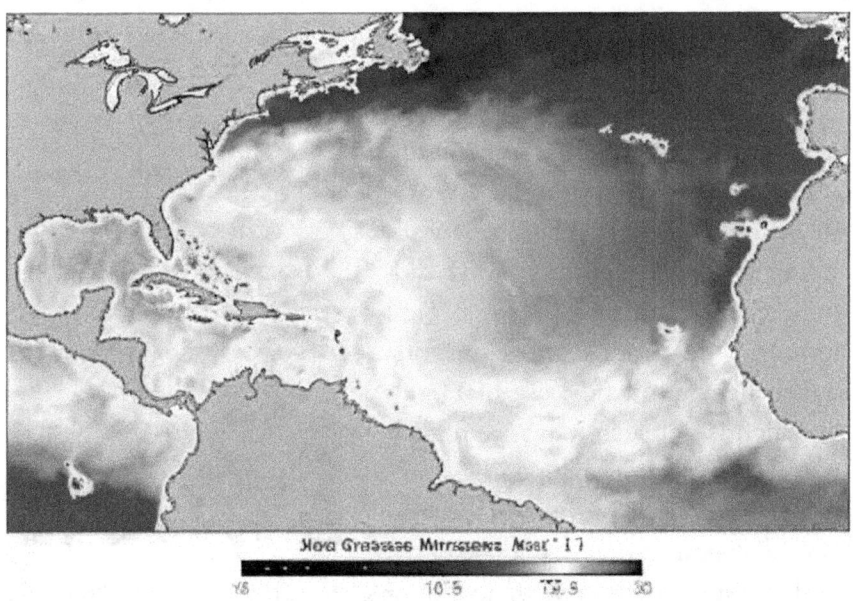

For example, yes the Bermuda Triangle is a place that produces several hazards to navigation, including sudden and severe weather (up to and including hurricanes), rogue waves, thick algae mats that can trap a vessel, and reefs in dangerously shallow water. It is also a very busy patch of water. Miami, which forms one of the three verticies of the Bermuda Triangle, is one of the largest ports on the entire eastern seaboard and definitely the busiest port for pleasure craft anywhere on the East Coast. Shipwrecks and sinkings are going to happen in such busy waters, and indeed, boats continue to go missing in the Bermuda Triangle. Many of the wrecks are attributable to inexperience or human error, even when the crew is experienced, as with Flight 19.

Another historical name for the Bermuda Triangle is 'hurricane alley'. In the 15th and 16th century, Spain lost several gold-laden galleons to unanticipated encounters with hurricanes in that area. First they would lose a rudder or mast in the hurricane, then they would get blown into shallow water and run aground, or get rolled by huge surf and demasted. It was said that Montezuma put a curse on the region with respect to the Spanish shipping traffic to avenge the plundering and slaughter perpetrated by Pizarro and his countrymen.

The name "Bermuda Triangle" was coined by Vincent Gaddis in an article about the place in Argosy Magazine in 1964. Then, a bestselling book by Charles Berlitz did quite a lot to increase public awareness. In both instances, the authors leaned heavily on the case of Flight 19, which is not seen today as indicative of paranormal happenings but rather a cascade of human errors. Another point that is raised by modern authors who wish to debunk the idea that the Bermuda Triangle is a paranormal hot spot is the correct contention that some of the weird and tragic nautical and aeronautical events that take place are disappearances that happen outside the strict confines of the Bermuda Triangle, they again improperly conclude that the concept of a Bermuda Triangle has no validity whatsoever. In truth, the name, the shape, and the area confined by the Bermuda Triangle were arbitrarily assigned by Vincent Gaddis and then repeated in Charles Berlitz's best-seller. Gaddis coined a catchy turn of phrase that stuck in the public consciousness. Gaddis invented a meme.

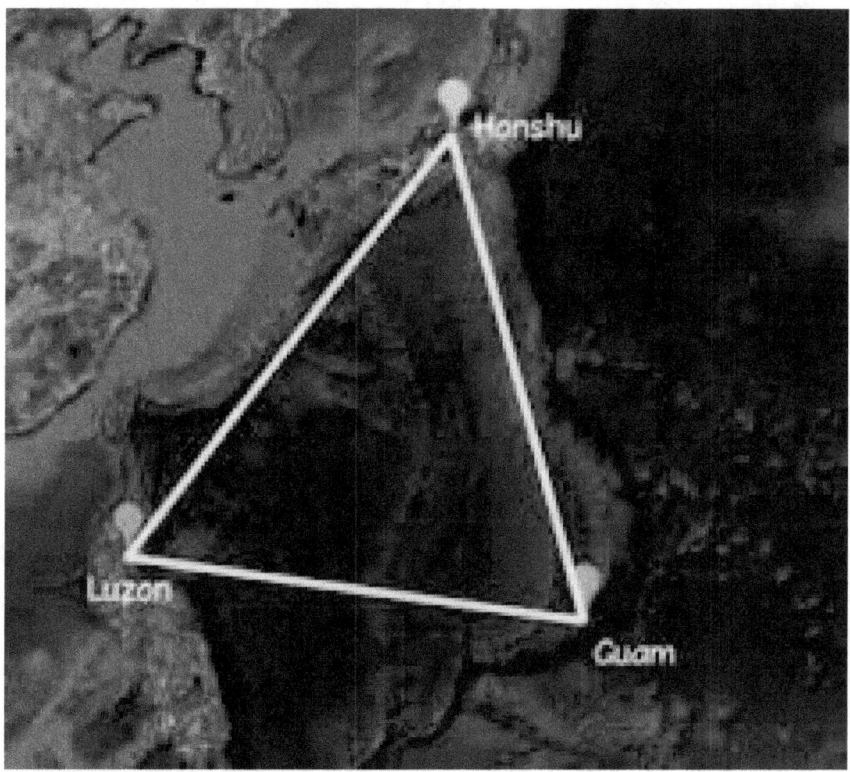

There is nothing special about a triangle's geometry; the mystery area is potentially much bigger than the 500,000 square mile triangle as delineated by Gaddis. The Bermuda Triangle is sort of a generalized reference to a larger region of the Atlantic that is disproportionately fraught with navigational hazards. Shipwrecks are so common in this general area of the Atlantic that the original settlers of Bermuda were the survivors of shipwrecks, beginning with a group of settlers who survived a shipwreck in 1609. The flag of Bermuda includes the image of a shipwreck. Many of the nautical disappearances, like the Cyclops, seem to have taken place after the ill-fated vessel successfully exited the Bermuda Triangle, per se. The ghost ship happened upon by Ellen Austin was found well north of the Bermuda Triangle. Many other ghost ships have turned up over the past two centuries, both in and out of the Bermuda Triangle. The Sargasso Sea is a vast bed of sargassum known to trap sailing vessels back in the day, adjacent, but still outside the strict confines of the Bermuda Triangle. This particular navigational hazard is thought to be responsible for many of the ghost ships that have been found, as is 'the doldrums,' an area around 33 degrees north latitude where sailing ships were famously beset by protracted periods of no wind. The doldrums extend across the whole of the Atlantic at 33 degree north latitude and the area was well understood to be a hazard to navigation in the days when all ships were sailing vessels. 'The Rhyme of the Ancient Mariner' is a famous piece of 19th-century epic poetry by Samuel Taylor Coleridge. He details the tribulations of a sailing vessel and her crew that was 'beset by calm.'

At the time, the doldrums were a region that was so notorious that the Bermuda Triangle of today pales in comparison. Thousands of people travel through the Bermuda Triangle every day without incident. If anything weird happens in the Bermuda Triangle, it doesn't happen often. Indeed, it seems incidents are incredibly rare, given the shipping and air traffic in that part of the Atlantic, making it very difficult to study whatever is said to go on there. It is also argued that planes and ships go missing all over the planet, and they do not happen with any greater frequency near Bermuda. It is counter-argued that not only is the Bermuda Triangle a paranormal hotbed, but it is also one of several so-called paranormal hot spots around the planet. There is one in the Great Lakes, especially Lake Michigan. The North and South Poles have a reputation, the Maldives in the Indian Ocean and the eastern Mediterranean. The most famous Bermuda Triangle counterpart is the 'Dragon's Triangle' that outlines a large part of the Pacific Ocean between Southeastern Japan, the Marianas Islands, and the Philippines. It has a reputation among local mariners for all the same mysterious events as the Bermuda Triangle: compasses spin, radios die, electronics fail, intense electrical storms and whirlpools in the water happen and, of course, ships go missing. In 1942, five Japanese warships went missing simultaneously. Even though a war was happening at the time, the United States was not yet active militarily in that part of the Pacific in early 1942. The Doolittle raid on Japan was the U.S.'s first response to Japan's raid on Pearl Harbor. That happened in August of 1942. In any event, the fact that a war was going on is ample justification for not building too much mystery around that incident.

According to Charles Berlitz's book *The Bermuda Triangle*, nine ships went missing between 1950 and 1954 in the so-called Dragon's Triangle. Berlitz claimed that in 1955, a research vessel was sent to investigate the place. It disappeared as well. Another author, Larry Kusche, wrote a book in 1974 called *The Bermuda Triangle Mystery Solved*, which obviously intended to debunk Berlitz' claims of paranormal happenings. He reached out to Japanese agencies and came up with the counter-claim  that the missing vessels were mostly fishing vessels operating in bad weather without radios, and not all of them disappeared in the confines of the so-called Dragon's Triangle. Kusche further claimed that Kaiyo Maru 5 was actually a research vessel sunk by an undersea volcano on September 24, 1952. Another author, Brian Dunning, was surprised to find no mention of any Dragon's Triangle in any Japanese newspaper or magazine, concluding that the term 'Dragon's Triangle' was not as ancient as was previously claimed. What Dunning did not do was check the Japanese phrase "Ma No Umi" which translates to "troublesome sea" or "dangerous sea." There is quite a bit of information to be found on the internet if that phrase is entered, but the term refers to any dangerous maritime location, of which there are several in Japanese nautical lore. Interestingly, the location of the Dragon's Triangle, is exactly opposite the Bermuda Triangle, although the actual boundaries of the Dragon's Triangle are a little fuzzier. It is also pointed out by debunking authors that undersea volcanoes are the biggest reason for labeling a location Ma No Umi. However, other events constitute known hazards to shipping, such as methane hydrates, which are big bubbles of methane gas that come from frozen deposits on the sea floor. If such a huge bubble were to rise to the surface beneath a ship, even a large ship could lose buoyancy and sink almost instantly. As with the Bermuda Triangle, advocates of the paranormal may tend to exaggerate the number of missing craft and overly dramatize the circumstances surrounding the disappearance.

On the other hand, the skeptics tend to debunk a few cases and call it 'case closed,' ignoring the larger number of cases they cannot debunk. Debunkers dismiss mysterious disappearances that happen outside of the somewhat arbitrary boundaries of these 'troublesome seas' location. Skeptics point out (correctly) that Bermuda Triangle-like disappearances happen all over. Most famously, Malaysia Air Flight 370 disappeared from the South China Sea on March 8, 2014. (Several pieces of debris from the plane have subsequently shown up on beaches around the Indian Ocean.) Amelia Earhart and co-pilot Ed Noonan went missing on June 2, 1937, somewhere near the so-called Dragon's Triangle, although there are several competing explanations that do not involve paranormal possibilities. Paranormal advocates do insist that there are definite concentrations of such disappearances, and one of those places is the waters east of Florida.

This is where it becomes necessary to dig much deeper than a TV show or magazine article has time to do, and ask the often-overlooked question of what else is said to go on in these locations. As it turns out, two other sets of phenomena are associated with the Bermuda Triangle. Once again, it must be stated that while these events may be associated with the Bermuda Triangle, they do not confine themselves to the Bermuda or any other triangle.

The first of these two sets of anomalous events is, of course, sightings of UFOs. Charles Berlitz says in his books that one cannot study the Bermuda Triangle without taking on the matter of UFOs and their submerged counterparts, Unidentified Submerged Objects (USOs). Some readers are surprised to learn that mysterious submerged objects of enormous size and sometimes traveling at incredible speed are often seen and reported, even by military personnel. It may come as no surprise that military personnel, like commercial pilots, are very reluctant, even forbidden, to publicly discuss unexplained objects they see in the ocean or in the air above it. It turns out that the Russian military is a lot more forthcoming about USOs. When the Soviet Union disintegrated in 1989, documents were declassified that discussed encounters between very fast moving USOs and nuclear submarines. One such account described an encounter between a nuclear submarine operating in the South Pacific and six disc-like objects moving toward the sub at a speed exceeding 200 miles per hour. The submarine surfaced and, through the periscope, Soviet mariners saw the objects emerge from the water and go streaking off at very high speed. UFO researchers Paul Stonehill and Philip Mantle have collected these declassified accounts and published them in a book entitled, *Russia's USO Secrets: Unidentified Submersible Objects in Russian and International Waters.*

As it turns out, the Bermuda Triangle, and the larger area surrounding it, has more than its share of UFO and USO sightings. Numerous sightings by pleasure boaters, fishermen, cruise ship passengers, private pilots, and military personnel come from the Caribbean, especially around Puerto Rico. The Bermuda Triangle, strictly speaking, is bound by San Juan, Puerto Rico which is on the island's north side. The real hotbed seems to be south and east of Puerto Rico. Once again, the reader cannot expect that paranormal activity will confine itself to the arbitrary boundaries of the so-called Bermuda Triangle.

In any event, no nation on Earth is currently in possession of a craft that can operate both underwater and in the air, yet there are numerous, maybe countless, sightings of typically disc-shaped craft that transition from submerged to airborne, or vice versa. Carl Feindt, a now-deceased UFO researcher, thoroughly catalogued USO sightings and published them on a website that can be found at wateru-fo.net. Charles Berlitz included a few USO sightings by fishermen in his book *Inside The Bermuda Triangle*. The submerged objects are typically huge, like 100 to 200 feet long, gray, smooth, no fins or windows, and moving very fast underwater. Berlitz cites one instance in February of 1963 in which a fleet of naval vessels performed anti-submarine maneuvers off Puerto Rico. An unexpected sonar return was picked up by several vessels. One submarine moved to intercept the submerged object but couldn't catch it. The craft plunged into the depths of the Puerto Rican Trench, an ocean feature that is also the deepest spot anywhere in the Atlantic ocean, some five miles deep. This trench is off the north coast of Puerto Rico, so it does cross one corner of the Bermuda Triangle.

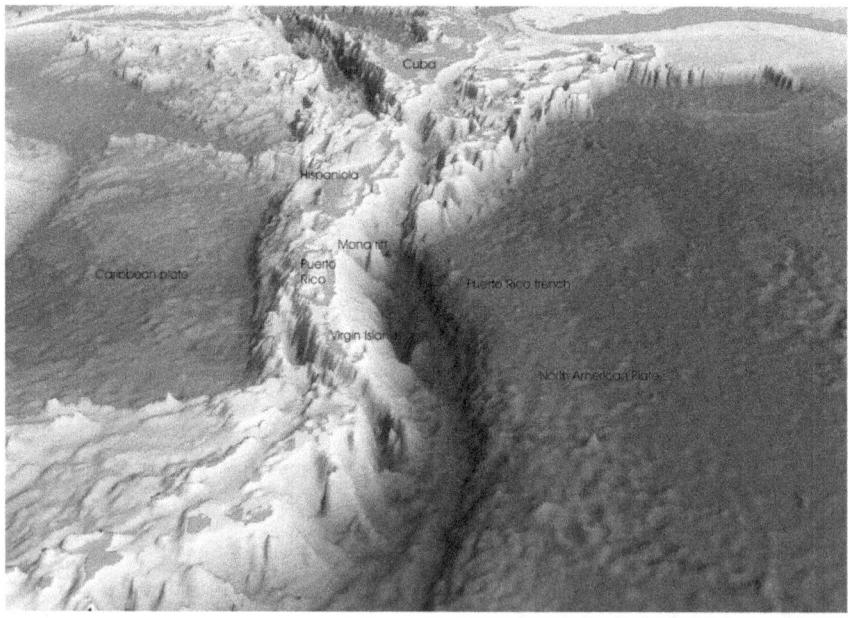

Space shuttle commander Story Musgrave captured video of one fast-moving object and a formation of three other slower-moving objects while orbiting the Earth. He was piloting the shuttle Columbia on mission STS 80 in December 1980 when he recorded a fast-moving object that appeared to be exiting the atmosphere just off the east coast of Puerto Rico. UFO researcher and Puerto Rican native Jorge Martin has identified unnatural geometric structures on the sea floor off the south coast of Puerto Rico. In his view, the structures and the concomitant UFO and USO activity that abounds in the area point to the presence of a subterranean or submerged alien base. Both Berlitz and Manson Valentine, Yale-educated Ph.D. and contributor to Charles Berlitz's book, would wholeheartedly agree. Dr. Valentine states that the Bermuda Triangle is a portal of some kind that is used by extraterrestrial inter-dimensional visitors. Dr. Valentine is aware of many USO sightings, often associated with a yellow fog that envelops them. Ships that encounter USOs also report radar malfunction, other electromagnetic anomalies, and sudden drops in ambient temperature.

In addition to the plethora of UFO and USO activity associated with places like the Bermuda Triangle, there is another paranormal phenomenon that never gets discussed by skeptics. The presence of gray or yellow fog has been reported in association with UFOs and by pilots whose planes are suddenly enshrouded by it. This particular phenomenon has been thoroughly documented by one author, researcher and pilot who had two personal and terrifying experiences with it while flying through the Bermuda Triangle.

Bruce Gernon is a West Palm Beach, Florida, resident who often flies to the Bahamas on business in his private plane. On December 5, 1970, Bruce, his father, and his business partner were returning home to West Palm from the Bahamas by way of Bimini. It's an easy 75-minute flight from the Bahamas to Miami, before it turns north for the short hop to West Palm Beach. Weather was calm with high clouds. Gernon's Beechcraft Bonanza took off from Andros Island and began the climb to cruising altitude. A few miles ahead, Bruce observed a low-lying lenticular (lens) shaped cloud low over the ocean. Ordinarily, such clouds would be found much higher in the atmosphere. This one extended from the ocean surface to about 1500 feet in altitude. It was peculiar; but was small and did not appear to pose any threat. Private pilots prefer to avoid flying through clouds and having already achieved an altitude of 1500 feet, Gernon calculated that his plane would clear the cloud if he just stayed level. To his surprise, the cloud began to rise vigorously just as they passed over it. He kept climbing and so did the cloud. Several times, the rapidly rising cloud enveloped the plane, then, owing to updrafts in the cloud, they would gain speed and rise out of it. Eventually, they thought they had outrun the cloud and began to relax, only to realize that the cloud had grown laterally and was rapidly surrounding them. They found themselves in the center of a donut-shaped cumulonimbus cloud that extended from the deck to the stratosphere. A small plane could not go high enough to fly over such a cloud; there was no room to fly under it because the cloud extended all the way down to the ocean's surface, so they would have to fly through it.

Bruce was flying by sight (VFR), not by instrument (IFR). Even instrument-rated (IFR) pilots avoid clouds when possible, but no pilot wants anything to do with the violent updrafts and downdrafts that one is certain to encounter inside a cumulonimbus cloud. The inside of a building thunderhead or cumulonimbus cloud is the rowdiest of all clouds. The powerful up and downdrafts of these atmospheric monsters can tear the wings off a small plane. Gernon was aware of his danger and made a ninety-degree turn to the south toward an opening between what was now two separate cumulonimbus clouds that were merging into a mega-cloud that surrounded his plane. One last opening was dead ahead, which continued shrinking as the plane approached it. Gernon hit the gas.

By the time he got the plane in the open space between the arms of the storm cloud, it had formed an ever-shrinking tunnel. There was now just enough room between the rotating walls of the tunnel to keep his plane in open sky. Gernon could see that the sides of the tunnel were rotating counterclockwise. There were circular ribbons of darker material rolling counterclockwise along with the rest of the cloud mass. There were also intensely bright flashes of light that were embedded  in the walls of the cloud, though he never saw any lightning bolts. They made it through the tunnel just before it slammed shut. As they emerged from the cloud, instead of entering clear skies, he was in a grey, all-enveloping fog. He could see no sky, no ground, and no horizon. Just grey fog. Suddenly, Gernon also noticed that none of his instruments were working and his compass was slowly spinning.

Surprisingly, the radio still worked and he radioed Miami flight control to inform them of their location just east of the Bimini island chain and, more importantly, to inform flight control of the sudden change in their flight plan. The flight controller in Miami countered that he had no plane on his radar in that vicinity. By this time, they had been flying for some thirty minutes and were still completely shrouded in a weird haze. Suddenly, the air traffic controller came back on the radio and excitedly told them he found their plane and they were right over Miami Beach. It seemed impossible because by this time, they had been flying thirty-four minutes, and, given the plane's maximum speed, it would have been a seventy-five-minute flight to Miami. The fog broke apart into ribbons of fog and eventually cleared. When it did, the occupants of the plane were stunned to get a clear view of Miami Beach below them. Everyone's watch and the one on the dashboard all verified that they had been in the air for thirty-four minutes; thirty minutes ahead of their calculated arrival time in Miami. When they landed, Bruce discovered, to his surprise, that they had ten extra gallons of gas that, by all calculations, should have been consumed in their journey from Bermuda. They were indeed relieved that their harrowing journey had ended well, but the fact that they had somehow jumped thirty minutes forward in time was something that Bruce could never forget. The inexplicable aspects of Bruce's flight motivated him to search for answers, leading him to his first awareness of this place, or thing, called the Bermuda Triangle.

Gernon was never shy about discussing his experience and despite frequent jokes and occasional ridicule, he kept talking, reading, and eventually writing about his paranormal experience in the Bermuda Triangle. He consulted with pilots, scientists, and even remote viewers. He produced two books, one called *The Fog* and another entitled *Beyond the Bermuda Triangle*. He was interviewed on several televised documentaries, meeting many other  researchers intrigued by the details of his story. One of these experts was the aforementioned Dr. Manson Valentine, who was so fascinated by the details of Gernon's account that he observed that Bruce was the only known person to fly through (and survive) "the heart of the storm, from its birth to its maturity and to exit through the vortex." Charles Berlitz included Bruce Gernon's story in his follow-up volume, <u>Without a Trace</u>, and Dr. Valentine confided to Bruce, "Always remember you hold the key to the Bermuda triangle."

When one puts oneself out there as a witness and an experiencer of a paranormal event, one thing that happens is that other people who have had similar experiences are motivated, even driven, to find you and share their own stories. I noticed this phenomenon while researching and writing about the Sasquatch phenomenon. If I spoke at a symposium, on a radio show, or even on a lowly podcast, people frequently sought me out and wanted, even needed to tell me the details of their own encounter. When one puts themselves out there, they become a magnet for other folks who carry similar feelings of bewilderment regarding their unexpected and often frightening experience. It seems that most people need to share these troubling experiences with someone who will take them seriously; someone who might also be able to provide some answers to their lingering questions. Experiencers of paranormal events are a bit traumatized by their experience. Sharing with someone who will listen without judgment or ridicule is a form of therapy. In studying Bruce Gernon's books, it was plain to see that for many other Bermuda Triangle witnesses/experiencers, Bruce Gernon was providing a very helpful service. For Bruce Gernon, there was also a certain benefit in fulfilling the role of the non-judgemental listener: as with me and the sasquatch biz, Bruce was in a position to collect quite a lot of useful anecdotes. These anecdotes, while not rising to the level of scientifically acceptable evidence, do verify that there are patterns that have a measure of statistical validity. I imagine Bruce Gernon has found, as I did, that by collecting and categorizing the admittedly unverifiable accounts of other experiencers, one can see the patterns and realize that they have predictive value. By collecting and sorting the sightings or encounters of others, one learns that :

1. There are a lot more people than you ever realized who have had paranormal experiences.
2. No one account has scientific value but by looking at a lot of accounts, very clear and sometimes useful patterns emerge.
3. One invariably feels a little less crazy and a lot more secure about the details of their own experience after hearing about the experiences of others.

4. Listening to the experiences of those who feel the need to share helps reassure those people that they really did experience it.
5. Even though no 'story' rises to the level of scientific evidence, 'anecdotal data' (stories) do have value and however spurious such anecdotal may be, it is likely the only kind of data one is ever likely to get.
6. The scientific method, in its strictest form, cannot be applied to paranormal topics or events since their occurrence cannot be predicted. When such events do occur, they have a somewhat random component that prevents empirical measurement.
7. Such events cannot be replicated in a way that enables them to be scientifically studied.

In Bruce Gernon's case, by putting himself out there, he was able to meet and interview other pilots who had experienced 'the fog.' Bruce was certain that he encountered a mysterious fog that attached itself to his plane because he had the benefit of being in the company of two other witnesses: his father and his business partner. This led to a measure of confidence when sharing his puzzling and slightly harrowing experience. As an outgrowth of his openness, he met other pilots and even military and law enforcement witnesses who had seen USOs and UFOs, often while working in professional capacities. For obvious reasons, such individuals are reluctant to share openly for fear of damaging their professional standing, but they will more likely share with a person who can help validate their experience. Gernon also met physicists who were able to provide science-based explanations for seemingly unexplainable phenomena like 'the fog' and the fact that Gernon and his passengers seem to have traversed some sort of temporary wormhole or ephemeral transit tunnel that was formed by the intense electromagnetic field that formed in the incipient electrical storm. Some sort of warp in the space-time continuum set up that sent him, his passengers, and his plane thirty minutes ahead in time.

As a result of his experience, Bruce could be sure that, however rare, such time slips do indeed happen. He had the gas receipts that proved he had a lot more gasoline at the end of his flight than he should have had, and he had the combined time measurements of three different wristwatches and a dashboard-mounted clock. Gernon then found that there were other sincere and honest souls who found themselves to have been unwittingly moved slightly forward in time and space (usually less than an hour but occasionally longer). Most were reporting moving ahead, but some were sure they had gone back in time. Bruce is emphatic in his view that this phenomenon is not restricted to the Bermuda (or any other) Triangle, although there does seem to be some peculiar energies associated with the Caribbean Sea.

Gernon further concluded that electromagnetism seems to be the force responsible for generating the fog and the associated wormhole. Thunderstorms, especially big ones, are producers of enormous amounts of electromagnetic energy, which is either drawn from or flows toward the Earth. The fog, whether it be yellow or grey, produces or somehow leads to the transit tunnel or time slip. One possible reason why this phenomenon may happen more frequently in the Bermuda Triangle may have something to do with the magnetite bedrock that occurs there. As much as 35% of the bedrock in the Bermuda Triangle is magnetite. There is more magnetite in the bedrock of that area than anywhere else on Earth. Magnetite is a rare bedrock that results from deeper-than-average volcanic eruptions. Magnetite is a combination of iron and titanium that originates some 400 or more miles or so beneath the earth. Such bedrock can transmit or even generate large amounts of natural electromagnetism. The reason such a dense rock is found in such abundance at the surface is probably because the Puerto Rican Trench is a subduction zone where crustal plates are colliding and dense, deeply buried rock types are brought to the surface by crustal movement and volcanic activity.

Overlay this intense source of geo-electromagnetism with a thunderstorm, which typically produces 100,000 to 200,000 volts per cubic meter of atmosphere. Or, combine it with the energy of mega-storms which produce 400,000 volts per cubic meter and a current of 200,000 amps. This powerful conduit of electromagnetic energy combines with, or grounds to, the highly charged magnetite bedrock, and you have the potential to move solid matter just like Tesla's ill-fated Philadelphia experiment.

A few other very useful insights came to Bruce Gernon as a consequence of his well-publicized interest in the Bermuda Triangle. Professor John Wheeler offered that the vortex or wormhole that opened up around Bruce's plane amidst the electrical storm is a phenomenon that occurs worldwide. Such vortexes or wormholes are much less powerful cousins of the famed black holes or Einstein-Rosen bridges that form amidst the collapse of super-massive stars. The vortex or transit tunnel, as it occurs on the surface of our planet, is (fortunately) much weaker than a black hole in space, and they exist only for a limited time. Gernon, and others, speculate that, if such transit tunnels could be generated at will and controlled, it would be a means of transporting matter or even people across potentially vast distances in mere seconds. A black hole, owing to its intense gravitational tides and radiation flux, is a one-way transit to nowhere, but a transit tunnel, as it may occur on the face of the planet, has both an entry and an exit. Owing to the energy of the electromagnetic storm that surrounded his plane, Bruce and his passengers unwittingly entered a transit tunnel that moved them some thirty minutes and one hundred miles ahead in time-space.

Bruce Gernon is perhaps the first person to notice that the grey fog (sometimes yellow) actually attaches itself to an object such as his plane. Once he and his passengers exited the electrical storm and the fog had attached itself to the plane, their immediate surroundings were foggy, but away from the plane, it was clear and sunny. Years after his first encounter with the fog, Bruce had a second experience with the fog on another flight. In this second encounter with 'the fog,' Gernon noticed that, while he saw no horizon, sky, or sea ahead of or beside his direction of travel, he could see a circle of blue sky straight above and straight below his plane. This patch of blue followed the flight path of his plane until it eventually dissipated over land. Others who had experiences similar to Bruce Gernon's were able to corroborate this observation. A commercial flight in August of 1976 was enveloped in yellow fog, and everyone aboard's watches stopped for thirty minutes. Jeff Butler, a private pilot traveling from Naples to Marathon, Florida in 1999, was flying at night when he lost his radio and compass. Meanwhile, air traffic control lost radar and radio contact with his plane. In 1978, a pilot traveling from Bimini to Opa Locka, Florida, in a Cessna 172 was enveloped by "gray, weird skies" and his compass began spinning.

A Ph.D. physicist named David Pares was able to provide Bruce with a helpful, albeit somewhat technical, explanation. He described Bruce's experience as a documented case of natural warping of space-time. As Pares described it to Bruce Gernon and as Bruce then described it in his book *Beyond the Bermuda Triangle*, ionized energy in the storm clouds was embedded in a dipole field that attached itself to the plane, forming a cocoon-like structure around the plane. What Bruce describes as an 'electronic fog' that attached itself to his aircraft was described by Pares as an external ionized confinement field that was generated by the electrical mega-thunderstorm he was trying to avoid. The ionized confinement field is drawn specifically to the carbon emissions from the plane's exhaust. When it attaches itself to the plane, it causes the instruments to fail because they are not shielded from the outside electrical interference.

Fortunately, in Gernon's case, the engine kept running because it was more effectively shielded by the engine cowling. It has been shown that a sufficiently strong electromagnetic field in close proximity to an internal combustion engine will kill the engine, though it seems that at least some pilots are spared this fate. There's no way to know whether it happened a little differently to some of the pilots who never returned. Gernon's radio continued to work, Pares speculates, because it was in the center of the instrument array on the dashboard, and the other instruments served to shield the radio. Compasses are the first to go, which rely on reading small amounts of Earth's magnetism. The altimeter would continue to work because it does not use any electricity. It works like a barometer, only reading physical changes in air pressure. The turn-slip indicator would also continue to work because it doesn't use any electricity either. All other instruments are electrically powered and would malfunction in the presence of strong electromagnetism.

Reconsidering the fate of Flight 19, one of the first problems the flight had was that both of Commander Taylor's compasses simultaneously stopped working. He may have been experiencing the same external ionized confinement field. This electromagnetic field may negatively affect the weak electrical impulses that power our brain and nervous system. Pilots who experience the field report a variety of weird sensations. The pilot in the Cessna 172 experienced a weird feeling that he had once before experienced at a sacred vortex site in Peru. Other pilots report feelings of weightlessness, mental distress, irritability, confusion, and a sense of panic. In Gernon's second encounter with the fog, his passengers temporarily lost consciousness. In the case of Flight 19, shore-based radio operators heard a certain amount of arguing among the pilots, and Taylor was perplexed about his whereabouts. He struggled with navigation and general decision-making. Another of the Flight 19 pilots got lost in some clouds. The rest of the squadron turned around. After making several turns without working compasses, confusion is understandable, even without mentally debilitating outside forces. It looks like Flight 19 may have been affected by Pares' external ionized confinement field, even if they ultimately ran out of gas.

As dangerous as an external ionized confinement field is, it may also explain why UFOs are associated with the Bermuda Triangle and other places like it. Electromagnetically-generated transit tunnels are being manipulated by the craft's occupants. Either they use the natural storm-generated electromagnetism to come and go from our realm or they can even generate such forces and use them at will. When Gernon related his entire experience, Dr. Valentine speculated that the original lenticular cloud Gernon saw may have had an extraterrestrial craft inside it. The whole hyper-energetic storm Gernon encountered may have been induced somehow by this craft for purposes of teleportation. Dr. Valentine goes so far as to speculate that all or part of the Bermuda Triangle may indeed be an interdimensional portal. If time is indeed another dimension, as Einstein said it is, then perhaps those who we think of as inter-dimensional travelers are really just time travelers. In this view, at least some of the UFOs we observe are visitors from our own future as opposed to alien visitors from some other world. They may be simply pleasure-cruising back in time to view the quaint events, places, and individuals of their own past.

And finally, if the Bermuda Triangle is all imaginary, why does the U.S. Navy maintain a secret base with its confines? Bruce Gernon has opened my eyes to the existence of AUTEC, a secret Navy installation on Andros Island in the Bahamas. The Atlantic Underwater Testing and Evaluation Center is not really a secret, but the base is off-limits and the work done there is highly classified. The base is not very big: only one square mile, but the location was chosen because it provides unscrutinized access to a very deep arm of the Atlantic known as the Tongue of the Ocean. Officially, the base is used for 'underwater acoustics' (submarine detection) and torpedo testing. Quite clearly, other 'black projects' are being conducted, which is why AUTEC is sometimes called the 'Underwater Area 51'. They allegedly have an underwater submarine dock. We can only speculate as to what else might be going on there, but it is a safe bet that its location on Andros Island in the Bermuda Triangle is not coincidental. Perhaps they are learning to tap into the sometimes manifest electromagnetic concentrations. Perhaps they are there because it is a UFO hotspot.

The UFO Hunters TV show did a spot about AUTEC, and they interviewed a researcher who felt that AUTEC is used to contact and communicate with the extraterrestrials (or interdimensionals). Perhaps they deliberately located the base in close proximity to the suspected underground base that Dr. Valentine, Charles Berlitz, and Jorge Martin write about. I do not expect to ever learn what AUTEC is doing in the Bermuda Triangle, but the fact that they are operating there, in secret, is enough to be certain that the Bermuda Triangle is a lot more than the punch line of a joke. The existence of underground realms here on earth is a recurring theme of this book so I am inclined to take seriously the view of Jorge Martin, who feels there is a subterranean or sub-aquatic base beneath the coast of southern Puerto Rico. Bear in mind that the coral-limestone bedrock of Puerto Rico is riddled with blue holes, caves, and chambers. Half the work of constructing a subterranean enclave would already be done by nature. I've even heard it said that part of Atlantis is down there, somewhere. I'm going to have to think about that one for a while, but one thing I've learned after researching these subjects: don't laugh.

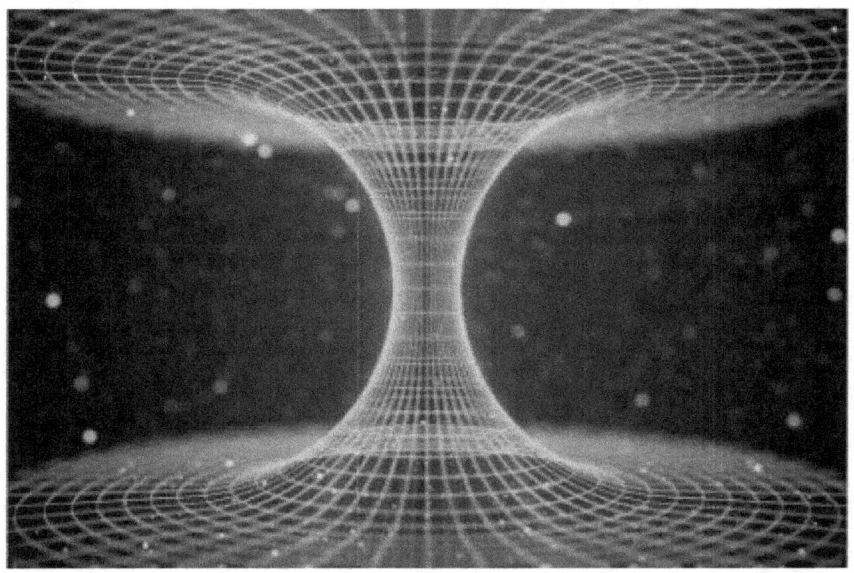

8

RED HERRINGS

Most, if not all, of the evidence of underground installations is indirect. There are witnesses to crafts coming and going through terrestrial or aquatic access points, but their claims are usually seen as unpersuasive or misinterpreted. I do not expect anyone to be invited to view such installations directly. Though still indirect, perhaps the most direct evidence we can access is the displaced earth that can be directly viewed all over the planet. On every continent, we can view mounds: piles of earth that have been moved around. Nowhere is it more evident than on the North American continent. Ever since the first European settlers arrived in North America, they could not help but notice the sometimes huge heaps of dirt and rock lying all over the place. Though many have since been destroyed by progress, the mounds that littered the landscape numbered in the millions. Sometimes, they were just hills of earth, but just as often, the mounds were arranged in geometrically shaped complexes. Others were shaped as huge animal effigies. In other cases, the mounds were so huge that they were assumed to be natural hills. Such mounds and huge stone works are found on every continent that isn't ice-covered. While every continent has these mysterious piles of earth, no continent seems to have more of them than North America.

Of the million or so mounds that were seen by the first European settlers upon arrival in the New World, nine-tenths of them have been eliminated to make room for farms, roads, and cities. In addition to being in the way, mounds were also a handy source of building materials, as were the rock walls that were often found in association with the mounds. It was discovered in the early 1800s that some mounds contained artifacts, even jewelry. People began digging into the mounds in search of these valuable antiquities and mounds as they occurred continent-wide were considered burial mounds. Before the twentieth century, there were absolutely no laws that protected mounds from being dug into or completely destroyed. The mounds and mound complexes were assumed to be the work of the same indigenous native populations that were being removed to make room for European settlement. The Midwest was being repopulated with whites. Revolutionary War soldiers were rewarded with large tracts of Indian land, often peppered with mounds. When artifacts started turning up, it was assumed that the mounds were burial sites of tribal leaders. Some mounds were found to contain interred human remains, but more typically, the human remains were unearthed near, not in, the mounds. In many cases, the remains were gigantic in stature, as discussed in chapter 2.

The geometrically shaped mounds were most commonly circular or semicircular, indicating that they could not be attributed to some natural process like glaciation. Other geometric shapes like squares and rectangles suggested that some mounds were built as fortresses, although the generally low height of the mounds did not seem to provide adequate defense from attack. Then there were the rare but impressive effigy mounds that were so big that the animal shapes were not even noticed from ground level.

Beginning in the 1830s, digging into the mounds became a

popular pioneer pastime. The first attempt to responsibly explore the mound phenomenon was conducted by Squirer and Davis, who surveyed and cataloged mounds throughout Ohio. The science of archaeology was still in its infancy, and most people who were digging into the mounds were nothing more than 'pot hunters' by today's standards. Most digs were not organized or recorded. Eventually, European immigrants and early archaeologists asked the surviving Indians who built the mounds and why. A large part of Ohio was the ancestral home of the Iroquois Nation, yet the surviving Iroquois historians insisted that they had no hand in building them; rather, the mounds were already there when the earliest Iroquois ancestors settled in the Midwest. The giant skeletons sometimes found in association with the mounds seemed to suggest a different native population, maybe even a large and very sophisticated population. This suggestion was at odds with the established dogma that there was no civilization in North America before the arrival of Columbus in 1492, so virtually all archaeologists discredited and ignored the evidence of ancient civilization in North America. Though cracks in this wall of archaeological dogma are appearing, the denial of ancient American civilization persists to this day.

Some mounds are so huge that they may be better described as earthen pyramids. One such earthen pyramid on the central Gulf coast of Mexico, La Venta, contains over one hundred thousand cubic feet of earth. Monk's Mound, on the banks of the Mississippi near present-day Collinsville, Illinois, is a flat-topped pyramid 100 feet high. Its base measures 775 by 955 feet, giving it roughly the same footprint as the Great Pyramid of Giza. It's the largest mound north of the Olmec behemoth at La Venta.

When discussing such earthen structures, the word 'enigmatic' is often used by archeologists and cultural historians who reluctantly admit that, when attempting to explain the mounds, mysteries positively abound.

One such mystery is the date of construction. 1000 A.D. is a number that is often suggested, based on radiocarbon dating of campfires and other remains, but clearly, not all mounds are of the same age. Some mounds, particularly in the lower Mississippi Valley, may be older than 5000 B.C.

The purpose of the mounds is most often said to be 'ceremonial,' but what the ceremony was and why it required earthen mounds is not known. Regarding how mounds were built, archeologists confidently state that mounds like the huge Monk's Mound in Illinois were built by Native Americans who transported the earth in baskets. Other questions surround the cultures that built the mounds and how they sustained what must have been an army of basket-carriers. Were they farmers or hunter-gatherers? Given the estimated time frame and the assumed sophistication of the cultures, most academics say the mounds were built by hunter-gatherer societies. This begs the question of how a culture of hunter-gatherers could muster enough manpower to transport and place such enormous quantities of earth, in light of the fact there is no survival value to all this work. The greatest enigma surrounds the question that is almost never asked: Where did all that dirt come from? For every large mound, not to mention the absolutely huge ones, there ought to be an equally huge hole in the ground. There never is. We are, therefore, told that the industrious natives scraped the earth evenly from the surrounding surface. Anyone who feels that this is a plausible answer has never tried to gather dirt in this manner. Huge mechanized graders perform this feat when roads and freeways are being built, but I am quite confident that a hundred thousand cubic feet of earth was not scraped from the earth to build the earthen pyramid at La Venta. Removing sod, much less forest or jungle, from many acres of land just to get at the underlying soil would require many thousands of otherwise idle laborers. Would they have burned entire forests or grasslands just to get at the underlying soil? Again, it would seem that any ancient culture, no matter how sophisticated, would have better things to do than to scrape millions or billions of baskets of dirt and then haul it to the job site.

Earthen mounds are inherently less impressive than immense stone structures like temples and pyramids. We grasp the difficulties of quarrying and moving extremely heavy blocks of stone. Moving equally large quantities of earth seems more achievable, but it may not be. Considering the amount of time and effort that would be required, not to mention the mind-boggling number of mounds as they exist continent-wide, the construction of the mounds and mound complexes is a mind-boggling undertaking that rivals the wonder of the pyramids of Egypt and Meso-America. Researchers like Graham Hancock contend that these early North American societies must have been larger and more sophisticated than we ever supposed if such enormous construction projects could have been supported. Hancock and others conclude that, based solely on their obvious physical achievements, North America was once home to some very large and very well-organized societies.

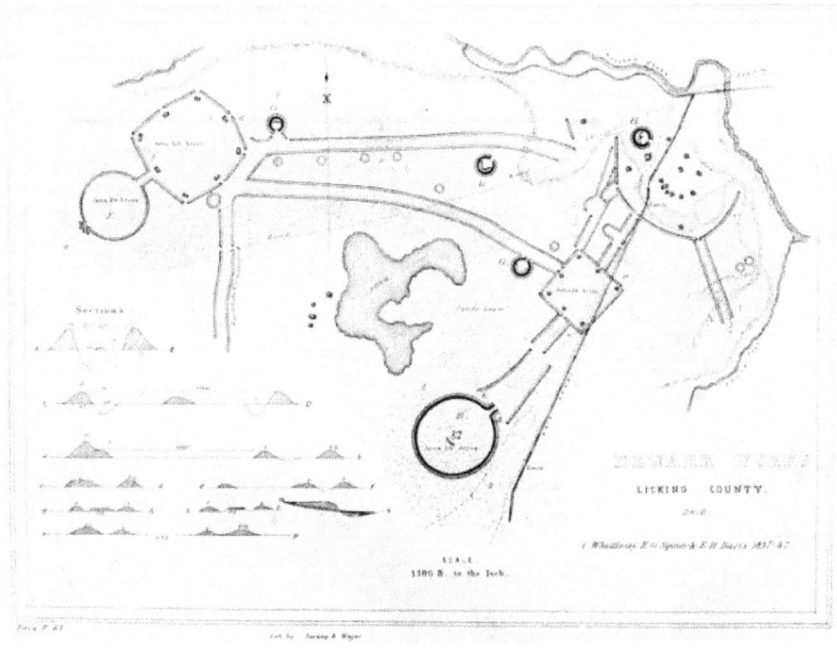

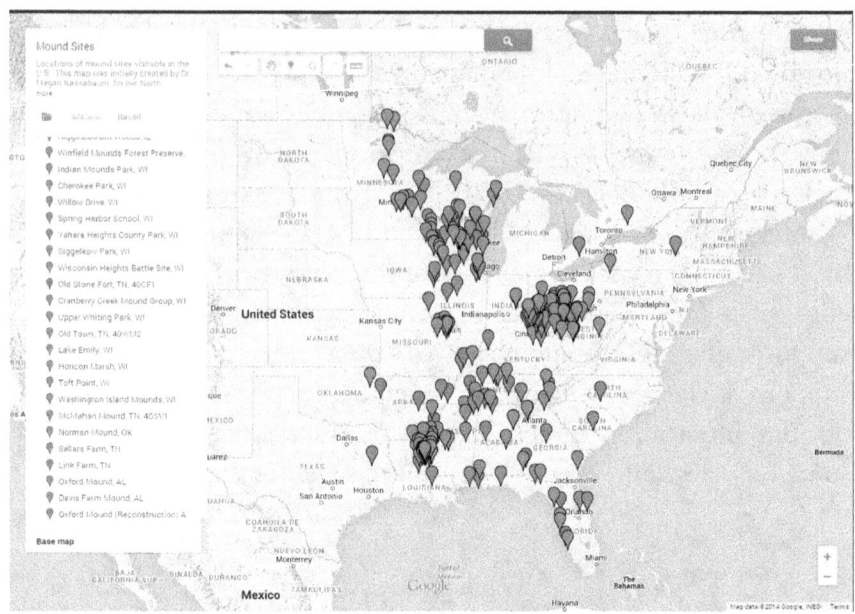

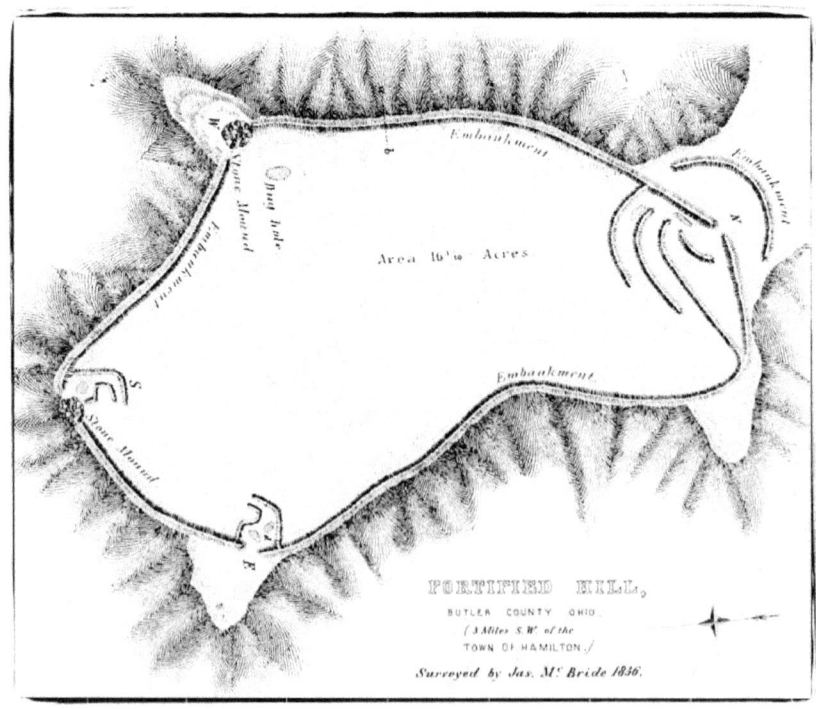

Rock wall in Ohio

Where did they go? We know that a great many Native Americans died of diseases they contracted from the first wave of European explorers. This tragedy began with the arrival of DeSoto in Florida in 1510. The tribes that DeSoto contacted and decimated were small, dispersed tribes that lived along waterways of the southeast U.S. These tribes of hunter-gatherers probably did not build the mounds, but they did live in the fertile valleys where the mounds had been located previously. What exactly happened to the culture of mound-builders is yet another enigma. No record exists of early contact between the highly organized civilizations that built mounds, and cities, the largest of which seems to be Cahokia in southern Illinois. It is estimated that in its heyday, Cahokia had between 25,000 and 30,000 residents, which would put Cahokia among the largest Middle Ages cities in the world. Where did they all go?

Historically, anthropologists and archaeologists have supposed that drought may have brought ruin to prehistoric cultures. More recently, speculation centers upon one or more natural disasters of epic proportions that acted as a huge reset button on prehistoric civilization continent-wide. The Ancient Puebloan (Anasazi) culture of the Four Corners region of the American Southwest also vanished quite suddenly, abandoning remarkable cliff dwellings and cities around 1100 A.D. In Mexico, the entire Aztec culture similarly 'left town,' abandoning huge stone step pyramids and thousands of smaller structures, as well as earthworks. Once abandoned, the jungle gradually overtook some large Meso-American cities that are now being rediscovered. If drought was the reason for large-scale abandonment, why did the inhabitants or their descendants not return when the drought abated?

While the residents of Central and North America were devastated by contact with Europeans beginning in the late 1400s, high cultures seem to have disappeared in Central and North America well before the first Europeans arrived. The Native Americans that contacted the first European arrivals are thought to have descended from Athabascans who migrated south from Canada in response to the abundant wildlife that was available in the then-unsettled lands of central North America. These tribes inherited a vacant landscape that was already blanketed with earthworks that, by their own admission, they did not build. Perhaps written records or oral traditions that reference a previous civilization were lost when Spaniards destroyed virtually all historical documents that were in the possession of Mayans and Aztecs. We don't have written records, but we do have physical evidence - in the form of temples, pyramids, and earthworks - that prove the existence of lost civilizations.

Graham Hancock is convinced that North America was the actual birthplace of humanity but that a natural disaster of epic proportions eliminated these early cultures. That event was the arrival of a comet swarm some 12,800 years ago, which we now call the Late Pleistocene Extinction Event or the Younger Dryas. The phrase Younger Dryas is derived from a kind of pollen found in ice cores. The pollen comes from a specific arctic plant that can survive in conditions that would be too cold for most other plants. The emergence of abundant Dryas pollen in ice cores would indicate a sudden plunge in worldwide temperatures. According to ice core data, there were two such sudden plunges in worldwide temperatures in the relatively recent past. The more recent, or younger of these two sudden plunges in global temperatures was the Younger Dryas.

Poverty Point

One of the largest single mounds found in the United States is found at a site in northern Louisiana known as Poverty Point. It gets its name from a plantation that sat on the site fifteen miles west of the Mississippi River in the northeast corner of Louisiana. There are so many mounds over such an enormous area that Poverty Point was not even recognized as a mound complex until the 1930s. Meanwhile, the area was being cultivated, the mounds had been degraded by plowing, and a highway was built through the mound complex. Indeed, the mound fields are so extensive that they can only be appreciated from the air. The largest complex on the site consists of a series of six concentric, semicircular ridges that measure ¾ of a mile in length. A series of larger mounds surround the six circular ridges. These mounds have been alphabetically labeled by archaeologists as Mound A through Mound F, with Mound A being the largest by far. In fact, Mound A is the second largest mound in the United States. The base of 72 feet tall Mound A measures 700 feet by 640 feet. It has a roughly "T" shape, which some interpret as a bird effigy. Mound A is so big that it was considered a natural hill for a long time. The volume of the earthen Mound A is a whopping 8,400,000 cubic feet of soil, which we are told was carried to the site one basket at a time between 1700 B.C. and 1000 B.C. Studies conclude that prior to the construction of the mounds, the site was burnt. The carbon residue from that site-clearing burn yielded C14 dates between 1400 B.C. and 1250 B.C. The only mound in eastern North America larger than Mound A is Monk's Mound in southern Illinois' Cahokia Complex. Mound B at Poverty Point is considered older than Mound A (1700 B.C.) but is much smaller (21 feet).

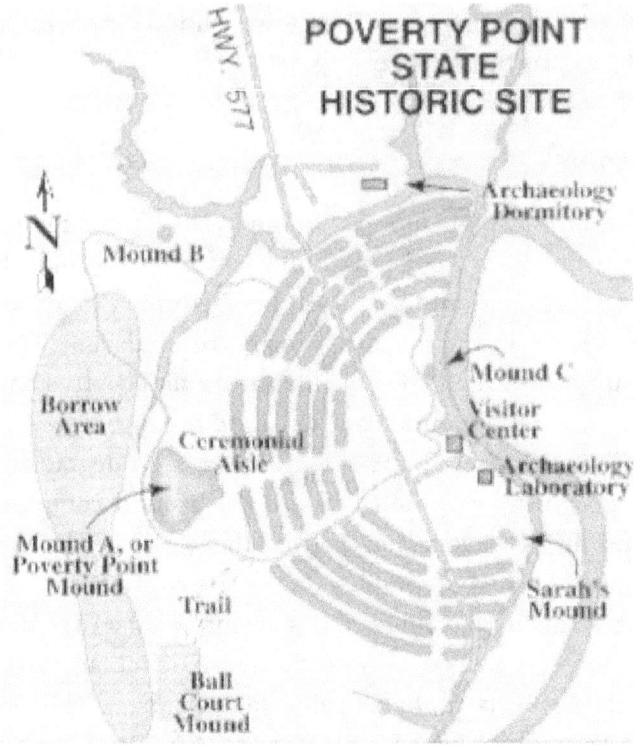

No one is sure why this mound complex was built. Some suggest it was a trade center, a settlement, and as always, a possible "ceremonial center." Predictably, no one has any idea what kind of ceremony would require the careful arrangement of so much earth. My first question when examining these sites is always the same: Where did they get all that earth, how did they move it, and why? In the case of Poverty Point, archeologists have identified a 'borrow area' (see map). 'Borrow' is a term that is still used today to refer to places where rock or earth is quarried. (The joke has long been that we take rock and dirt from 'borrow pits' but we never put it back. Shouldn't they be called 'take pits'?)

The problem is in the math. The volume of the borrow pit in no way corresponds to the enormous volume of material that was applied to the construction of the collective mounds of the whole 400-acre site. Archeologists are quick to add that material was borrowed "elsewhere" without offering any specifics. They also state that the mounds, especially Mound A were built 'quickly,' although we are offered no estimates of the available manpower that would have been available. We are further told that the Late Archaic Culture, which is generally credited with building these mounds, were, again, nomadic hunter-gatherers, not sedentary farmers. Such a society would be subsistence-level, hunting and fishing for meals and living in dirt-floor structures. Yet, as with so many other mound sites, this population of hand-to-mouth hunter-gatherers somehow had enough spare time and available manpower to create massive earthen structures with no clear benefit for their primitive existence, other than 'ceremony.'

Graham Hancock and others have taken a wider look at the site and found an alignment between Poverty Point and other mounds that were considered to be part of the Poverty Point site. Lower Jackson Mound and Motley Mound are both about a mile away from Poverty Point. Lower Jackson has radiocarbon dating that estimates it to be fifteen hundred years older than the oldest mounds at Poverty Point. Lower Jackson Mound aligns perfectly with mounds A, B, and E to form a straight, perfectly aligned north-south line. Astro-alignments are often found at other ancient mound sites, leading researchers like Hancock to conclude that the intended purpose of the mounds were to mark calendar events like equinoxes and solstices. It is then offered that the mound builders were very aware of a connection between the events in the cosmos and events that took place on Earth. Despite their presumably primitive existence, the mound builders were aware of a duality between the sky and the earth. It is often proposed that the knowledge of equinoxes and solstices would be important for planting crops, although the site's inhabitants are thought to have been hunter-gatherers.

Even if they were keeping track of planting dates, I question the value of marking celestial events like equinoxes for that purpose. Weather varies from year to year and that variability directly affects soil temperature. Nor do mound orientations seem necessary to keep track of equinoxes and solstices. Unlike planting schedules, solar alignments do not vary from year to year, so we can easily keep track of them with a piece of paper (a calendar). Even without paper, marks on a wall or sticks in the ground would serve to keep track of important solar alignments. There are wood circles (called henges) that are found in the immediate proximity of Poverty Point, illustrating the fact that they had alternative means of tracking the movement of celestial objects, like the sun. In light of this, building large earthen mounds for this purpose would seem redundant and unnecessary. The mounds must have been put there for some other reason, and to me, the simplest and most obvious reason to build mounds would be to get rid of large quantities of unwanted earth.

Where did all this earth come from? Why was it carefully placed so as to form linear alignments with celestial objects and events? In Louisiana alone, there are 97 surviving mound fields. They haven't all received radiocarbon dating estimates of their age but the ones that have yield dates of as far back as 5000 years B.C. (7000 years ago).

The Lower Mississippi mound complex that has been studied the most, outside of Poverty Point, is Watson Brake, Louisiana. It happens to be the oldest mound site in the lower Mississippi Valley, and one of the oldest mound sites in the country, also dating back to the Middle Archaic period, but some two thousand years earlier than Poverty Point. Watson Brake is also attributed to a hunter-gatherer culture called the Evans Culture. Based on spear points and other artifacts from the site, the Evan Culture is thought to have been particularly advanced compared to other contemporaneous cultures. Evidence and artifacts suggest that they lived at the site for 500 years without building any mounds, then they suddenly began building mounds, around 3400 B.C. The elliptical configuration of a dozen mounds at Watson Brake contains no evidence of burials. The configuration of mounds strongly resembles another mound field at Caney, Louisiana. As with most mound complexes, some convoluted interpretations of the configuration of mounds at Watson Brake suggest a connection to astronomical events, particularly solstices and eclipses. If this is true, that would make Watson Brake among North America's oldest celestially aligned mound complexes.

The Serpent Mound in Ohio is also thought to have multiple celestial alignments. That famous and impressive effigy mound is thought to be two thousand years younger than Watson Brake. The burst of Middle Archaic mound building, then, began (suddenly) around 3400 B.C. and continued for 700 years. Then, it all stopped, and no mounds at all were built for the next thousand years. Then, with the emergence of the Poverty Point culture, mound building resumed in the Late Archaic period between 2700 and 1700 B.C. No mound can be found anywhere in the Lower Mississippi Valley that dates to the 1000-year interval between mid-Archaic and Late Archaic. To explain this, archaeologists suggest climate change, social unrest, or other possibilities, but they have yet to consider what I see as the most obvious possibility: they lost their source of loose, transportable earth.

It stands to reason that any culture, especially a primitive one, would have to have three things in place in order to undertake such a non-essential task as mound building. First, they would need a nearly limitless supply of loose earth. Digging earth in enormous quantities from beneath sod or forest seems to require an enormous set of robust metal tools that they just did not seem to have. One reason it is alleged that the soil for mound building was carried in baskets is that no digging tools are found by archaeologists in the proximity of mound complexes. Digging small holes in the ground to plant seeds is one thing. Excavating enough soil to build mounds that approach a million cubic feet in volume, without metal tools, is improbable in the extreme.

The second prerequisite that would have to be in place for a culture to undertake a protracted program of mound building would be a desire to devote multiple lifetimes of human effort to the creation of a set of structures that have no clear benefit to the builders. To this day, no one knows why the mound complexes were built at Watson Brake, Poverty Point, and elsewhere. In most sites, the mounds have not produced interred human remains. They weren't burial mounds, but even when bodies are found in mounds, the possibility remains that they were put there at some time after initial construction, maybe because the mounds were sacred, and maybe digging in the mounds was that much easier.

The third element that must be in place if a hunter-gatherer society will undertake a large public works project is a large labor pool. If the population of these ancient societies numbered in the millions, they might have been able to dedicate a large labor force to mound-building, but it is by no means demonstrated that these cultures were anywhere near that large. Pre-contact population estimates for all of land north of Mexico range from 5 to 50 million. Those are continent-wide estimates circa 1400 A.D. What the population was one to three thousand years before that is anybody's guess. Cahokia is estimated to have had a population of 35-40,000 at its most prosperous time. Populations in areas distant from this center of commerce could not have been greater than 10,000, and even that number seems high for a hunter-gatherer society. How could a local community muster a labor pool capable of such an enormous yet non-essential task? And, this mound-building appears to have been going on at numerous locations at once. They must have had help. There must have been a way to get the work done with a smaller labor pool, and that would require technology to reduce the workload.

It all boils down to one big question: How did an Archaic Culture acquire the means, materials, and motivation required to accomplish a whole series of formidable undertakings? In my view, this implies that all three essentials, the means, the materials, and the motivation came from an outside source, and that would be either off-planeters or highly sophisticated Earthlings, or both. I can think of no other possibilities. These early cultures were indeed visited by highly sophisticated beings who schooled them in the ways of advanced earth-moving physics, or more sophisticated beings did it themselves with a minimum of local help.

The idea that all that earth was moved by primitive means, basket by basket, is patently absurd. It is an idea that could only come from individuals who do not have much personal experience with moving large amounts of earth by hand. Even if baskets were used, many, many shovels would be needed to load the baskets and however many laborers were put to the task, there would need to be a support system of twice as many people to maintain food, clothing, and shelter for the workforce. I also doubt that baskets per se are an effective way to move millions of cubic feet of earth. Baskets would degrade to the point of collapse after a few trips. Lifting heavy loads to the shoulder for carrying seems to be more work than is really necessary. Buckets would better serve the labor force. Lifting one five-gallon bucket full of dirt is about the limit of an average-sized person. Two buckets, one in each hand, makes the most sense in terms of balance, but if both buckets were full, one would not get very far with that load. Two half-full pails make more sense, especially if one were doing it all day. Multiple days of hauling heavy loads, whether with buckets or baskets, is a fast track to shoulder and elbow injury. Loading the buckets (or baskets) would be even more work than just carrying them from place to place. How was all that earth dug up in the first place? And from where? It would have to be very nearby.

Off-planeters would benefit from a god-like status among the archaic hunter-gatherers. The indigenous people would be more likely to help if they were asked or told to do so by a deity. The deity or deities would, in all likelihood, bring to bear some advanced technologies that also rendered the project less labor-intensive. The word 'aliens' comes up because it involves a short, familiar label and an easy concept to grasp. It may not be the best choice of monikers, though, especially if the beings already resided on or under the Earth.

If the choice is between beings from space or beings from underground, it seems that space-faring beings are easier to imagine. When questions become difficult to answer, it is usually because the problem is being oversimplified. What if it is not an either/or solution but rather a combination solution. The beings came from elsewhere, but they had a very terrestrial mission: to construct subterranean redoubts intended for future use. Large amounts of earth were being brought to the surface and had to be stashed somewhere, preferably a place that did not give away the presence of these enclaves meant to be secret.

Radiocarbon dating of the mounds of the lower Mississippi Valley seems to point to an on-again-off-again construction interval punctuated by hundreds or thousands of years. This scientific observation is consistent with the admittedly un-provable hypothesis that, every thousand years or so, the extraterrestrial job bosses showed up and construction of subterranean enclaves resumed. Every millennium or so, more large amounts of earth and rock were brought to the surface as a consequence of ambitious subterranean excavations. Initially, the piles were placed haphazardly, just the way mining companies dump their mine tailings right outside the mine's opening. The oldest mound fields, which date back ten to fifteen thousand years, are haphazard mound configurations like the Mima Mounds of Washington and elsewhere. But highly intelligent beings, whether they are space-farers or not, would not be content to solve problems one at a time.

Solving only one problem at a time really isn't helping; more than likely, you're just trading one problem for another. This is particularly true in mining operations. As previously stated, highly intelligent beings would presumably apply solutions that solve multiple problems simultaneously.

Now consider a super-intelligent, super-powerful group of beings that show up on Earth and make a plan to establish themselves on this jewel of a planet without overly disrupting the development of primitive cultures that currently reside here. Subterranean enclaves would also afford protection from extreme climate swings, which periodically happen when large chunks of rock and ice from space impact the Earth. If one could make them comfortable, underground enclaves are the ideal refuge from dangerous radiation as well as impact events. Plans to establish colonies on Mars do include identifying and exploiting existing subterranean enclaves to protect our astronaut crews.

With this in mind, look around on the surface of planet Earth. We find countless examples of impossibly large amounts of rock and earth that have been transported at impossible distances and configured in even more impossible ways. In the case of dams, freeways, and other public works, we bear the expense because the project has an intrinsic value. But where on Earth are technologically capable humans using our advanced earth-moving capabilities to create enormous mounds, pyramids, and temples whose only value is ceremonial? Even the Great Wall of China had a specific utilitarian purpose, though that purpose ultimately failed.

Mounds, pyramids, temples, and earthworks are found on every continent. Their origin and means of construction often cannot be explained. The volume of material is impossibly great, the individual blocks are too massive, and the shaping and fit of the stones is so perfect that one cannot insert a piece of paper into the joint between stones. Such enormous blocks that fit together perfectly can be found on multiple continents. It invites, I think, some outside-the-box thinking. The mound phenomenon, that is, the enormous piles of rock and earth that exist world-wide can be interpreted as evidence that underground excavations have been happening or did happen for a long time. But if the underground excavations are to be concealed, then the tailings must be relocated to somewhere far away from the entrance. That, or the tailings could be repurposed to form some structure that looks important. Creating effigies and designs with large amounts of earth may serve as a distraction that keeps us wondering about the intended purpose of a structure. Really, such structures were put there to get rid of a lot of unwanted earth. Making it look ceremonial keeps us from asking the bigger question of where all that dirt and rock came from in the first place.

We do not KNOW the Egyptians built the pyramids. We only know that they were built in Egypt. We assume the Egyptians built them, but we have no witnesses and no one signed their work. Similarly, we do not KNOW that Middle or Late Archaic North American natives built the mounds. We have no witnesses. We only know that the mounds were built during a certain time frame between a few and several thousand years ago. Even that is not a certainty. Newer thinking suggests that at least some of the mounds are much older, but they were modified or renewed periodically in the more recent past. Either way, we have no baskets, shovels, or other tools that are attributable to an enormous public works style mound-building effort to show.

We are often told the mounds and effigies were ceremonial but we don't know what kind of ceremonies entailed the building of mounds. The mounds numbered in the millions when white settlers first arrived on the continent. That's a lot of ceremonies. Human burials are most often suggested, but very few of the mounds that have been excavated contain interred remains. The challenge we face is to become more sophisticated in the questions we ask and in the potential answers we consider. One generation's 'out-there' ideas have a way of becoming the foregone conclusions of the next. The whole history of geology, to name but one discipline, centers on the eventual acceptance of ideas that were too radical to be taken seriously when they were first suggested.

From the perspective of the masterminds of the mound-building phenomenon, they may not object to the destruction of the mounds by us surface-dwelling humans. They may have been meant to be used to create more fertile farmland or building materials. The material may have been put there for our use if we want it. Whether we revere it as a sacred site or tear it apart for building materials, we participate in multiple problem-solving strategies that underpin their existence. Super-intelligent beings produce large amounts of earth and rock. They move it to the surface, first dumping it, then disguising it as mysterious earthworks that leave only vague hints as to its true origin, but also providing a ready supply of fertile soil and rock that can be used by an emerging humanity to provide for themselves.

Admittedly, this is all very far-fetched but it is not implausible. Anyone who doubts that there are intelligently-piloted extraterrestrial crafts that come and go from under or inside the Earth should refer to this book's Bermuda Triangle essay (Chapter 7).

Maybe the ideas proposed above are without merit. It is easy to mock their absurdity from a purely scientific perspective. Yet, abject ridicule also supports the cover-story that there are no super-powerful visitors, that we are the sole intelligent beings on the planet, and maybe even that we are alone in the cosmos. In that case, all this earth moving was done without super-advanced technology. I cannot blame skeptically-minded individuals for doubting the veracity of my narrative. I may have lines of evidence to point to but I do not have absolute proof. Yet, certain earthworks worldwide hint at the veracity of the seemingly implausible view that enormous quantities of earth and rock were moved around by non-human intelligences.

The Serpent Mound

As previously stated, it is one of the most striking examples, if not THE most impressive animal effigy mounds in the entire world. It is seen by many as the greatest Native American artwork of all time, even though the modern descendants of Native Americans deny that their ancestors had anything at all to do with its creation.

Author Graham Hancock agrees that the Serpent Mound is the finest prehistoric animal effigy in the world. It is, of course, the effigy of a semi-coiled snake. If the coils were straightened, it would be a 1,348-foot-long continuous mound. The mound is four feet high and twenty-four feet across at its widest point. The age of the mound is a matter of some debate, with estimates ranging from one to five thousand years old. If it is one thousand years old, its creation is credited to the Adena Culture, and if it goes back five thousand, it would be attributed to the Fort Ancient Culture.

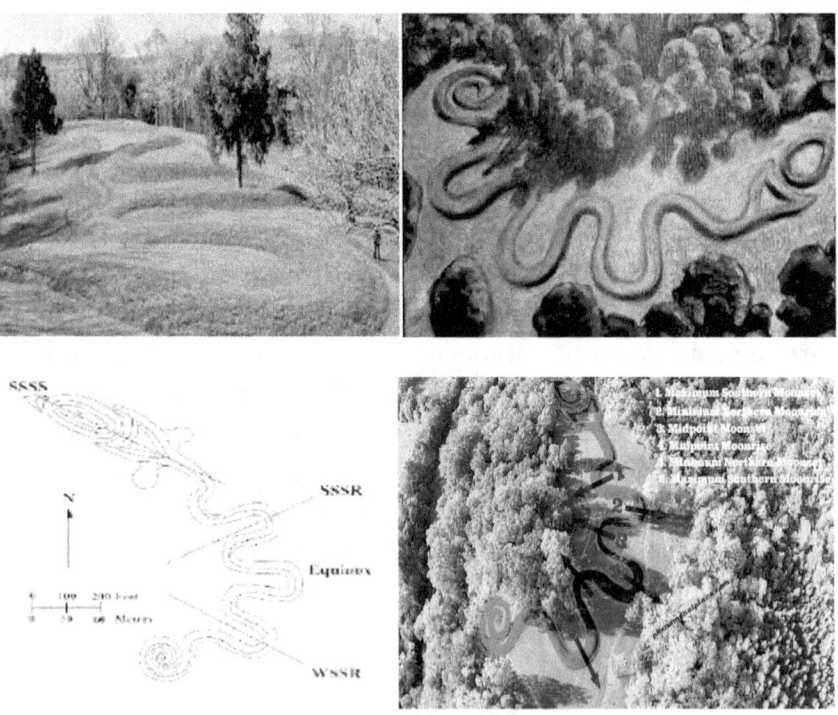

Ross Hamilton has studied the Serpent Mound as much as anyone and he favors the five thousand year date, making the Serpent mound contemporaneous with Watson Brake, the oldest of the lower Mississippi Valley mound complexes. Graham Hancock supports the previously stated possibility that the mound is much older than radiocarbon dating indicates. He and Ross Hamilton would agree that the mound was improved or restored a few times over the millennia, leading to discrepancies in the radiocarbon dating. The original iteration of the mound may be even older than 5,000 years B.C., but there just isn't any way to be sure.

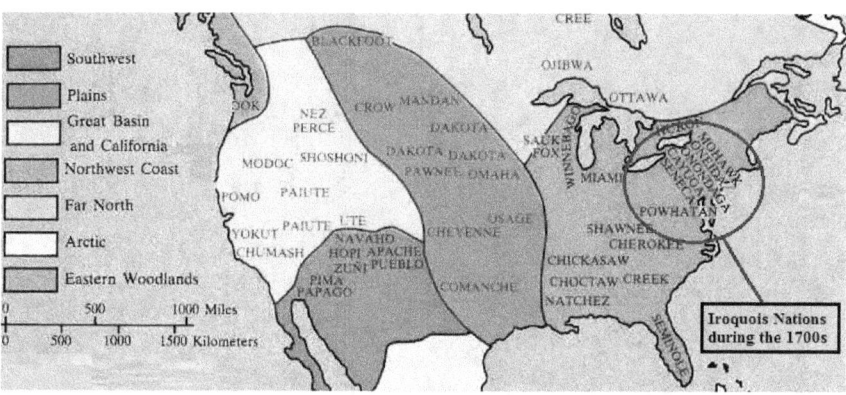

What makes the Serpent Mound so impressive, beyond the sheer volume of material, is the intricate alignments of the effigy with true north as well as significant points on the horizon. Again, Graham Hancock and Ross Hamilton have studied these alignments in every detail. They have come to find that vectors extending toward the horizon from the long axis of the partial coils point precisely to points on the horizon where the sun and moon rise and set at both summer and winter solstices. In contrast, other coil axes align with the Sun and Moon rise and setting points for both equinoxes. The long axis of the entire mound orients perfectly north, and the open mouth faces almost exactly at the setting sun on the summer solstice. Specifically, the alignment of the open jaw is 2.05 degrees off the precise point on the horizon where the sun sets on the summer solstice. Interestingly,

Graham Hancock attributes the discrepancy to the procession of the Earth's axis over time. He finds that twelve thousand years ago, the orientation of the mouth would have been exact, and Hancock suggests that the orientation may be a way of encoding a significant date. Might that be the date when the first Serpent Mound was created? Might it also indicate that something significant took place at the time of exact orientation, even if the mound was built much later? By now, the reader should recognize the 12,800 years before present as the circa of the Late Pleistocene Extinction Event, also known as Younger Dryas.

The remarkable precision of multiple celestial alignments is one of the most impressive features of the Great Serpent and it speaks to a surprising degree of sophistication and determination on the part of the builders, whoever they were. But the surprises do not end there. The Serpent Mound rests on a narrow limestone ridge one hundred feet above nearby Brush Creek. The ridge accommodates the sprawling form of the serpent so perfectly that most feel that we are dealing with a sacred site that was known to the ancients even before the mound was constructed. Moreover, the Serpent Mound site rests within the confines of an ancient meteor crater known as the Serpent Mound Crypto-Explosive Structure. For a long time, it was debated whether it was a volcanic feature or an impact site, but eventually, as other impact sites were identified and studied, the meteor crater view became more widely accepted.

Serpent Mound Crater, Ohio

~8-11 km D., exposed
<320 MYO, complex crater, sub-aerial or shallow marine (?)
39° 2′ N. Lat., 83° 24′ W. Long.; Adams, Highland, & Pike Counties, Ohio
Data from: PASSC Database; Hester (2010); Google Earth; Duncan et al., (2010).

Most agree that the mound represents a serpent but some see a spermatozoa. If it is a serpent, then it appears to be swallowing (or regurgitating) an egg. The first scientists to study the Serpent Manitou (spirit), as it is sometimes called, were Ephriam Squirer in the 1830s and Edwin Davis, who surveyed and cataloged mound complexes throughout Ohio in the 1840s. They were both suitably impressed by the enormity and complexity of the Serpent effigy mound. They also noted that the serpent is an often-featured symbol for many primitive cultures, particularly in Central and South America. The serpent deity they were referring to is a lot more well-known today. It would be Quetzalcoatl, a serpent deity that appears on Aztec and Mayan temples. There is a whole temple in Peru that is dedicated to Quetzalcoatl.

Interestingly, Quetzalcoatl was a very Christ-like entity, both in appearance and in disposition. He or she is often represented on bas-reliefs as a winged serpent. In Mayan legend, Quetzalcoatl arrived by boat a long time ago and helped to reorganize Mayan culture in the wake of some catastrophe (like the worldwide destruction following the Younger Dryas). Quetzalcoatl is remembered as being very tall, fair-haired, and with very king-like wisdom. He was a bearded man amidst a culture where men did not generally possess facial hair, and most importantly, he was very, very smart. He instructed the culture on how to self-govern, build, and farm. Once he got things up and running, Quetzalcoatl returned to his 'boat that had no oars' and sailed off. In another Jesus-like move, he promised to one day return.

It is also interesting how many other native cultures share a similar, if not identical, legend. Many North American tribes tell of a tall, white, bearded entity who espoused virtuous behavior and helped reorganize their society after a cataclysm. Indeed, the tale is so pervasive that several authors, including Graham Hancock, speculate that, such entities were part of a remnant population of highly advanced humans that inhabited North America and were almost completely wiped out by the series of comet impacts that eliminated a very advanced, almost Atlantis-like high culture. Their disappearance corresponds to the Mass Extinction Event or Younger Dryas between 12,800 B.C. and 11,600 B.C., but their extinction was not total.

The surviving remnants of this population of advanced humans spread out with the goal of restarting humanity worldwide in the most benevolent of manners. Many cultures throughout the world revere these mythical beings, and always for the same reason. They taught useful skills to populations in need of assistance, as well as teaching the need for virtues like kindness and charity. Shared cultural lore also described the Christ-like Quetzalcoatl entities as being able to perform miracles (much like Jesus in New Testament Scripture). One of Quetzalcoatl's most impressive miracles was his ability to move really heavy things. He showed the local shamans how to duplicate this feat. He was exceptionally clever in all ways, as well as being good-natured and playful. His moniker, or nick name in Mayan lore, was 'The Trickster.'

I mention this because when I look at the Serpent Mound, I notice two small wing-like structures that are just behind the head. When the Serpent Mound is drawn or photographed, the two diminutive structures are not always shown in the representation but are indeed there. Having studied the Quetzalcoatl legend and myth as it manifests throughout Central, North and South America, it suddenly occurred to me: The Serpent Mound of Adams County, Ohio, is a depiction of none other than Quetzalcoatl.

When Europeans arrived in North America, one of the tribes that inhabited the central U.S. was the Dhegihan Siouan. According to Brad Leppert, an Ohio Historical Society archaeologist, the ancestors of this tribe told of a character in their lore called "Toothy Mouth," lord of the Beneath World, who impregnated the first woman to emerge from the underworld. When I came across this item of ancient lore, a whole bunch of things suddenly began to fit together. Over and over, we are told that the ancients viewed the mound complexes, and specifically the Serpent Mound as a portal; an entrance to the underworld. It would not be mere coincidence, then, that the Serpent Mound is built upon limestone bedrock. Geologically, limestone bedrock is known worldwide for facilitating the development of Karst topography. Groundwater seeps and trickles through cracks in the water-soluble limestone bedrock. The cracks gradually become larger, eventually joining with other 'solution openings' as a geologist would say, and the result is cave country. Unique features of limestone or Karst topography include sinkholes and subterranean caverns which, over time, can become quite large, as in the case of Mammoth Caves in Kentucky, Meremec Cave and Picture Cave in Missouri, and Carlsbad Caverns of New Mexico to name a few examples. All of these cave systems exist because they formed from the gradual dissolution of the native limestone bedrock due to the action of groundwater.

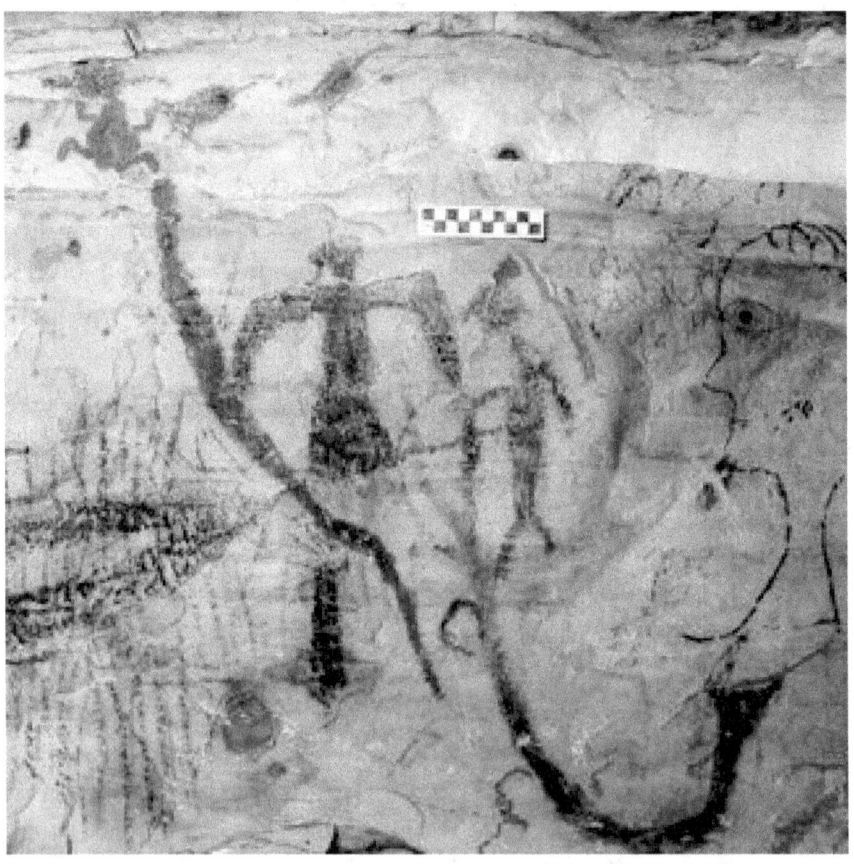

Picture Cave in Missouri has petroglyphs that are thought to trace back to the Fort Ancient culture around 1000 A.D. The serpent motif is seen below in the petroglyph from Picture Cave. Mammoth Caves is the largest cave system in the U.S. and new sections of cave are being discovered in that cave system from time to time. It is often said that for every cave we know of, there are ten more that have yet to be discovered. The longest-known cave in Ohio is in Adams County. Cave Hill cave is only a couple miles distant from the Serpent Mound, which also resides in Adams County. In addition to the presence of caves, the Serpent Mound site is unique in that it sits within a crypto-explosion feature, also called an impact site. Such features are sprinkled throughout the face of the globe and identified by their concentric circles of uplifted and down-dropped circles of bedrock. Another diagnostic feature of impact sites is the presence of rare earth elements like titanium, uranium, platinum and iridium. Such heavy metals are found within the seven-mile circular structure that contains the Serpent Mound.

The whole picture leads me to conclude that the Serpent Mound rests where it does for several reasons, and the mound itself is an effigy that evokes not just of a generic snake but Quetzalcoatl, The Trickster. Perhaps the site is sacred because it identifies the site that was chosen by a powerful being or group of beings to take up residence. The limestone bedrock, which is not very common in Ohio, provides caves and caverns where subterranean enclaves could be established. The presence of rare earth elements is another unique feature of the site. Remember, super-intelligent beings logically favor multi-purpose solutions.

The work of establishing or expanding large underground citadels would generate large volumes of rock debris that would have to be hauled to the surface, just like mining operations do. Even if creating livable places was the top priority, one might as well separate valuable ore from the unwanted tailings. Excavating caves for living in an impact crater might achieve two objectives at once.

In the lower Mississippi mound complexes, each mound-building episode appears to be separated by intervals of 700-1000 years. Same with the Serpent Mound. Whenever work did resume, more crushed rock and earth would be brought to the surface and added to the serpent effigy mound. This is consistent with the on-again off-again manner in which the Serpent Mound appears to have been built. Efforts have been made to determine the composition of the Serpent Mound. No one is allowed to dig into such a treasured site, but ground penetrating radar has been put to the Serpent Mound, resulting in the effigy being composed of soil and large, angular rock fragments. There are mounds in Louisiana that have been found to contain rocks that are only found at considerable depths below the surface. This is consistent with the view that some mounds are comprised of tailings, also known as spoils.

Was the Serpent Mound built for a purpose? Is there a message that is being conveyed? Indeed, there are astronomical alignments with respect to solstices and equinoxes. I think it is oriented toward events in the lunar cycle as much as the solar cycle. The Serpent Mound is a reference to the cosmos from whence the tall blonde Quetzalcoatl beings originated. They came to Earth and, among other things, undertook a program of subterranean excavation and construction.

If Quetzalcoatl is indeed the entity or entities being portrayed, and I think he is, then his reputation for trickery must be remembered. The alignments of the Serpent Mound were encoded to recognize the sacred aspects of the geographic site, as well as the motions of the heavens. The Serpent Mound then invokes the duality of the heavens and the Earth, and memorializes the trickster, Quetzalcoatl, who was or is a deity who established or re-established humanity. It's also an address marker for an underground establishment. Yet all of those considerations are just a 'red herring' intended to disguise the fact that the Serpent Mound is also a mining dump, and if we finally realized it for what it is, we might conclude that there must be a sizeable subterranean installation either beneath the effigy or somewhere nearby. Astronomical and geometric alignments were encoded to hint at the origin of the builders, and also to keep us from asking the most important question: Who put all that earth there, and how could a small population of hunter-gatherers muster the free time, tools, and manpower required to build something that had no practical value to them?

If there was but a single mound or mound complex, I could accept the view that the site was constructed by members of some Fort Ancient Culture five thousand years ago, the Hopewell, or the Adena Culture of 1000 years ago, or both. But there are so many other sites throughout the Ohio River Valley, not to mention the lower Mississippi Valley. The overall commitment of time and manpower simply boggles the mind. Fort Ancient, the site from which the culture draws its name, is a positively immense mound complex near Lebanon, Ohio. The Newark Earthworks is the most sprawling of all mound sites in Ohio. There are many more in southern Ohio, Kentucky, West Virginia, Indiana, Wisconsin, Minnesota, and beyond.

Remember that 90% of the earthworks have been destroyed to make way for farming, road building and general development. Even if we look at only what remains, the number of mound complexes and their sheer size defies the capabilities of even the most industrious of ancient cultures. I question the assumption that Hopewell or Fort Ancients ever hauled meaningful amounts of earth to any of these sites. As in Louisiana, I doubt they were ever in possession of the means, the material, and the motivation to undertake such daunting and unnecessary tasks.

One expert on the mounds of Louisiana, Joe Saunders, suggested that perhaps the reason for building mound sites, whether it be Poverty Point, Watson Brake, Serpent Mound or any of the other countless mounds, was simply for the zen-like purpose of building mounds. It reminds me of my parents' reply when I asked why it was so important to clean my bedroom every week. "It's good for you," was the only reply I ever got.

Suppose the gods, extraterrestrials, or super-advanced sea-faring terrestrials were able to command the local hunter-gatherers to do their bidding. In that case, the practicalities alone of obtaining, moving, and carefully placing such enormous quantities of material might not be that good for them. Injuries and fatigue, maybe even accidental deaths, might result. Moving so much material would be quite an imposition upon any unmechanized labor force. It is exactly the same conundrum one faces when trying to explain the building of the Great Pyramids with conventional tools and human labor. No Bronze-age culture was capable of accomplishing such spectacular feats of earth moving. There must have been some kind of advanced, relatively effortless means of quarrying, transporting and placing enormous amounts of material.

There are a couple of credible suggestions for how so much earth-moving was accomplished. One is a Tesla-like plan to electromagnetically charge the earth, then charge the earthen block or masses of earth one wished to move with a like charge, creating a magnetic repulsion between the building material and the ground upon which it rested. Once accomplished, a ten-ton stone would be free of ground contact friction and a single person could push the block across the ground. Another equally far-fetched possibility for achieving the same friction-free suspension is with resonant sonic tones. I cannot blame anyone for doubting this if for no other reason than it is humbling to consider that ancient folks had amazing tricks at their disposal that we still do not have.

Maybe our great awakening is not so far off. Just because you or I are unaware of how to apply these physics-bending technologies doesn't mean no one ever has. One person in the recent past left us clues that he did indeed figure out how to move super heavy things all by himself.

The world's only modern megalithic structure was built in Homestead, Florida, between 1923 and 1951 by a Latvian immigrant named Ed Leedskalnin. He bought a piece of property between Miami and the

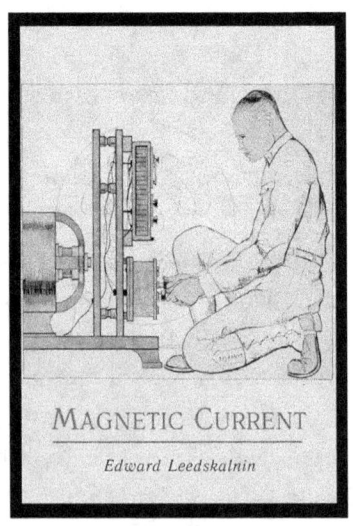

MAGNETIC CURRENT

Edward Leedskalnin

Everglades and single-handedly built what is now known as the Coral Castle. Built out of massive blocks of coral rock (coquina) that he quarried on site, somehow a five-foot-tall man with simple tools and no known advanced technology was able to quarry, move, and place five-ton stones, raise a twenty-ton obelisk, hang a nine-ton stone door so that it could be opened with one hand, and artistically place some two million pounds of quarried coral rock to create the remarkable Coral Castle in Homestead, Florida. His tool set, as far as is known, consisted of a few pulleys, a tripod of three telephone pole-sized logs, a chain rated for five-ton loads, and a single block and tackle with a ten-ton rating. He worked only at night, always alone. He was sometimes seen at the library studying Egyptians and Egyptian pyramids, as well as other megalithic structures, worldwide. He never divulged his building secrets, and he left very few writings, but he did state that he had solved the mystery of the pyramids. Whatever he learned from his research, he was able to apply his knowledge to the task of quarrying, moving, and placing at least one twenty-ton stone using a five-ton block and tackle! He lifted and placed stones that were wider than the base of the tripod that was ostensibly used to lift them. He moved and placed an obelisk that was taller than the same tripod. To this day, dozens of architects and engineers have visited Coral Castle and have no idea how a single man could have assembled such a modern megalith. He was somewhat cryptic in the few notes he left, saying only that he was using 'reverse energy' and 'anti-gravity' to accomplish his seemingly impossible feat.

He did write a booklet entitled *Magnetic Current,* where he mentioned a device he called a perpetual motion holder. From what little we know, it consisted of a mile of copper wire wound around a 1 ½ inch U-shaped steel bar with another bar connecting the two ends of the U-shaped, copper-wound steel bar. When a current was applied, it would run through the device forever. Since his death, no one has ever been able to produce a working model of the device he described, but it seems to have had superconducting properties that enabled him to single-handedly lift super heavy objects.

Returning to the puzzle of the mound phenomenon as it occurs continent-wide, it begins to appear that either a highly advanced terrestrial culture or a highly advanced extraterrestrial culture had an understanding of the same electromagnetic feat accomplished by Edward Leedskalnin. As with Tesla's secrets of free energy, Leedskalnin's secret of achieving some sort of electromagnetically induced weightlessness has been lost to history. Based on observation of their mounds and megaliths, it does appear that somebody in prehistoric times had access to both of these highly useful engineering principles. Whether it be the Great Pyramid, Stonehenge, Tiwanaku, Kalasasaya or other megaliths as they occur worldwide, the ancients apparently had access to the same or similar engineering technologies that enabled them to lift and transport super-human loads.

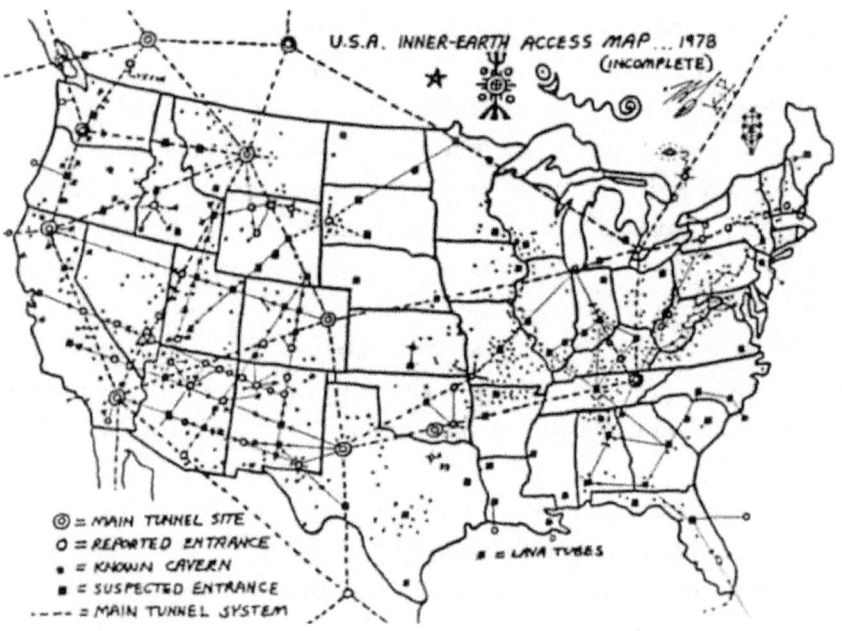

Recall from the Luna chapter that the ancient Mayan calendar at Tiwanaku tells of a time when the Earth had no Moon. Zulu legend describes a race of intelligent, lizard-like extraterrestrials that inhabit a hollow moon. Now, return to the Serpent Mound and note the elliptical object perched between the open jaws of the serpent mouth. The builders of the Serpent Mound went to some extra trouble to shape a hollow earthen oval protruding from the mouth of the Serpent Manitou. I think that was not an accident. It seems to suggest a thought-provoking possibility: the object in the jaws of the winged serpent Quetzalcoatl is the moon, complete with an internal void, being towed into position by the clever and all-powerful Quetzalcoatl.

In a bit of circular logic, I contend that if all the material used in pyramids worldwide could be moved into position with relatively little effort, then moving an entire moon becomes possible as well. Or, if they could move a moon, then building pyramids, not to mention earthen mounds, should be child's play. And if these beings, whoever they were, could move either of those sets of materials, then they should be capable of excavating enormous subterranean cavities, and connecting them with subterranean passages. Interestingly, in Ross Hamilton's magnum opus, *Mysteries of the Serpent Mound*, he relates a metaphysical experience he had with remote viewing. He was given a vision of a whole series of subterranean enclaves that were arranged in concentric circles and connected with linear passages like spokes on a wheel. Granted, it can be dismissed as hallucination, but it begins to look like he is describing details of the same underworld that has been described by many cultures dating back to antiquity. Not only do ancient legends and tribal lore, Judeo-Christian scripture, modern shamans and mystics all refer to an underworld, but it can be argued that we are in possession of physical evidence that such a subterranean realm actually exists. That evidence is lying all over the landscape, with the mounds, the stone pyramids, and the earthen pyramids, as they occur worldwide.

Curiously, the effigy mounds and the geometrically arranged mound complexes do not occur in the western United States, but that is not to say the western U.S. has no mounds. They have thousands that remain and millions that once existed, just as was the case in the eastern U.S. before European settlement destroyed most of them. Mounds, as they manifest in the western U.S., are more haphazardly placed, even though the volume of the individual mounds is very uniform. The mounds of the West are best represented by the mound field in western Washington, where the phenomenon was first studied by University of Washington geologist J Harlan Bretz. Best known for his groundbreaking work in eastern Washington's Channeled Scablands, Bretz did not have far to travel from his campus office in Seattle to a vast mound field of extremely uniform twenty cubic yard earthen mounds that still number in the thousands, though there used to be far more. More than half of this spectacular mound field was bulldozed to accommodate a Weyerhauser tree farm.

The Mima Mounds consist of rock and fertile soil that rests upon a very much less fertile glacial outwash plain. Because the mounds sit upon a glaciated surface, Bretz concluded the mounds were created by retreating ice, although he could not envision a means by which soil containing organic matter could originate from a glacier. Over the years, other large tracts of uniformly spaced and uniformly sized mounds have been discovered throughout the West. Since the time of Bretz, numerous geologists have undertaken to explain the mounds using known natural processes. Earthquakes, glaciers, floods, and gopher activity have all been applied and all explanations have been found wanting. Glaciers and earthquakes have been convincingly disputed, and right now, believe it or not, the most accepted theory for the origin of the mound fields across several states is gophers.

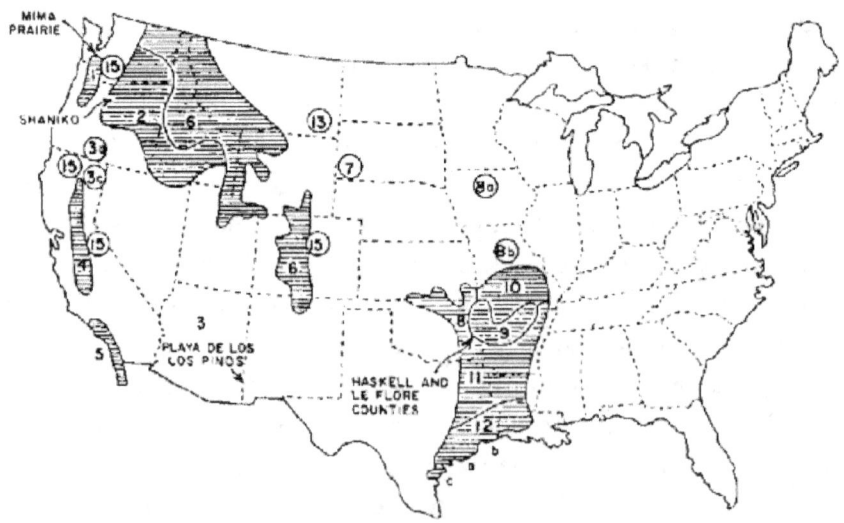

The town of Mima is gone, but Bretz and others used the mound field near the former town as the 'type locality' when studying the phenomenon. A large tract of those mounds has now been preserved in the Mima Mounds Natural Area a mile north of Little Rock, Washington. Many geologists have come to study them and attempt to explain their origin. Whole symposiums have been convened, and resulting monographs have been published to summarize the conclusions of geologic scholars. One such monograph is <u>Mima Mounds: The Case for Polygenesis and Bioturbation</u>, by Burnham and Johnson. While the conclusions were not unanimous, the upshot of Special Paper 490, published in 2012 by The Geological Society of America, is that the mounds are the result of gopher activity, specifically pocket gophers *Thomomys talpoides*.

Several curiosities surround this tentative conclusion: No gophers currently reside in the mound fields that were studied. They ostensibly built the mounds by piling up available earth to build colony nests, and then they all left at some time in the past, just like the

Anasazi. Pocket gophers still inhabit ranch country in many states of the western U.S. I have them on my five-acre property in western Oregon. But nowhere can we find gophers inhabiting immense mounds consisting of the equivalent of two dump trucks of earth and rock. Many of the rocks in the mounds are too big to pass through the digestive system of gophers. One geologist disputed his colleagues' conclusion, observing that gophers are better at tearing down mounds than building them up. I have abundant mole populations on my property as well as gophers and voles. They all tunnel and dig, but the only mounds I observe are tiny versions of the much more impressive Mima-style mound fields. The mounds I observe are no more than ankle-high. Nothing head-high or even knee-high. I did build a shoulder-high mound on my property out of fill dirt, rocks, and bricks. Burrowing squirrels (California ground squirrels) promptly moved in, but they certainly didn't help build it. The more one looks at the scientific conclusion and the logic behind it, the more it begins to take on the appearance of a misapplication of science; that is, selecting only certain facts to support a preconceived conclusion, and discarding the facts that do not fit.

Curiously, throughout the eastern U.S., there is absolute agreement that the Ohio Valley and the Mississippi Valley mounds are anthropogenic in nature (human-built), even though no currently existing Indian tribe is claiming that their ancestors built the mounds. The only questions about the mound phenomenon as it manifests in the eastern U.S. surround which culture can be credited with building them and how long ago they were created. Even the question of 'how' the mounds were created is not in dispute, although, if you've been reading the earlier parts of this essay, you will know that I think this question is not so easily dismissed. (Baskets. Right.) The uniformity of opinion about the origin of eastern mounds clearly stems from the geometric shapes and animal effigies portrayed, which cannot possibly be attributed to any natural process. Out west, however, the mounds are all conical or hemispherical piles of dirt and rock. There are no effigies, no geometric shapes, no bones, and no artifacts. Nothing to even help with radiocarbon dating, just thousands of uniform mounds, spread mostly over open areas in Washington, Oregon, and California, with some smaller patches in Oklahoma and other central states.

It might help resolve the issue if one could excavate a few mounds but the ones that weren't obliterated to make way for farming are now preserved and protected. There are literally thousands of remaining mounds within the boundaries of the Mima Mounds Preserve, but you'd better not get caught digging into one of them. To my knowledge, there is exactly one mound within the boundaries of the preserve that has been opened up so that one can view the entire cross-section. It lies at the southern end of the preserve, near a borrow pit off of Bordeaux Road.

The excavated cross-section seems to show that at least the one mound that has been opened up is composed of different material than the glacial outwash plain upon which it sits. The excavated mound contains a darker, richer, less rocky soil than the soil of the surrounding terrain, which is why Weyerhauser bought, then leveled half of the original Mima mound field. The more fertile soil was perfect for growing tree seedlings by the millions.

Even more puzzling is the fact that the base of the excavated mound sits more deeply in the substrate at the center of its mass. That is, the base of the mound is convex with respect to the substrate. Recall the observation of Christopher O'Brien with respect to cattle mutilations. There is often a corresponding dent in the ground that suggests that the carcass was dropped from height. It is as though the whole twenty cubic yard mass of soil was similarly dropped from a height upon the local landscape by an aerial dump truck. Until some more mounds are opened up, we must assume that the one mound cross-section is representative of all mounds at the site. Again, only one mound has been opened up so one cannot be certain that all mounds display this downward-curving base. If it were true of the whole mound field, then it is tenable, even necessary, to assert that the whole mass of each mound (and there are thousands) was dumped at once, onto the landscape from a height of ten feet or so above the ground. It is worth noting that mound fields are always found on treeless landscapes, making it much easier to approach the site and dump material from the air.

In the symposium monograph, there is an aerial photo of another mound field on Vandenberg Air Force Base in California. It shows strings of mounds that are arranged like pearls on a necklace. Another photo shows the same thing even more plainly in an aerial photo taken of Morehouse Parish, Louisiana, on the floodplain of the Ouachita River. In case the reader is unfamiliar with the local geography, the mound field on the floodplain of the Ouachita River is seventy miles from Poverty Point. That juxtaposition seems a bit suspicious. Poverty Point is a mound complex that is clearly anthropic (human-caused) yet seventy miles to the north is another mound field that is attributed to gophers, even though the mounds are arranged in peculiarly organized curvilinear fashion. In the central valley of California is another mound field near Merced, with hundreds of low mounds that appear in straight lines. If they were created by a population of gophers, then we have an indication that gophers can do Euclidean geometry. Or, we have the 'smoking gun' evidence that the Mima Mounds are intelligently created.

Of course, I am arguing for the seemingly far-fetched notion that the mound phenomenon is at least sometimes not as natural as we are led to believe; that intelligent beings are carting soil from the depths of the earth to the surface where they are getting rid of it in such a manner as to conceal its origin. It may be that the strategies employed to conceal the origin of the tailings have evolved with time.

Making geometric mound fields was done for a while, as we see more random dumping in most mound fields in the West. Later, someone figured out that they were being too obvious with their dumping strategies. They probably had a meeting. They came up with a better plan moving forward: make designs and effigies that look like the work of industrious, spiritually inclined humans. That should keep the prying eyes of future scientists thoroughly confused. One author, Jim Brandon, wrote a book about earth mysteries entitled, *The Rebirth of Pan*. He humorously observes that the mound phenomenon as it manifests continent-wide is so confusing that it begins to appear that the whole phenomenon is configured in a way that is deliberately intended to confuse scientists. He may have been joking, but I think he's right.

The Mima Mounds monograph, Special Paper 490, included one paper by an author who attempted to determine the date of formation of a few mound fields in the Columbia Basin of eastern Washington and Oregon. Roald Fryxell of Washington State University came up with estimated dates of formation between 14,000 years and 7,500 years ago. While the dates of earliest formation (14,000 years ago) are a little variable depending on the exact mound field in question, all the mounds he examined ceased to form at the very same time: 7,500 years ago. Compare that to the date of Poverty Point and Watson Brake, where the oldest dates are 5000 years ago at Watson Brake, and somewhere around 2,000 in the case of Poverty Point.

Center hill is composed of loose fertile material allowing for tree and shrub growth. Hill at right is volcanic bedrock that lacks fertility, How was the hill of loose earth formed?

While it is no doubt a bold assertion that the mound phenomenon as it occurs continent-wide points to the work of super-intelligent, and maybe extraterrestrial 'gophers,' there is one more location where everything comes together so extraordinarily that it almost removes all doubt that such a far out assertion is indeed the case. That important location is one that is probably already well known to serious student of the paranormal: Mount Shasta.

Are mounds found in large numbers around Mount Shasta? You better believe it, and it doesn't stop there. But to begin with, even the science-minded folk who contributed to the Mima Mounds Symposium have a lot to share about Mount Shasta. The Modoc Plateau, a hundred miles to the east of Shasta, is described as 'abundantly mounded.' A researcher named Mason identifies mound sites on three sides of Mount Shasta. To my knowledge, all the mound fields around Shasta are the Mima-style mounds, sometimes called pimple mounds or pimpled prairies. No effigies and no geometric shapes. From the air, the locations look exactly like the pigskin on a football: very evenly spaced and evenly sized mounds extending for a considerable distance.

Much has been written about a mythical race of lizard-like beings called Lamerians that are said to reside in subterranean enclaves in the vicinity of Mt. Shasta. UFO sightings positively abound in the vicinity of this picturesque mountain with a deep history of paranormal events. You name it. If it's paranormal, it has been reported in the vicinity of Mount Shasta. The list includes UFOs, aliens, sasquatches, ghosts, and spirit beings. I had some free time one fall, so I drove down to visit a friend who lived in the shadow of that magical mountain. I fished for the famed trout of the McCloud River, then visited my good friend Alyssa Alexandria. She was kind enough to show me around and I was very surprised that she knew of some of the local mound fields. She led me to one mound on the edge of Shastina Lake that was positively huge. Curiously, it was located right next to a small volcanic cinder cone of the exact same size. The closer we examined the two adjacent features, the clearer it was that one had the stratigraphy of an ancient but extinct cinder cone, and the one right next to it was a big pile of unconsolidated and unstratified dirt. It was as though the pile of loose dirt was situated right next to a natural volcanic feature of the exact same size so that the loose material in the artificially constructed pile blended right in with the natural volcanic feature.

Mt. Shasta.

Then, things proceeded to get even more peculiar. Alyssa escorted me to some private ranchland, where she had permission to hike. First, we stumbled upon an impression in the pasture grass that looked like a small crop circle for the whole world. Then, she led me to a curiosity that I had never before encountered.

The California Stone Lines

We hiked through pasture grass and cheat grass, then climbed out of the cattle-grazing lowlands and onto sagebrush and juniper forested hills. Numerous bedrock outcrops revealed the dark, iron-rich volcanic rock that is so typical of Northwestern U.S. volcanic land-scapes. We encountered low rock walls at irregular intervals that would wend their way around the landscape and often right up a hill-side to the 800-foot summit. I assumed we were looking at some feature that a rancher put there to define and contain different tracts of grazing land. Then, with a wry smile, Alyssa asked me if the walls looked like they were capable of confining grazing cattle. Clearly, they were not. The walls were low, often with sides that sloped up at an angle that a cow could easily negotiate and a goat or sheep could effortlessly negotiate. The walls sometimes had openings like windows with header stones spanning the top of the portal in a manner that it looked a bit artistic.

Alyssa spared me the rest of the guessing game and explained to me that they are indeed a local mystery that pops up in other locations around the Golden State, specifically in the hilly ranch country east of San Francisco. In the Bay Area, the features bear one of several names, including the East Bay Walls, the Berkley Walls, and the California Stone Lines. The latter name is perhaps the most accurate because the structures, whatever they are, are too low to function as walls. They are completely ineffective if their intention is or was to keep livestock in or out. They are usually comprised of dark, iron-rich volcanic rock; the same rock that is seen lying all over the landscape, and the walls or lines wend around the landscape for miles. Sometimes, the lines intersect other stone lines at seemingly random angles.

Over the years, curious people have queried the local tribes as to the purpose and origin of the stone lines. As with the mounds back east, the local tribes make no claim to having built them. That invites others to speculate that they are the product of Chinese laborers. It is true that large numbers of Chinese laborers were brought to California in the mid-nineteenth century to do the back-breaking work of railroad building and gold mining. Many a railroad or  mining area bears the mark of this large and underpaid labor force, but the stone lines, which extend for hundreds of miles, have no discernible connection to either of those industries. They may have been woefully underpaid, but considering their paltry wages, Chinese laborers didn't build things just for the heck of it. In some places, the walls are artistically assembled with peepholes and smaller openings that are not consistent with retaining walls or the stone fences of New England. In other cases, the rocks that cap the walls are far too big for even two people to muscle into place. In other places, the lines look like messy piles of rock. They do not follow any clear property lines. Sometimes, they end abruptly and then resume further up the hillsides. The surviving descendants of the indigenous Ohlone Indians take no credit. Like the earliest Spanish settlers and explorers, the Ohlone insist that the walls were there when they arrived.

There are about 800 miles of stone lines in California alone. They are also found in other states, including Delaware, parts of New England, Ohio, and more. They also occur in many other countries throughout the world. There is very little research on the subject, and I could not find a single book on it. There is a website that does a reasonable job of cataloging the phenomenon as it manifests statewide. It can be found by Googling 'California Stone Lines,' although the title of the webpage is Relics of the Gods. The sponsors of that website offer that, indeed, the Shasta area has the highest concentration of these enigmatic structures. The stone lines inventory webpage identifies 200 miles of stone lines in the area surrounding Mt. Shasta. Another of the most curious concentrations surrounds the extinct volcano of Sutter Butte, California.

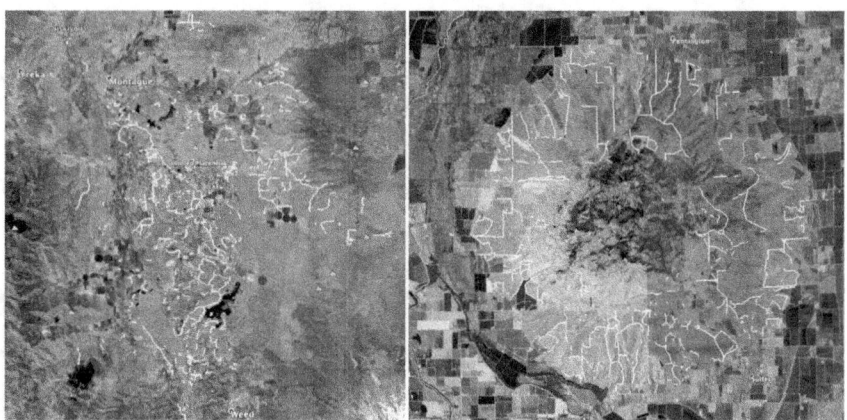

Stone lines in vicinity of Mt. Shasta (left) and Sutter Butte (right).

Studying the aerial photo of Sutter Butte with the overlain outline of the known stone lines clearly illustrates the fact that the walls are not laid out with any obvious purpose in mind. Property boundaries and livestock containment are the most obvious possibilities. Neither of these possibilities stands up to careful scrutiny. It does seem that the mystery of the origin of the California stone lines parallels the mystery of the mound phenomenon. In several places, the mound phenomenon seems to intersect the stone line phenomenon, inviting us to devise a reason to feel that seemingly separate enigmas do bear some currently unknown connection.

I stared at the map of the rock lines, especially the ones around Sutter Butte, for a very long time. I thought about it as I lay in bed, trying to fall asleep. I tried to reconcile it with my suspicion that there were underground citadels here on Earth that are being occupied by very intelligent and capable beings, perhaps beings whose origin was somewhere else in the galaxy or somewhere else in dimensionality, or both. I kept asking myself what a group of subterranean occupants might need or want that the rock lines would provide. I came up with two possibilities: energy and communication. Both of these infra-structures would require wires or other conductive materials. I kept revisiting the thought that the stone lines do look like wires. I can't speak for all stone lines, but the ones I saw around Shasta were made from igneous rocks that are high in iron and magnesium, or what a geologist would call mafic rocks. (As rocks go, such rock types would be relatively good conductors of electricity.)

I factored in the way the stone lines are concentrated in an area rather than spread out evenly throughout the landscape. Where had I seen patterns like that before? It hit me: *They could be antennas.* They could be purposed for collecting or possibly transmitting very large amplitude radio waves. Some of the stone lines I saw went straight up the side of small mountains to the summit. What would be the purpose of a conductive rock 'wire' that extended to the top of a mountain? Lightning? If that rock wire was struck by a bolt of light-ning, it might be able to capture and transport some extremely high voltage current. Again, I remembered that intelligent beings would devise multi-purpose solutions. Perhaps the rock lines do a little of both. Perhaps some are intended to transmit signals and some collect ambient sources of terrestrial or atmospheric energy. Perhaps the builders of the lines are clever enough to devise a system that can alternate between both purposes. The curious arrangement of gaps and holes in the stone lines may have a purpose, but perhaps they are put there only to confuse us, just like the geometries, alignments, and effigies that are integrated into the mounds. It began to look like everything I looked at separately fit together in a neat package. I showed the map of the lines around Shasta and Sutter Butte to my neighbor and electrical engineer, Jonathan.

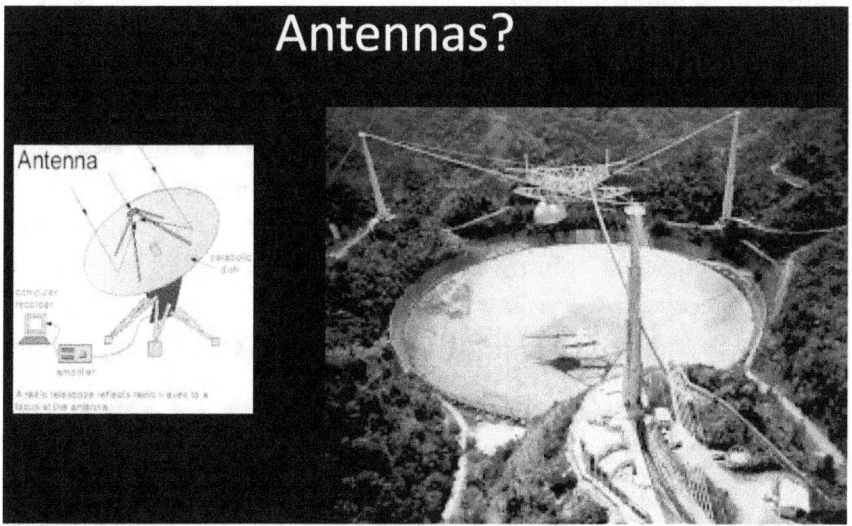

Jonathan made a very useful observation: even if the rocks that comprise the walls have enough conductivity to transmit current, they would all have to connect if current was expected to flow. Wires in a circuit of any kind cannot just end. Then he produced a circuit board and showed me tiny electricity pathways that do appear to abruptly end. That is because, he explained, a circuit board consists of five or six layers, and the wires connect to other levels of the circuit board by way of structures called sleeves. If the stone lines connected to other buried stone lines, or the bedrock itself, there would be a chance of creating a closed circuit that could collect or transmit some kind of electromagnetic energy.

A third possibility must be considered. Like the mounds, they may not do anything at all except serve as a means of stashing a whole bunch of unwanted bedrock in clever designs that leave us scratching our heads and looking for a purpose that isn't there. In this case, like the Serpent Mound, we have a clue that Sutter Butte and Shasta have large subterranean openings that were constructed by beings who are capable of moving very large loads of unwanted bedrock to the surface.

Return to Serpent Mound

The big benefit to studying a wide range of paranormal topics, as opposed to just one or two, is that you begin to see connections. And when those connections emerge from the fog of misunderstanding, you finally feel like you might just be getting somewhere. That 'somewhere' is a realization that these seemingly separate topics might just be connected, even inter-woven. Could there possibly be a paranormal 'theory of everything'? When I look at the serpent mound and all of its implications, I begin to see a Theory of Everything.

Skeleton of Mound Builder, 7 ft. in length, Serpent Mound. Peebles, Ohio.

It starts with the fact that the Serpent Mound is located in a 200 million-year-old meteor crater. It also sits on the only limestone topography in Ohio, and limestone naturally produces large underground open spaces. The volume of soil and rock is suspiciously large, and there is no obvious source of the 'midden' used in its making. The theme of the earthwork may or may not evoke the image of the cosmic trickster and saving grace, Quetzalcoatl.

Recall that in the 1890s, Frederic Ward Putnam excavated some of the mounds next to the Serpent Mound and brought to the surface a skeleton that was seven feet in length. Everything below the knees was lost in what was surely a fairly clumsy exhuming, but the skeleton still measured 7 feet.

Like so many others, the skeleton disappeared in obscurity, probably at the behest of the Smithsonian Institute. Yet, it seems like the Mound is connected to the man, just like the sky is connected to the earth.

Recall from Chapter Two that Tree Pruit was grooving on a summer evening near the sacred Serpent Mound on August 24, 2003, when she saw a UFO, which she attempted to report. I'm not sure how hard she pursued it, but she produced a drawing of the aerial craft she saw in the immediate vicinity of the Serpent Mound.

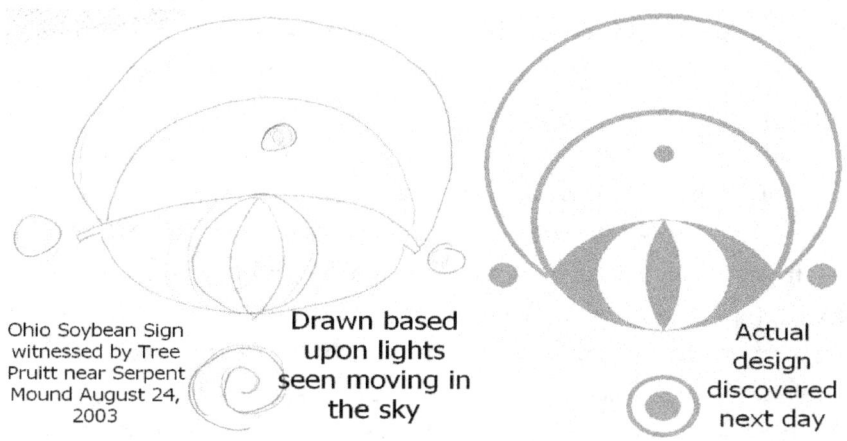

Ohio Soybean Sign witnessed by Tree Pruitt near Serpent Mound August 24, 2003

Drawn based upon lights seen moving in the sky

Actual design discovered next day

The following day, this crop circle appeared in a field of soybeans on a ridge on the opposite side of Brush Creek from the Serpent

Mound. Fortunately, someone got into a plane and photographed it from the air and even took a photo showing the glyph and its proximity to Serpent Mound (see below).

Naturally, skeptics will claim that Tree Pruit had something to do with the appearance of the crop glyph. She said she didn't know anything about crop circles. She was just enjoying a nice August evening in rural southern Ohio. The glyph looks to be as geometrically perfect as anything we see in the grain fields of southern England. Legitimate crop circles do occur in many places outside of southern England. Which brings us full circle to a reconsideration of crop circles (glyphs) as they continue to manifest in the grain fields of southern England: I think the English crop circle researchers have done a superior job of distinguishing between the truly mysterious crop glyphs that sometimes manifest, and the bogus crop circles created by disreputable pranksters. (Please revisit Chapter 2 if this point is unfamiliar.)

It gets even better. Let's go back and inspect the full catalog of crop glyphs that have been so assiduously cataloged by heroic researchers like Lucy Pringle, Freddy Silva, Colin Andrews, and others. We find that a few images bear a stirring reference to the Great Serpent Manitou half a world away. In the glyph seen below, the coiled serpent interacts with a series of circles, which hearkens to the constellation Hercules. When we overlay the constellation of the glyph as it appeared in England, it appears that the serpent is pointing at a specific star. That star is below and to the left of epsilon-Hercules, one of the stars that form the rough square at the center of the Hercules constellation.

A clear signature of the "feathered serpent", known also as Quetzalcoatl to the Mayans or Aztecs

On the left is another crop glyph that appeared in a field adjacent to Barbury Castle in August 1999, which clearly references Serpent Mound. If the crop glyphs are attributable to off-planeters, these glyph makers connect themselves to the Serpent Mound. We are being shown where Quetzalcoatl hails from in the first glyph seen above. Quetzalcoatl is again referenced in the Serpent Mound in the crop glyph on the left. Obviously, these indications stop well short of being absolute proof of anything. There will always be those who dismiss any and all crop circles as hoaxes. I see it as unverifiable information we are being handed by the highly intelligent (and tricky) off-planeters.

English crop circle researchers have long maintained that there is a bona fide connection between genuine crop circles and extraterrestrials. If we take that claim seriously, then we are getting indications that Quetzalcoatl is not only still a player, but that we still are being given, in modern times, the same clues that the ancients were getting, as to the origin of this set of beings who were watchful of earlier humanity and who continue to be a watchful presence to this day.

Quetzalcoatl, or Jesus, didn't die. We are still, in modern times, being given indications of his presence.

Bruce Gernon (Chapter 7) heard from the former director of the secret AUTEC installation that when it comes to civilians being in possession of secret information, the agency people don't care what you know; they only care about what you can prove. I think our off-planeters feel the same way about our knowledge of them and their agenda. They don't mind giving you hints and other unverifiable indications of what they are up to, where they come from, and so forth, but they will not give you proof. The same is true for the mound phenomenon in general. They will not tell us outright that they are the work of off-planeters, but they do not mind leaving clues. They'll give us evidence, but they won't give us proof. They will always leave room for doubt and, at times, they deliberately confuse the issue. They know that some of us are studying them, they seem to enjoy leaving clues, but they will not offer any proof.

A red herring is, of course, a fish, a very smelly fish. It was ostensibly used by escaping convicts to throw the bloodhounds off their scent. In a sense, the mounds, as they manifest worldwide, are the biggest clue. They imply the presence, or former presence, of a group of powerful and sentient beings. But in another sense, they are red herrings, throwing empirically-minded scientists off the scent of the subterranean redoubts where the off-planeters are comfortably ensconced. We are deliberately left to wonder about the mounds' true origin, which was the plan all along. Bill Grimstad is right. They were configured so as to confuse the researchers, both amateur and professional. They want professional archaeologists and paleontologists to attribute the mounds to ancient cultures, gophers, or anything other than them. In this sense, the mounds are the red herrings. The Trickster abides.

9

PLANET STRANGE

eople who read many scientific papers know there is a trick to getting through a long and detailed scientific paper in short order: you read the abstract on the first page and then skip to the conclusion. Leave everything else to be combed through by those who are part of the peer-review process. If one is not concerned with verifying the myriad details of the experimental procedure, data collection and data interpretation, you can skip the whole rest of the paper, at least as long as you don't have any serious truck with whatever the author has concluded. Applying that strategy to this book, it becomes possible to understand this book in a shorter time by reading the introduction to get a rough sense of where I was going, then skip right to this final chapter in which I summarize all the other ones. If one doesn't have any serious truck with my conclusions, one could skip the rest of the book. If a reader does skip right to this chapter, they will either throw the book at the wall after reading it, or go back and look at the other chapters in an attempt to understand what the hell led me to articulate such a wacky (I prefer to say 'outside the box') view of what did go on and what is still going on beneath our feet.

The introduction explained the thesis of the book: that there exists a subterranean 'netherworld' down under that is inhabited by intelligent living beings who generally avoid humans and human affairs. Few of us have spent much time below the surface of the Earth, so it is perhaps a difficult environment to fully comprehend. While miners do spend a lot of time underground, theirs is a world that is filthy, loud, and dangerous. Another group that spends as much or more time than miners inside the Earth are the engineers and laborers who construct and maintain DUMBS, which is an acronym for Deep Underground Military Bases, of which there are many.

Perhaps the first to establish underground military installations were the Nazis during World War II. They assembled their V-1 and V-2 rockets in underground facilities where their secret work could not be seen from the air and where they were safe from Allied bombing raids. Of course, during the Battle of Britain, the residents of London also spent a lot of time in crowded and uncomfortable bomb shelters. Then came the atomic bomb at the end of the war. Stalin and the Soviets were suddenly not our allies, and they were eagerly developing their own atomic bomb. Military planners and government officials suddenly had a vulnerability that never before existed: the possibility of getting suddenly and totally bombed into oblivion. By 1947, it was painfully clear that the highest levels of the federal government were concentrated in one city. If that city was annihilated by just one or two atomic bombs, the whole of the federal government would cease to exist. In response to this concern, the concept of the Continuity of Government (COG for short) became an important and previously unaddressed concern. First of all, it became apparent that the whole national government was vulnerable because it was too concentrated. The centers of government needed to be spread out so as to make it tougher to eliminate, and the most important government and military individuals needed secure places from which to operate in the event of a nuclear attack. Clearly, the safest place was underground.

Planners fanned out and searched for subterranean places that could be improved to create subterranean citadels. Because of its proximity to Washington D.C., military men began surveying the caves along the Blue Ridge Mountains of West Virginia. Other teams toured the subway systems and explored around Europe to learn how ceilings were strengthened and supported. By 1948, plans were being made to construct a subterranean command center, an "alternate Pentagon" if you will, outside Washington D.C. A particularly suitable spot was identified in Adams County, Pennsylvania, just over the state line from Maryland, on an 1100 acre parcel known as the Beard Lot. The engineering firm that built the Lincoln Tunnel under the Hudson River connecting New York and New Jersey was hired. By January 1951, P.J. Healy, Inc. began work on the site, which had a code name of 'Site R' but eventually became known as Raven Rock. The plan was to excavate five parallel caverns and put a three-story building in each one. This would be enough room for 6,000 military planners and support staff. Round-the-clock work concluded on June 30, 1953, and the military now had its 'alternate Pentagon.'

Meanwhile, in 1951, the 50-ton hydrogen bomb, code-named 'Mike,' was tested and proved to be 500 times more powerful than the atomic bomb that was dropped on Hiroshima. The threat of nuclear Armageddon was suddenly far worse. The Soviets weren't going to be stopped from developing their own thermonuclear device, and by 1953, they tested their first hydrogen bomb-like device. By 1954, the COG initiative was in high gear. Resolution NSC-5408 was adopted, which allowed for the relocation of the entire legislative and judicial branches of government in the wake of a Soviet attack. A large instal-lation was constructed beneath the luxurious Greenbriar Hotel in West Virginia, and another facility in Virginia called High Point was to be constructed 300 feet below the top of Mount Weather. The High Point facility would be able to house 3000 high-level government offi-cials. By the end of the Eisenhower administration in 1960, some fifty-eight relocation sites were arranged in an arc around Washington D.C., as well as the strictly military DUMBS like Raven Rock. There are now an additional 250 underground bunkers in Canada. The Strategic Air Command built one in Massachusetts under Bare Mountain, and NORAD built the huge facility under Cheyenne

Mountain in Wyoming. In the 1960s, there was a big increase in the construction of 'relocation centers' (bomb shelters, really) as the Cold War intensified, and events like the Cuban Missile Crisis made nuclear war seem inevitable. Many cities used their own funds and matching federal dollars to build relocation centers for local governments. In Portland, where I live, $670,000 was spent hollowing out Rocky Butte six miles east of town to create 20,000 square feet of living and office space in an extinct volcano; enough room to accommodate 250 VIPs. Many underground bunkers and converted salt mines were created just to store valuable records. Some of the bigger DUMBs have been further enlarged. The High Point site under Mt. Weather now contains 900,000 square feet of office space. Many underground bases connect.

DUMBS are constructed through a process known as 'shaped-charge mining,' a technique that was adapted from rock quarrying. Shaped-charge mining is also used in oil and gas exploration. Explosives that concentrate their force in a certain direction fracture the rock, after which it is removed. Tunnel boring machines (TBMs) are also used when linear tunnels are needed for underground railways and highways. They consist of huge, cylindrically shaped machines with a rotating face that grind away at the rock and dirt, which is then conveyed to the rear of the machine for removal. The biggest ones are fifteen to seventeen meters in diameter and over a hundred meters in length. They are typically made in Germany; they cost hundreds of millions of dollars and can tear through fifteen to twenty meters of rock per day. The machine is braced to the sides of the tunnel so the grinding surface can push forward and tear into the end of the tunnel that is being excavated. As the debris is carried away, another part of the machine lines the cylindrical tunnel with concrete pieces.

While actual underground bases have only existed since World War II, underground military activities like tunneling under fortified positions are nothing new. Before the use of shaped charges, tunneling was done with mining equipment, dynamite, and lots of human labor. During World War I, in an attempt to break the stalemate of trench warfare, both sides tunneled under enemy positions so as to plant explosives and inflict mass casualties. The Germans may have been the first to employ this tactic during the Battle of Givanchy in December of 1914. They tunneled under the French and British trenches and mined the tunnels with a dozen 110 lb. charges. Eight hundred or so Allied soldiers were killed when the charges were detonated. At first, the British didn't have engineers who were experienced in underground warfare. Then, along came John Norton Griffith. He owned a mining company that was employed to rebuild sewer systems in Manchester. His employees, called moles, were generally small in stature and very accustomed to working in the cramped, cold, and dangerous conditions of underground job sites.

"Hellfire Jack" as Griffith was known, wrote to the British military command and suggested using his crews to tunnel under German positions and set charges. For two months, his letter went unheeded even as the Germans continued to blow up Allied trenches from below. Finally, in 1916, General Herbert Plumer took another look at Norton's letter and gave the go-ahead.

Meanwhile, the German's were holding an L-shaped ridge north of Mesen, Belgium, that gave them a commanding view of British-French positions. Trying to take the ridge by charging uphill across a no-man's-land proved futile. Messine Ridge, as it was called, was a heavily fortified, 200-foot high ridge that had been held by the Germans since 1914. The British developed a plan to dig 22 tunnels (known as galleries) under the ridge and plant charges. Two companies of Canadian tunnelers (called 'Beavers'), one company of Australians (who called themselves "Diggers"), and three companies of British tunnelers were put to the task, as well as volunteers from all over the British Iles. By 1916, there were 25,000 workers constructing tunnels all along the Western Front. Known as 'clay kickers,' the workers were usually small in frame (often shorter than five feet), over 40 years old, and possessed no military training. They got paid more than the soldiers, but their working conditions were abysmal. Candles were their only source of illumination. Trench foot was a perpetual concern as the tunnels were often partially flooded. Death by carbon monoxide poisoning was the biggest threat of all. The miners would bring along the proverbial 'canary in the coal mine' though they also used caged rats or mice to determine when the carbon monoxide level was getting perilously high. Some tunnels were so oxygen-poor that a breathing device known as a 'protoman' was developed. It had a breathing tube connected to canisters of oxygen that enabled a clay kicker to work for up to two hours in a no-oxygen environment.

The miners spent eight-hour shifts in a sitting position, digging using mostly leg muscles. Braced against a backrest, they would push the shovel into the earth with their legs, filling one bucket at a time, then passing it back where other members of the team hauled it rearward and out. Back problems were commonplace. The Germans used picks and mattocks to dig their tunnels, which made for a noisy affair. The British method of 'clay kicking' was not only four times faster, but also a lot quieter. The clay kickers worked their entire shifts in absolute silence. Both sides used geophones or seismophones to detect the subterranean activities of their adversaries, and when they did detect enemy tunneling, they would plant a charge in the vicinity and detonate it. Occasionally, a tunneling team might experience the terror of breaking through into an adjacent enemy tunnel. A fight would ensue among unarmed tunnelers who battled each other with nothing but fists or digging tools.

The German position on the high ground of Messine Ridge did present a disadvantage when it came to tunneling. They had to tunnel vertically much farther before they could start digging horizontally. Still worse, the terrain around Messines Ridge was underlain by a thick layer of fairly loose sand that was prone to collapse. The English engineers devised a stout, stackable ring system that reinforced the vertical shafts' sides to prevent cave-ins. Once the clay kickers got below the sand layer, the stratigraphy turned to clay, which was seen as the ideal material to tunnel through, hence the name 'clay kickers.'

By early June of 1917, an amazing 22 galleries had been constructed under Messine Ridge, each one being over a hundred feet down and over a thousand feet long. Only one of the 22 galleries was ever discovered by German forces. The rest of the galleries were packed and wired with an astounding 500 tons of TNT. Charges were primed and wired to British trenches a safe distance away. The last mine was finally placed and primed on June 6, 1917. A coordinated detonation time was planned for 3:17 a.m. on the morning of June 7th. The night before the planned detonation, General Charles Harrington in England, hinted at the coming cataclysm when he was quoted as saying, "I do not know whether we will change the world tomorrow, but we will definitely alter the geography."

How right he was. At 3 a.m., Allied shelling stopped and an eerie silence fell over the battlefield. At 3:17, nineteen mined galleries exploded over a twenty-second interval. It shook the Earth so violently that scientists at nearby Lille University thought they were experiencing an earthquake. It was heard as far away as Scotland, and the explosive energy instantly killed 10,000 German soldiers, and injured another 7,000. Witnesses described German soldiers flying through the air like rag dolls, and then being buried beneath the debris that rained down upon them after they hit the ground. It was the largest man-made explosion ever created up until the 1945 Trinity atomic test was detonated in New Mexico.

Immediately following the explosion, the German positions were shelled, followed by an infantry attack. The Germans were predictably dazed and confused. Allies took Messine Ridge in less than a day, continuing to advance in what became a pivotal point in the war. The initial explosion and the ensuing offensive produced a total of 25,000 German casualties. A German historian published *Der Werthkrieg* in which he cited the mining of Messine Ridge as the second biggest reason Germany lost that war. British General Grant Grieve similarly observed that, "Never before in the history of warfare have miners performed such an important role."

While it is an amazing story of weaponized tunneling, the clay-kicking episodes of World War I in no way resemble the techniques used to construct DUMBS. As previously mentioned, shaped charges are used, as described by Phillip Schneider, a now-deceased resident of Wilsonville, Oregon, who claimed to have worked on DUMBS.

Both Phil and his father before him were employed by Morrison-Knudsen, a large construction firm that was contracted by the government to build DUMBS. How off-planeters do it, I do not know. Scientist/author Henry Franzoni has described a physics concept he calls 'superforce' that, when harnessed, can render enormous amounts of matter essentially weightless.

If large subterranean excavation projects are taking place, and I think there is, one wonders whether engineers like Phil Schneider had unintended encounters with off-planeters, the way the English clay kickers sometimes had surprise encounters with their German counterparts.

Phillip Schneider claimed he worked on a seven-story DUMB beneath Archuleta Mesa outside Dulce (pronounced DULL-say), New Mexico. Schneider frequently spoke at UFO conferences and was a regular attendee at Ray Crowe's monthly meeting of the Western Bigfoot Society in Portland. Schneider claims they did indeed encounter off-planet entities while constructing the Dulce base and a battle ensued. Schneider had three fingers missing from one hand, which he claims to have lost in the kerfuffle. Peace was eventually restored and a deal was struck to share the underground base. Naturally, it was never possible to verify Schneider's claims, but he was missing three fingers.

Between 1993 and 1996, Henry Franzoni got to know Schneider pretty well through Ray Crowe's monthly meetings. Henry recalls that even though the theme of the Western Bigfoot Society meetings was definitely bigfoot, Phil's principal interest was UFOs. At the meetings, Phil did often rail on about wasteful government spending on 'black (secret) projects', and he was known to pass around bits of metal that he felt were alien in origin. I asked Henry about Phil's claim of encountering off-planeters while building the DUMB outside Dulce. Henry offered that Phil probably did work for Morrison-Knudsen building DUMBS, but Phil was also a bit of an embellisher. Henry thinks the subterranean encounter with off-planeters probably did happen, but maybe not to Phil. Further, Phil was dying of terminal bone cancer, although the cause of his 1996 death was ruled as suicide. He allegedly strangled himself with rubber tubing. While his cause of death was a bit suspicious, Henry feels it does not stand to reason that shadowy forces would take action to assassinate a person who was already at death's door. Nor does it make total sense that Phil's outspoken opinions about government spending at a small gathering of bigfoot enthusiasts would be seen by someone as so threatening that Phil would have to be permanently silenced.

Dulce does continue to be a place where certain paranormal topics intersect, specifically, underground bases presumably inhabited by off-planeters, bigfoot encounters, cattle mutilations, and unidentified aerial phenomena (UAPs). Other such places where multiple phenomena intersect are Mt. Shasta (CA), Mt. Adams (WA), Sedona (AZ), Skinwalker Ranch (UT), the Bermuda Triangle, and the agricultural fields of southern England. It is this intersection of multiple phenomena at certain places that really got my attention and motivated me to search for connections and explanations. Each chapter in this book addressed a separate phenomenon, and at this point in the book, I am speculating as to where it all points.

The first chapter explored Zechariah Sitchin and his pioneering attempts to decipher the cuneiform tablets originating from Syria and elsewhere in the Middle East. Sitchin felt that these tablets could be used to assemble a human history that began with off-planet entities arriving on Earth after their home planet, Nibiru, developed serious environmental problems. In Sitchin's books, he reports that Anu, a ruler on said planet, had two highly capable sons whom he dispatched to Earth to round up a supply of mono-atomic gold that was needed to repair the atmosphere of Niburu. This would have taken place some 100,000 to 200,000 years ago. Enlil and Enki found what they were looking for, but the process of extracting it proved to be overwhelming. In order to generate a labor pool, they got busy and gene-spliced their DNA with that of the indigenous primates, specifically Homo erectus. This was the dawn of humanity. The Anunnaki, of which Enlil and Enki were two, may have been the same as the race of tall, pale-skinned Jesus-like characters that are mentioned in several cultures' oral histories, though other descriptions of Enlil and

Enki have them looking scaly and lizard-like. In any case, they allegedly gene-spliced off-spring that would become the ancestors of humanity, beginning with Adamu, or Adam and Eve, as in the Book of Genesis.

Eventually, the humans got a bit too intelligent and uppity for their own good, and Enlil decided that, with the difficult mining work winding down, humans had to be eliminated. At least one of the brothers began to plot their demise. These guys had mastered access to the superforce that enabled them to move huge amounts of material and they weren't done making improvements to the planet, so Enlil found a large planetesimal somewhere, maybe in the asteroid belt between Mars and Jupiter where the pieces of a destroyed planet remained in orbit around the Sun. They hauled our future moon into its new position. The good news is that it stabilized the motions of our planet and ameliorated our climate. The bad news is that it also pulled a bunch of other interplanetary debris with it, and the Earth got pummeled, maybe on purpose.

Laugh if you want to. Certainly, Sitchin's accounts will be seen by some as the most dubious and unverifiable material that I present in this book. The Book of Genesis supports elements of Sitchin's account (Cain and Abel, Adam and Eve, the great flood). Hauling a moon into orbit around the Earth is another eye-roller for anyone applying a scientific viewpoint. We cannot be sure there was once a time when the Earth had no moon. Still, it has become increasingly certain that the Earth did indeed get pummeled 12,800 years ago. A catastrophic worldwide flood did ensue as the comets or asteroids repeatedly pummeled the continental glaciers that covered much of the Northern Hemisphere. No one can prove the Enlil-Enki-Anunnaki bit, but there is little doubt that the worldwide cataclysm DID happen, and it was a repeated pummeling that lasted as many as 1100 years. What was left of humanity was forced to hunker down in caves for a thousand years. Finally, the global cold spell abated, and after a long period of living underground, the 'cave men' emerged from their underground refuge to re-inhabit a somewhat sterilized landscape. Meanwhile, most of the Anunnaki left the planet, maybe to take up residence a safe distance away in their pre-arranged Winnebago-in-the-sky that we know as the Moon. And they're still there. Some of them returned, led by Enlil, the more soft-hearted of the two brothers. (Yes, they apparently live a really long time.) Anyway, the tall ones fanned out around the planet and, in an act of benevolence, did what they could to restart and reorganize the frail vestiges of humanity that came crawling out from subterranean shelters.

Zulu legend describes the arrival of the Moon some 12-13,000 years ago, which coincides with the Late Pleistocene extinction event, or Younger Dryas. If there is any truth to this legend, perhaps the Moon's arrival was the cataclysm's triggering event. It stands to reason that a somewhat large gravitation center might drag a whole bunch of smaller bits with it as it traveled or was somehow towed across the solar system. As previously stated, the moving of a moon is scientifically dubious at best, yet one scientifically valid point must be re-stated: wherever it came from and whenever it arrived, the Moon had to be moving very slowly and on a very precise trajectory for it to be captured into Earth's orbit. The alternative theory that the Moon formed in place, perhaps from shattered Earth debris, is not as tenable as was once believed. As explained in the Moon chapter, scholars cite multiple reasons why the Moon could not have formed from the debris of a large collision.

Further, objects in space do not ordinarily travel so slowly that they can be captured, especially by a planet of such similar size. The Moon should not be there, but there it is. The Moon should not be hollow, but it is. The fact that the Moon is 1/400th the size of the Sun *and* exactly 1/400 of the distance to the Sun is seen by many as a nearly impossible coincidence. As a result of this alleged coincidence, we on Earth are the only known planet to witness perfect solar eclipses. In my view, this strengthens the case that the Moon did not end up orbiting the Earth by natural processes alone.

The question arises as to whether the pyramids were built before or after the Younger-Dryas cataclysm 12,800 years ago. If the pyramids pre-date the Younger Dryas event, they reflect a high degree of technological sophistication among some of the Earth's inhabitants before this cataclysm. Other indications that Earth's inhabitants at that time were highly sophisticated come from evidence uncovered by Graham Hancock and others. Hancock maintains that early humans were regularly crossing oceans, as evidenced by genetic markers of South American natives that indicate Southeast Asian ancestry. Native North Americans also show a haploid-x marker that is shared by residents of the British Isles and the Middle East. In any event, the Younger Dryas cataclysm pushed a big reset button on civilization.

If the capture of the Moon, either naturally or artificially, destabilized the orbits of asteroids or comets that then pummeled the Earth, this might explain the multiple collisions that brought about the Younger Dryas cooling event and the accompanying sudden rise in worldwide sea levels. In chapter 3, we learned that the gravitational influences of the Moon were a key force that was indirectly tapped by the pyramids to produce power. If the Moon arrived only 12,800 years ago, as Zulu legend states, then energy production in pyramids could not have happened prior to this date. If the pyramids pre-date the Younger Dryas and were built to produce power, as Christopher Dunn asserts, then the Moon arrived earlier than Zulu legend states. If the moon only arrived 12,800 years ago, then the pyramids must be younger than that. No Moon, no pyramid power. I favor the view that the pyramids are much older than currently accepted estimates, so the Moon is probably older as well. I like the creation stories of Sitchin and they bear strong similarities to Old Testament scripture, but the dates cannot be reconciled with certain known events like Younger Dryas.

This inconsistency does not trouble me too much. Zulu legend is hardly authoritative. Nor are the translated cuneiform accounts produced and published by Zechariah Sitchin. Still, I find these sources to be useful. I am heartened by the numerous similarities between Sitchin's translations and other potentially historical documents like the Bible. A great flood was found to be referenced in the cuneiform tablets, which can, indeed, be confirmed. At least some of the time, Sitchin's translation proved to be accurate. He may not have been right about everything, but Sitchin's work is very worthy of serious consideration. Similarly, the other authors referenced in this book may not be able to provide unassailable proof of their somewhat radical ideas, but I find their evidence to be compelling nonetheless.

Paranormal Pioneers

Among the earliest of the paranormal pioneers mentioned in this book is Charles Fort. His research and writing dates back to the turn of the Nineteenth Century and it was he who first supposed that aerial phenomena may have origins on other planets. He was also the first to see a connection between seemingly unrelated paranormal events, whether they be hairy bipeds, aerial phenomena, vortexes, spirit entities, and more. Bill Grimstad courageously added a layer onto the ideas of Charles Fort by suggesting in the early 1980s that the Earth is a living being that is generating these phenomena. This idea has been advocated by others and it has become known as the Gaia hypothesis.

Sitchin's work was published about the same time. He asserts that off-planeters showed up and transformed a somewhat sterile planet into a cradle for humanity, even if their motive was resource extraction. Michael Tellinger's Slave Species of the Gods contains research that seems to verify the suggestion that Bronze-age humans were indeed involved in deep-earth gold mining in southern Africa, even though they should not have been in posession of such a technologically advanced skill set. Graham Hancock's multiple works, including *America Before,* help support the view that early humanity, prior to the Younger Dryas cataclysm, was much more sophisticated than what is currently accepted. His historical research finds multiple reasons to take seriously the view that a population of very tall, pale, and very sophisticated beings existed before being largely eliminated by the Late Pleistocene extinction event that also wiped out numerous species of mammals, not to mention the island nation of Atlantis. Randall Carlson, Graham Hancock, and Antonio Zamora have all done admirable work that supports the view that the Younger Dryas cataclysm did indeed happen and it was a big setback in the development of human civilization. The highly speculative work of Zechariah Sitchin is supported by the work of these more mainstream authors.

In *Giants on Record*, Hugh Newman and Jim Vieira have done spectacular work that essentially verifies the existence of the same race of tall ones that I discussed in Chapter 2, and that Graham Hancock discusses at length in *America Before*. Another author, Richard Dewhurst published *The Ancient Giants Who Ruled North America* a year earlier than Newman and Vieira in 2014. Bill Grimstad discusses evidence of a giant race in *Rebirth of Pan* (1983) that Newman and Vieira presented in much more detail in *Giants on Record* (2015). Their stature notwithstanding, Christopher Dunn does a magnificent job of showing that some highly sophisticated beings built the pyramids as power plants, not tombs. This radical revision of Egyptology is finding favor with every passing year since the publication of *Giza Power Plant* in 1998. There are now countless books and TV productions that build on this once boldly radical idea.

And when it comes to making boldly radical statements in print, nothing exceeds the venturesome assertion of Don Wilson (*Secrets of Our Spaceship Moon*, 1979) as well as Christopher Knight and Alan Butler, who contend in *Who Built The Moon?* (2005) that the Moon is as hollow as it is artificial. The fact that the Moon is not just of very low density but actually somewhat hollow is again a very venturesome assertion that continues to be supported by subsequent research. Even astrophysics icon Carl Sagan acknowledged that the Moon is not only curiously low in mass but also that there is no such thing as a natural satellite that is largely hollow. As was mentioned in Chapter 6, Knight and Dunn conclude that the Moon was indeed put into place, though not by aliens, per se. Rather, they submit yet another venturesome conclusion that it was built by sophisticated Earthlings who traveled back in time from Earth's own future. In any event, the installers of the Moon display the same mastery of moving massive objects as the beings Dunn references in *Giza Power Plant*.

Regarding the question of who is moving massive objects around with relative ease, the mound phenomenon as it occurs worldwide supports the view that this concept is firmly based in fact. Bill Grimstad is the first author I am aware of who, in *Rebirth of Pan* (1983), ponders who or what is moving all this Earth around. He credits the Earth itself as the only entity capable of such a feat. Graham Hancock investigates the mound phenomenon at length in *America Before,* and he favors the view that a race of super tall, super capable giants built them; the same guys Vieira, Newman, and Dewhurst discuss in their books. Hancock also boldly factors in the numerous references in Mayan and Aztec lore that offer the name Quetzalcoatl as the being or set of beings who do the moving, and the monitoring of humanity. After the Younger Dryas catastrophe, he (they) took pity on humanity and fanned out around the globe with the agenda of restarting and re-civilizing humanity. These entities demonstrated how to harness the superforce of physics that enabled humanity (with some help) to build impossibly massive and impossibly precise structures. Even if one doubts this admittedly far-out idea, no one can deny that very large amounts of earth and rock are lying all around the surface of the Earth in a manner that is not consistent with any known natural process. Graham Hancock has also noted that there are impossibly large tracts of impossibly fertile soil in South America. They are known as the Amazon Dark Earths (ADEs) or terra pritas. They are vast in scale but locally placed only in certain areas that are not consistent with any known natural process. With respect to the ADEs, Graham Hancock sees them as clear evidence that someone or something in the past did humanity a huge favor by moving vast amounts of material intended for agricultural use.

Lest we assume that whoever performed these colossal feats has since left the planet, we must consider the crop circle evidence as an indication that they or he is still around. The dedicated work of a slew of mostly English researchers indicates that mighty entities are still around. Lucy Pringle, Freddy Silva (Portugese), Colin Andrews, Richard Hoagland (Australian), and others have studied crop glyphs for decades and they generally agree that crop glyphs are otherworldly in origin. Messaging is indeed happening in the glyphs, with specific entities such as Quetzalcoatl sometimes being referenced. These may even be the crop circle creators. Perhaps Quetzalcoatl is still around, and it is my supposition that such entities reside, at least partially, right here on planet Earth. Not only do other-worldly phenomena like crop circles continue to occur every summer in southern England, but other indications, like the mounds, suggest they emanate from underground citadels. According to Chris O'Brien, they not only live here, but they share our food supply. In his book, O'Brien logically concludes that the cattle mutilation phenomenon is real and otherworldly, and implies that there is a concern that Earth's food supply is being jeopardized by careless and ill-considered scientific research and experimentation. This was a fairly radical assertion in 2014 when Chris published *Stalking the Herd*. In the post-Covid world we now inhabit, who could still argue that we have anything but a "Faustian bargain with Mephisthophelean Sci-tech" as Bill Grimstad said in *Rebirth of Pan*?

In his book, *Mysteries of the Serpent Mound*, Ross Hamilton recounts an experience he had with remote viewing, in which he actually got a view of extensive underground complexes which were arranged in a rough wagon wheel orientation, with the 'spokes' of the wheel being tunnels that connected separate chambers that were cavernous in size.

Further support for the view that 'they' are still here and inhabit an underworld can be drawn from another courageous paranormal author, Bruce Gernon. In *Beyond the Bermuda Triangle* (2017), Bruce Gernon and Rob MacGregor do an admirable job of trying to get to the bottom of a subject that has intrigued other authors like Charles Berlitz and Brian Dunning. Gernon persuasively argues that the vortex phenomenon provides a means by which beings can come and go from this world, but that it is also a conduit to some kind of under-world that is accessed through land-based portals as well as through oceanic access points. Gernon and MacGregor lay the UFO/vortex phenomenon at the doorstep of subterranean-based off-planeters. They do not take the Bermuda Triangle absolutely literally, but rather, they see it as one of many places where energy and physics combine to provide a means for sophisticated beings to cross realms.

Toward the end of *Beyond the Bermuda Triangle*, Gernon and MacGregor do something more courageous than most: they make predictions. Not only do they espouse the view that off-planeters are behind the phenomenon, but they offer five fairly bold predictions:

1. Humans will make contact with extraterrestrial life by the year 2030
2. The electric fog that he encountered while flying in the Bermuda Triangle will be harnessed by 2050 to create a warp drive propulsion system.
3. Time travel will be understood by 2060.
4. Near-light speed interstellar travel will happen by 2070.
5. By 2100, we will be meeting with aliens and hopefully traveling the galaxy with them.

I don't know about hitching a ride with them, but I think meeting up with aliens will happen much sooner than Gernon predicts. I suspect it has already happened. Still, I cannot help but admire their willingness to stick their neck out, perhaps because I am also doing the same thing. I'm sticking my neck out a country mile just by attempting to unify all of these seemingly separate paranormal subjects into this one coherent idea: off-planeters come and go from our world and they reside, at least partially, in a subterranean realm. They leave clues about their existence, but they do just as much to deliberately confuse the situation. They live here, they watch us, they are concerned by some of our (military) activities, but they largely stay out of sight. They have been comfortably ensconced in a subterranean realm for thousands of years, but they continue tunneling beneath the continents and oceans.

These off-planeters, or whatever they are, aren't the only ones who are tunnelers. We humans are tunnelers, too. The Younger Dryas forced us to be. If we hadn't been tunnelers, we never would have, as a species, survived that Late Pleistocene Extinction Event, which brought the world population of almost all animals (and people) to the brink of extinction. Caves and underground excavations were critical human habitat for at least 600 years, maybe twice that long. Maybe someday we will return to the underworld. If Bruce Gernon's predictions are true, we may someday get invited to go down under to dialogue with the off-planeters (or under-planeters, as the case may be). I do not expect that this opportunity will happen in my lifetime. I hope I am wrong. It may have already happened. I know of several people who are actively searching for ways to dialogue with off-planeters. Henry Franzoni says it happens all the time and has been happening for many years. Henry, who bears some Native American ancestry, rhetorically asked me, "What do you think goes on in those sweat lodges?"

Exactly where do these beings reside that we are trying to contact? They may be on planets that orbit other stars. They may exist in some other realm or dimension. At least some of the time, they are probably a lot closer to home. It may be another realm, but that realm is a subterranean one right here on planet Earth. It may be very difficult to scientifically verify, but it is a realm that humans have suspected to exist for a very long time. Vikings felt that their god Thor lived beneath a volcano in a subterranean realm that Scandinavians knew as Asar. The Egyptians called it Amenti. Persians called it Aryana. Tibetans and Mongols called it Erdami. Celts called it Dananda. Greeks called it Hades. Whatever the name, it is a place we will someday understand. When we do, we will finally have explanations for the many mysteries we encounter right here on Planet Strange.

AFTERWORD

Go to <u>hangar1publishing.com</u> to learn more about the Authors and stay up to date with their newest releases.